The Making of the OCTOBER CRISIS

THE
MAKING
OF THE
OCTOBER
CRISIS

CANADA'S LONG NIGHTMARE
OF TERRORISM AT THE
HANDS OF THE FLQ

D'Arcy Jenish

Doubleday Canada

Doubleday Canada and colophon are registered trademarks of Penguin Random House Canada Limited

Library and Archives Canada Cataloguing in Publication

Jenish, D'Arcy, 1952-, author
The making of the October Crisis / D'Arcy Jenish.

Issued in print and electronic formats.
ISBN 978-0-385-66326-7 (hardcover).—ISBN 978-0-385-69019-5 (EPUB)

1. Québec (Province)—History—October Crisis, 1970. I. Title.

FC2925.9.O25J46 2018   971.4'04   C2018-901226-9
C2018-901227-7

Jacket design: Andrew Roberts
Jacket photograph: *Montreal Gazette*
Printed and bound in the USA

Interior image: (man) Manifesto, Front de libération du Québec, from the William Ready Division of Archives and Research Collections, McMaster University

Photo insert credits: Page 1: ZUMA Press, Inc./Alamy Stock Photo; Pages 2, 8: *Montreal Gazette*/CP; Pages 3 (top and bottom), 5, 7 (bottom): Montreal Police Service/private collection; Page 4 (top): The Canadian Press/Peter Bregg; Page 4 (bottom): AP Photo/ *Montreal Star*; Page 6 (top): The Canadian Press/CP; Page 6 (bottom): Sûreté du Québec/ private collection; Page 7: Frank Prazak/Library and Archives Canada.

Published in Canada by Doubleday Canada,
a division of Penguin Random House Canada Limited

www.penguinrandomhouse.ca

10 9 8 7 6 5 4 3 2 1

Penguin
Random House
DOUBLEDAY CANADA

To Hélène. For all your support over all our years together.

CONTENTS

Prologue

———

THERE HAD BEEN OVER TWO HUNDRED BOMBINGS, dozens of
bank robberies, six deaths and two kidnappings, all committed in the
name of the Front de libération du Québec, all in the space of seven and
a half years, and then this—one of the hostages brutally murdered at
the hands of his abductors. The other victims of FLQ terrorism had
been ordinary citizens—a night watchman, the vice-president of one
of Canada's largest firearms stores, one of the employees, a secretary,
an Ottawa grandmother who worked for the Department of National
Defence and a sixteen-year-old youth who had died when the bomb he
was planting exploded in his hands.

The latest casualty—Pierre Laporte—was strangled. He was forty-
nine years old and a prominent Quebecker. He had been the legislative
correspondent for the Montreal daily *Le Devoir*—the newspaper of
choice for Quebec's political, cultural and intellectual elite. He had also
been a member of two provincial Liberal governments and a cabinet
minister in both. He was well liked by his constituents and respected by
his colleagues, one of whom described him as "the best parliamentarian
in the National Assembly."

Laporte was murdered on a Saturday evening, amid the October
Crisis of 1970, and the services held to honour him reflected his stature.
From midday Sunday until midday Tuesday, his body lay in state in an
open casket in the grand, marble-walled lobby of the Palais de justice
courthouse on Notre-Dame Street in Old Montreal. The flag of Quebec
was draped over the casket and four members of the Sûreté du
Québec—the provincial police force—stood guard.

Pierre Trudeau and Robert Bourassa were among the first dignitaries to pay their respects. They walked the short distance from City Hall flanked by machine gun–wielding soldiers, mounted the broad stone steps of the Palais de justice, stepped past the twenty-foot-high burnished-brass doors and stood before the casket for a few moments with heads bowed.

Thousands upon thousands of ordinary citizens waited their turn in unseasonably chilly autumn weather and in streets thick with soldiers dressed and armed for combat. The lineups stretched for blocks, and when their moment came, men, women and children swept silently past the casket and through the lobby and back to the street.

Premier Bourassa offered a state funeral in Old Montreal's ornate and magnificent Notre-Dame Basilica, but Madame Laporte insisted on a simple requiem celebrated without organ or choir or dirge, and open only to family and friends and her late husband's peers from the realm of politics. Parishes across Montreal and throughout Quebec held commemorative masses, similar services were held in Ottawa and Toronto, and all Quebec government offices were closed on the afternoon of the funeral.

It was set to begin at 4 p.m., but long before that the authorities had taken every precaution to ensure the safety of those attending, and that included the prime minister, most of his Cabinet and at least one hundred MPs from all parties, the premier of Quebec and every member of the National Assembly, Montreal's mayor and city councillors, and municipal politicians from the Montreal area.

The streets for several blocks around the basilica were barricaded. Soldiers armed with rifles—and bayonets attached to the barrels—kept motorists out. Army snipers were posted on rooftops. Troops manned a machine-gun nest between the two massive towers that soared above the front doors of the basilica. Police had earlier searched every inch of the interior. Barricades had been erected around Place d'Armes—the square in front of Notre-Dame—and they held back onlookers six to seven deep.

The dignitaries arrived in limousines, aboard school buses and on foot. Once everyone was seated inside the basilica, three police officers on motorcycles slowly made their way through the onlookers, followed by the hearse bearing Mr. Laporte's body. "The hush that fell over the crowd was so absolute that a policeman's footsteps echoed loudly across the square," one journalist noted, and others reported that an air of silence fell over much of the city as the service was about to begin.

It lasted forty-five minutes. Maurice Cardinal Roy of Quebec City presided and was assisted by Archbishop Paul Grégoire of Montreal and two parish priests. Afterward, pallbearers carried the casket to the hearse, followed by Madame Laporte, whose face was covered by a thick veil, and her two children, twenty-year-old Claire and ten-year-old Jean.

The family had barred reporters and photographers from attending, but one worshipper told a journalist, "I've never known anything like it. There was this enormous church and not a sound. Not a whisper. People didn't talk to each other, rarely shook hands and kept their eyes on the floor. I suppose there was nothing to say. We were stunned."

WHAT LED TO THIS

THE SEEDS THAT PRODUCED seven and a half years of terrorism were sown in 1960, in the provincial election campaign that began on May 8 and ended on June 22 when 2.4 million Quebeckers cast their votes. A slender majority turned their backs on the past and embraced a bold new vision of the future. They rejected the tattered, worn-out Union Nationale government and its promise of more of the same and turned to the Liberal Party and its platform of fundamental reform.

In the days leading up to the vote, Union Nationale candidates complained that the Liberals had resorted to lies, deceptions and calumny. The Liberals were guilty of the usual distortions that occur during a hotly contested election, but that wasn't why they won. They had campaigned on the slogan *"C'est le temps que ça change"* (It's Time for a Change), and they had tapped into the mood of the majority. The Union Nationale had won four consecutive elections starting in 1944, and the party had been in power sixteen years, but for all intents and purposes one man—Maurice Duplessis—had governed Quebec.

Duplessis was a masterful politician but a peculiar human being. He was a native of Trois-Rivières and maintained a residence there, but he lived for the most part at the Château Frontenac hotel in Quebec City, and he lived alone since he was a lifelong bachelor. For years, he walked each morning with his bodyguard through the cobblestone streets of the centuries-old walled city, up the Grande Allée and into the

Legislative Assembly building. He believed firmly that "a man's home is his castle," and he ran the Assembly as though it were his.

His ministers delivered texts he had had prepared, and he interrupted them if they went on too long. When one Liberal deputy was criticized for not adhering to the rules of the Assembly, he replied, "How do you expect me to follow the rules? We play by Mr. Duplessis's rules around here and he's never published them." Ministers rose when he entered the Cabinet room and waited until he took his place at the head of the table before sitting down. He reviewed each ministerial order-in-council at the weekly Cabinet meeting and approved or rejected each—no matter how minor. He scrutinized the province's half-billion-dollar annual budget line by line, took note of such things as the recommended salary increases of individual civil servants—all of whom were poorly paid anyway—and sometimes crossed out one number and inserted another.

He knew by name party officials and prominent citizens in every parish and township. He appointed old college friends to the chairs of Crown corporations and rewarded the contractors, tavern keepers and other businessmen who contributed to the party coffers, but punished and sometimes publicly humiliated those who crossed him. He had opposition members expelled from the Assembly, barred hostile journalists from attending his Friday press conferences and blocked appointments to Quebec's French-language universities.

Duplessis's opponents viewed him as ruthless and vindictive, but many Quebeckers revered him. They referred to him as "le Chef"—the chief. They were charmed by his wit and generosity and awed by his accomplishments. Duplessis was the architect of a remarkable post-war economic transformation. He was a staunch advocate of free enterprise. He maintained cordial relations with Montreal's English business community and kept a tight rein on organized labour. He courted investors from English Canada, the United States and to a lesser extent Great Britain, and they poured hundreds of millions of dollars into the development of the province's primary and secondary industries.

Government revenues soared, but rather than allow government to expand in lockstep with the economy, Duplessis used tax windfalls to pave roads, build schools, create new hospital beds and extend the electrical grid to all but the remotest rural routes. Most Quebeckers prospered through these happy economic times. Those working in new or growing industries earned good wages, their taxes were low and they had the disposable income necessary to acquire the latest appliances, entertainment systems and other consumer goods.

Quebec and Quebeckers advanced materially, but their society remained bound to the past, and this too was Duplessis's doing. He was a firm believer in the three pillars of the Old Quebec—ancestral traditions, the French language and Roman Catholicism—and, under his rule, "the state was an instrument not so much of progress as of preservation," as the historian Dale C. Thomson put it.

Roman Catholic clergy were pervasive and powerful, though not as powerful as le Chef. "The bishops eat from my hand," he boasted privately, and there was truth in this. Priests, lay brothers and nuns ran the hospitals, the schools, the French-language universities and many of the province's social assistance programs. They were beholden to Duplessis and his government for funding, and any who crossed him had to plead for their parishes or their institutions. Relations between church and state were sometimes contentious but never broken. Each needed the other to resist the forces of secularization that were reshaping post-war North America. Education was seen as the first line of defence. Faith, language and traditions could all be perpetuated if religious orders ran the schools and instructed the next generation.

This suited the majority of Quebeckers, who were conservative in outlook and steeped in the faith, and they faithfully returned Duplessis and his Union Nationale deputies in election after election. Duplessis also commanded the loyalty of moderate nationalists with his policy of provincial autonomy, which he sold as a sensible compromise between assimilation and separation. Autonomy meant opposition to any real or perceived federal infringement on provincial jurisdiction. It led to stormy and confrontational relations with the Liberal governments of

William Lyon Mackenzie King and his successor, Louis St. Laurent, and left Quebec on the sidelines when other provinces accepted hospital insurance, federal funding for universities and the construction of the Trans-Canada Highway.

Quebeckers had been content with their authoritarian premier through the immediate post-war years and most of the 1950s. He governed, he delivered and they adhered, and even after four consecutive mandates, there seemed no reason to believe that the Union Nationale could go down in the 1960 election. Some wondered about Duplessis's health. If anyone asked, he replied, "I am dangerously well." But he wasn't. Duplessis died suddenly of a stroke on September 7, 1959. He was sixty-nine. The death of le Chef, with an election mere months away, came as a shock, but well before his demise, Duplessis had anointed a successor—Paul Sauvé.

Sauvé was a popular minister and the only member of Cabinet who was allowed to speak for himself. He was the son of a prominent Conservative politician who had served both federally and provincially. He was first elected in his father's former constituency of Two Mountains, northwest of Montreal, in 1930 at age twenty-three, and except for one brief interlude, he had held the seat since then. *Désormais* ("henceforth") became the watchword of Sauvé's administration. Henceforth, things would be different, and he swiftly implemented reforms that might have saved the Union Nationale, but on January 2, 1960, he died of a heart attack.

Antonio Barrette, who had served as minister of labour since 1944, led the Union Nationale into the 1960 election. Barrette took the reins of a party that was well financed, tightly controlled and fuelled by a corps of dedicated organizers and workers on the ground. Furthermore, the economy was booming.

Barrette campaigned on the slogan *"Vers les sommets"* (On to New Summits) but for many voters that merely meant more of the same, and they were in no mood for that. The populace had changed in ways that were not always apparent. Quebeckers had been able to travel outside the province more frequently. Television had given them more exposure to the world. Prosperity had raised ambitions and led to discontent. It was often said that the Quebec economy ran on foreign capital and French-Canadian muscle. Many Quebeckers resented the fact that the managerial class was almost entirely English-speaking and that most of the profits from the mining and manufacturing boom landed in the coffers of the outside companies that financed these enterprises.

They wanted change, and Jean Lesage and his reinvigorated Liberals offered a clear alternative as well as a clean break from the past. "The people deserve this victory," a jubilant Lesage told supporters on election night. "They have wanted—despite the chains that bound them—to rid themselves of a regime that held them in serfdom. The province has been liberated." And in his first press conference after taking office, he declared, "This is more than a change of government. It is a change in our way of life."

The Liberal platform contained two hundred clearly defined promises and a vision of a reformed, modernized and creative Quebec. The party committed to creating three new departments—Cultural Affairs, Natural Resources, and Federal–Provincial Affairs—and an expanded Department of Family Affairs and Youth. Compulsory school attendance would be extended from age fourteen to age sixteen, and education would be free at all levels, including university.

The new government would appoint Royal commissions on education reform and the province's financial system. Government contracts would be awarded by public tender, not at the whim of ministers or the premier, and civil service positions would be filled on the basis of merit, not party loyalty. There were measures to improve agriculture; family housing loans; and pensions for the aged, the disabled and the blind, as well as widows and unmarried women over sixty.

The Lesage Liberals began implementing their program at a pace that left journalists and many voters breathless. *Le Devoir* described the government's first month in office as "thirty days that shook the province." A *Globe and Mail* writer called it "a quiet revolution," inadvertently coining the term that would come to describe this pivotal moment in Quebec history. The revolution may have been quiet, but the repercussions were unpredictable and frequently unnerving for the Lesage Liberals. Midway through their term, they circulated a questionnaire to party members. This pulse-taking proved an unpleasant surprise. Things were changing too fast, particularly for older, rural and more traditionally minded Quebeckers—or in ways that weren't benefitting them.

The Lesage Liberals also unleashed a new brand of nationalism that was less manageable than the old nationalism that Duplessis had so successfully manipulated. Old and new shared the same goal—the preservation of the language and the culture—but otherwise they differed radically. Traditional nationalism had been conceived in the nineteenth century, when Quebec was predominantly rural and community life was centred on the parish. It was cultural rather than political, bound to and defined by the Catholic faith, inward-looking and resistant to outside influences. It survived the great transition of the early twentieth century, when thousands of sons and daughters of habitants left the farms and rural communities of their childhood and migrated to Montreal and other cities to work in plants and mills and factories owned and managed by English-Canadian or American companies. Quebec became an urban, industrialized society, but the old nationalism persisted until the middle of the century, when a new generation chafed at the heavy-handed rule of Maurice Duplessis and the stifling influence of the Church; the domination of the English-Canadian business class; and the pre-eminence of the English language in business, industry and commerce.

The reforms of the Lesage government opened new, hitherto unimaginable possibilities for ambitious, well-educated Quebeckers. They could build a dynamic and creative state that would defend their language and culture and reflect the aspirations of the people. Having been held back and down for so long, and denied opportunity in the federal government as well as the Anglo-dominated business world, they now asserted themselves not as French Canadians but as Québécois, and not as one strand of a broader, geographically dispersed French Canada but as proud citizens of the Quebec nation.

But no matter how grand their achievements, their reformed and modernized Quebec would remain a province of Canada, one partner in a confederation of ten provinces and subservient to a federal government dominated by the interests of the other nine English-speaking provinces. Furthermore, their government would always be subject to the rules of the market and the capitalist economy, and would be compelled to keep foreign investors and bond-rating agencies happy.

These were the failings of the Quiet Revolution in the minds of some members of this freshly liberated generation. They dreamed of independence and drew inspiration from the liberation movements that were transforming Asia and Africa. Three dozen states gained their independence between 1945 and 1960. Seventeen African nations became independent in 1960 alone—big, populous, potentially rich and powerful nations such as Nigeria and the Democratic Republic of Congo, as well as tiny nations with poor prospects such as Togo and Burkina Faso. If such nations could take their place on the world stage, why not Quebec with all its industrial might and economic prowess, and its wealth of human and natural resources? Such was the thinking of thirty-odd lawyers, intellectuals, artists and civil servants who gathered at a resort in the Laurentians on September 10, 1960, to launch a sovereignty movement.

They called their movement the Rassemblement pour l'indépendance nationale (RIN). They elected a president, André d'Allemagne, a translator, and an executive that included Marcel Chaput, a biochemist at the Defence Research Board, Jacques Bellemare, a lawyer and future dean of the Faculty of Law at the Université de Montréal, and the writer Yves Préfontaine, and in October they drafted and issued their manifesto. "At the present time," it stated, "when peoples throughout the world are throwing off the colonial yoke and nations are demanding full independence, French Canada cannot willingly remain under foreign economic and political control. The ideal of national independence . . . is as valid here as anywhere else."

Several other organizations dedicated to the independence of Quebec sprang up in the early 1960s, but the RIN eclipsed them all in membership, public profile and importance. Members organized public lectures, supported striking workers and distributed literature. One hundred delegates from across the province attended the RIN's first congress in October 1961, and they approved a number of ambitious measures. They demanded that the Lesage government declare Quebec a unilingual French state, that the fleur-de-lys provincial flag fly above all others on every building in the province and that the government establish a free school of diplomacy and public administration to prepare for independence. Youthful members of the movement took nationalist agitation in a different direction. They painted pro-independence graffiti on English-only traffic signs and the walls of buildings in Montreal, Ottawa and Hull.

The RIN could be dismissed as a nationalist fringe group, but Lesage could not ignore or control the nationalists within his own caucus and Cabinet, and René Lévesque, his minister of natural resources, was the most troublesome. In the winter of 1962, Lévesque launched a campaign to nationalize the mish-mash of forty-six private power companies, the forty-eight co-operatives and the thirty-four municipalities that generated electricity throughout the province. Lesage was opposed, his Cabinet and caucus divided, and Lévesque unstoppable.

The nationalist cabinet minister embarked on a speaking tour of the province and drew full houses wherever he went. Prior to entering politics, Lévesque had hosted the Radio-Canada television program *Point de mire (Focal Point)* and nearly every French-speaking family in the province that owned a TV tuned in weekly. Lévesque the television host connected viscerally with Quebeckers. He used simple language as well as maps, a blackboard and a pointer to explain the complex world beyond their borders. Lévesque the politician used the same folksy, down-to-earth approach to explain nationalization to ordinary Quebeckers—a plan that would cost some four hundred million dollars, nearly equivalent to the entire provincial budget a few years earlier—and Lesage was unable to rein him in. Two years after the triumphant election of June 1960, the premier presided over a divided government.

The dispute festered over the summer, but had to be resolved before the government faced the opposition in the fall. The Cabinet and a few senior members of the party met in early September 1962 at a government-owned retreat north of Quebec City. No amount of reasoned debate or arm-twisting could yield a consensus or a compromise. Everyone needed a way out and Lesage provided it. He called a snap election.

The Liberals campaigned under a slogan tailor-made for the times: *"Maîtres chez nous"* (Masters of Our Own House). Lévesque went on the road with his pointer and blackboard to sell the plan to the electorate, and the Liberals won a resounding victory in the November election. But this did nothing to quell nationalist fervour, and one intemperate remark by Donald Gordon, the sixty-one-year-old president of the government-owned Canadian National Railway (CN), caused an eruption.

In late November, Gordon appeared before the House of Commons Railway Committee to present the corporation's 1962 annual report and the budget for the coming year. At the conclusion of the hearing, Social Credit MP Gilles Grégoire, a relentless advocate for bilingualism in the federal government, observed, "I note one president, seventeen vice-presidents, ten directors and not one of them French-Canadian." Gordon replied that the railway hired and promoted on the basis of merit alone, and then added, "As far as I am concerned, as long as I am president, promotions are not going to be made because the person is French-Canadian."

The RIN immediately organized a demonstration in Place d'Youville square in Quebec City. Some three hundred people participated. They chanted slogans: "Death to the Traitor!", "We Want Liberty!" and "Save Our Rights!" They burned the Red Ensign and hung and burned Donald Gordon in effigy. One young man jumped onto the roof of a truck and urged the "white negroes of Quebec" to launch a revolution.

Gordon issued a 450-word public statement aimed at clarifying his remarks. He pointed out that 13 percent of the railway's upper-middle and senior management were French-speaking and held key techni-cal, professional and administrative posts. André Laurendeau, editor of *Le Devoir*, responded with a front-page editorial. He noted that French Canadians constituted one-third of the population but held only 12 percent of upper-level administrative positions in the federal civil service. His compatriots were excluded from such posts in twenty-three of seventy-eight departments and agencies. "Since this is the case," he concluded, "to isolate Mr. Gordon and to speak of him as if he were mainly responsible for the situation is unjust and could even become repugnant."

But Gordon was an irresistible target and he was burned in effigy once more, this time in downtown Montreal. On December 11, students at the Université de Montréal held a mass protest—despite the sub-zero temperature and high winds. A thousand or more demonstrators con-verged on Place Ville Marie at around 4 p.m., causing a huge traffic jam, blocking the entrances to Central Station and preventing commuters from catching rush-hour trains. Some of the protesters tried to force their way into the Queen Elizabeth Hotel, but police held them back. The crowd made way when a truck arrived bearing a dummy with a pig's head affixed to it and the label "Donald Gordon." Protesters low-ered the Red Ensign from the flagpole in front of Place Ville Marie and then raised the dummy. Then they lowered it, doused it with kerosene, ignited it and hoisted it again—"flaming into the evening sky," one newspaper reported, "while students danced beneath it."

Three months later, in the spring of 1963, a new movement appeared—the Front de libération du Québec (FLQ). The young men behind it belonged to the RIN, but they had lost patience with the democratic pro-cess. They were inspired by the Cuban Revolution, which had cata-pulted Fidel Castro and his small band of followers from exile to power in a matter of months, and by the Front de libération nationale (FLN), which in 1962 had freed Algeria from the clutches of its French imperial masters after a violent, sometimes barbarous, eight-year insurgency.

The founders of the FLQ had come to see Quebec as not a province but a colony, and French-speaking Quebeckers as not a minority but a colonized people, and the English not as fellow citizens but occupiers. They had lifted this template from the book *The Wretched of the Earth* by Frantz Fanon, a psychiatrist from the French colony of Martinique who had studied in France and then worked in Algeria and joined the FLN. "National liberation, national resistance, the restoration of nationhood to the people, commonwealth," Fanon wrote, "whatever may be the headings used or new formula introduced, decolonization is always a violent phenomenon."

Dozens acted in the name of the FLQ, and most resorted to violence: bombings, bank robberies, murders and, finally, in October 1970, the kidnappings of the British diplomat James Cross and the Quebec cabinet minister and former journalist Pierre Laporte, hurling Canada into a peacetime crisis unlike any that came before or after.

One

BOMBERS AND SABOTEURS

ON THE MORNING OF MONDAY, October 5, 1970, Detective-Sergeant Robert Côté of the Montreal police department (MPD) had an early-morning appointment at the Canadian Pacific Railway's (CPR) Windsor Station. He had been asked to address a contingent of railway police officers and had just launched into his remarks when a bellboy interrupted him to deliver a note from headquarters. At 8:30 a.m., it said, armed gunmen had abducted British trade commissioner James Cross. Côté looked up, turned to his audience and said, "Gentlemen, the FLQ has adopted a new tactic in their war against us—kidnapping."

He had been in that war from the start—since the spring of 1963. Initially, he had been a foot soldier in the conflict with the movement's shadowy, constantly metastasizing clusters of bombers, bank robbers and saboteurs, but for the previous four years he had been the tip of the spear.

Côté was commander of the seven-member technical unit of the MPD—the bomb squad, in plain language. People often asked why there were seven men and he always had a ready answer: "Well, if they have to hold a civic funeral for one of us, the other six can serve as pallbearers." He had dismantled twenty-four FLQ bombs. He worked with his hands, his mind focused, his anxiety palpable, his face mere inches from sticks of dynamite bundled together and the tick-tock, tick-tock, tick-tock of the timing device—usually a cheap alarm clock—clearly audible.

His job was to find the wires that connected the detonator to the timer, or the battery that provided the jolt of electricity required to set the whole thing off. Then he would reach for the nail clippers attached to his belt and he would snip the wire.

Some of these bombs were small. Some were big, and the last one— planted under darkness in the early hours of July 12, 1970—was huge. A Pinkerton security guard making his rounds at the Bank of Montreal head office complex on St. James Street had alerted police. The guard's suspicions were aroused by the salmon-coloured Volkswagen Beetle left unattended in the enclosed, tunnel-like alleyway that ran through the four buildings in the complex. Côté discovered two large sticks of dynamite under the passenger seat. John Meloche, another member of the squad, spotted a fifty-pound box of dynamite behind the passenger seat. Meloche lifted the hood of the trunk and found a second fifty-pound box. "Your heart rate goes off the chart when you find something like that," Côté said years later. "Had I failed that day, they would have scraped our remains off the walls and sent them to three or four funeral homes."

Côté had joined the force in September 1959, at age twenty-three, and had been assigned to Detachment No. 11 in Pointe-Saint-Charles, a rough-and-tumble neighbourhood of working-class, French- and English-speaking Montrealers. The area known locally as the Point was wedged between the St. Lawrence River and the Lachine Canal southwest of downtown. It had once been a booming industrial centre. Many men and women in the community found employment at the Redpath Sugar refinery, the Sherwin-Williams paint plant and the eight-storey Northern Electric factory, where employees assembled phones, radios and small appliances. Others worked at the massive, thirty-acre CN shops, where the locomotives and freight cars for much of the nation's railways were repaired and painted. Côté was *"un gar de la Pointe"*—a guy from the Point. He was born and raised there but left at age sixteen, joined the army and served for four years before trading his army khaki for police blue.

The Point's economic fortunes were in decline when Côté returned there as a constable with the MPD. He and his fellow officers spent a good deal of their time dealing with alcohol-fuelled misconduct, domestic violence, petty theft, burglaries and illegal gambling. Early on a long-serving sergeant offered Côte some advice: "Young man, if you want to be successful in the force, you have to do three things: catch thieves, issue tickets and keep your mouth shut."

That was before the spring of 1963, before the advent of the FLQ, before bombs began exploding, before property was destroyed, people were maimed or killed and the MPD was compelled to respond to wave after wave of politically-inspired violence unlike anything ever seen in Montreal or, for that matter, in Canada.

The first bombs were hurled rather than planted, and they hit the armouries of the Royal 22nd, the Victoria Rifles and the Royal Montreal regiments. The perpetrators struck on the evening of March 8, 1963, while Montrealers were digging out after a heavy, late-winter snowfall that had left traffic snarled and congested. Their bombs were Molotov cocktails—narrow-neck glass bottles filled with gasoline. They stuffed gasoline-soaked rags in the bottle mouths, lit the rags and hurled their bombs. One broke a window but otherwise caused no damage. Another shattered against a wall and scorched it. The third landed in a stairwell and failed to ignite.

The attacks had amateur written all over them, but the perpetrators succeeded in attracting attention to their cause and that was their objective. They typed a communiqué, printed it on a mimeograph machine and sent it to the city's newspapers and the radio and TV stations. It included a flag crudely sketched in crayon with two panels, blue and white, and a red star imposed on the white panel. The communiqué was addressed to "the people of the State of Quebec." It described the FLQ as "a revolutionary movement composed of volunteers ready to die for the economic independence of Quebec." The authors proclaimed themselves "suicide commandos" and declared that their goal was "complete destruction by systematic sabotage of:

(a) all the symbols and colonial institutions
    of the federal government, in particular
    the RCMP and the armed forces,

(b) all media of the colonial language that
    holds us in contempt,

(c) all enterprises and commercial establish-
    ments which discriminate against the
    Quebec people, which do not use French as
    their first language and which have signs
    in the colonial language,

(d) all factories which discriminate against
    French Canadian workers.

The bombings and communiqué may have struck some as a roar of the Lilliputians, but who could ignore it? On March 12, a signed editorial in *La Presse*, Montreal's largest French-language daily, took stock. Editor-in-chief Gérard Pelletier, friend and confidant of Pierre Trudeau, as well as a future member of Parliament, cabinet minister and ambassador, wondered, "Should we laugh? Should we cry? Should we shrug our shoulders and tell ourselves that it was a ridiculous incident?" Pelletier thought not. He anticipated that there was more to come, noting, "If the first three bombs went off like wet firecrackers . . . there's nothing to say that the next three will be equally inoffensive. If one explosion kills someone, even the most modest night watchman at the most insignificant public building, we're swimming in different waters."

All was quiet for three weeks. Then came April and there were more bombs and attempts at sabotage, and someone was killed. The attacks began on the first of the month. They coincided with the last frantic days of a federal election campaign, the second in the space of ten months. John Diefenbaker's minority Progressive Conservative government had been defeated in the House of Commons. Lester B. Pearson's Liberals were campaigning hard to oust the Tories. Tommy Douglas's New Democrats added an unpredictable element to the mix.

On the morning of April 1, Prime Minister Diefenbaker was scheduled to travel by train from Montreal to Quebec on CN's main line on the south shore of the St. Lawrence. Overnight, saboteurs went to work at the tiny, isolated village of Lemieux, about one hundred kilometres southwest of Quebec. They placed beside the track a bomb made from five sticks of dynamite, then hid behind a concrete building and detonated it. They'd hoped it would do enough damage to cause a derailment. Instead, it merely sliced through the track as cleanly as if it had been severed by a saw, leaving behind a three-foot gap. Otherwise, track and bed were intact. At 3:30 a.m., CN freight train No. 423 rolled through Lemieux without incident, although the engineer reported to the stationmaster, a Mrs. Eva Doucet, that the track had been rough and bumpy.

Later that morning, an anonymous caller phoned the headquarters of the MPD at 750 Bonsecours Street. He warned that a bomb was about to explode at the ten-storey Department of National Revenue building at the corner of Dorchester Boulevard and Bleury Street.[1] It had been placed in an air vent adjacent to the side entrance, after which it slid to the basement, struck a metal grate and blew a hole in the ceiling of the maintenance staff locker room. "We thought it was some kind of April Fool's joke," an officer later told the *Gazette*. "But it certainly wasn't. Someone could have been killed."

The next attack occurred on Saturday, April 6, two days before the federal election. The target was a 360-foot communications tower on the summit of Mount Royal. A CBC technician was inspecting construction at the site around 2 p.m. and spotted a suspicious-looking package placed at the base of the tower. He noticed the word *"Liberté"* and the letters "FLQ" crudely painted in red on the tower and immediately called police, who discovered two twelve-stick bundles of dynamite timed to explode at 5 p.m. The saboteurs intended to topple the tower and cut the radio transmissions of the Montreal police, the provincial police, the fire department and the provincial transport department. The French and English CBC, as well as the city's two private TV stations, relied on the tower as well.

It was the third attack in the space of a week, and the police hadn't made a single arrest. Special measures were required. The criminal investigation bureau of the MPD joined forces with the Quebec provincial force—the Sûreté du Québec (SQ)—and the RCMP and launched an operation to break up the FLQ. At 6 a.m. on April 12—Good Friday—officers executed search warrants at a dozen residences in the city. They seized a grenade, a revolver, several briefcases full of personal papers and ten typewriters, hoping to match the fonts with the type used in FLQ communiqués. They detained and questioned fifteen men between the ages of twenty and thirty.

The operation yielded nothing, but it did produce a backlash. First there was a street protest, and then more bombings. On the evening of Friday, April 19, several dozen students and other young people demonstrated outside the Montreal detachment of the RCMP on Wood Avenue. They burned a Red Ensign, and later that night someone tossed a stick of dynamite at the building. It bounced off a wall, landed in a flower bed and blew out the windows of several offices and those in homes across the street.

Roughly twenty-four hours later, at 11:45 p.m. on April 20, a powerful bomb exploded in a garbage bin behind the five-storey Canadian Army Recruiting Centre at the corner of Sherbrooke Street West and McGill College Avenue. The blast did no damage to the building itself, but shock waves shattered windows five floors up and in nearby apartment buildings. Stunned onlookers quickly gathered in the street. Police and fire vehicles arrived with sirens wailing and lights flashing. In the smoke-filled alley, police officers found the broken, twisted, face-down body of a night watchman—ten feet from where the blast had occurred. It had incinerated most of his clothing and he lay scorched and nearly naked. The victim was Wilfrid O'Neil. He was sixty-five and due to retire in a month. He had arrived for work half an hour early. The building superintendent who was on duty could not say why O'Neil had gone to the rear of the building. "He must have heard a noise," the superintendent said. "There is no other explanation."

Condemnation came swiftly and from all quarters. "It had to happen," André Laurendeau wrote in *Le Devoir*. "One does not play with fire unpunished. This time, they've done it. A man has been killed. . . . These are the fireworks of hate." The perpetrators responded with a communiqué. "During a nocturnal raid against the centre of the Canadian Army in Montreal," it read, "something unforeseen happened, causing the accidental death of an English-speaking person. The press of the collaborators immediately spoke of murder and assassination. Unfortunately, no revolution takes place without bloodshed."

O'Neil's funeral was a modest affair. Two dozen mourners attended. The weekly newspaper *La Patrie* reported that among their surnames were Duguay, Lévesque, Moreau, Leblanc, Cyr and Legouff. The night watchman may have had an Irish surname, but he was more French than Irish. He was a native of Gaspé. His mother was a Duguay and he had married a Lévesque.

O'Neil was just the first casualty in the FLQ's seven-and-a-half-year campaign of terror. There were others, either killed or grievously injured, and they were Walter Leja, Leslie McWilliams, Alfred Pinisch, Thérèse Morin, Jean Corbo, Jeanne d'Arc Saint-Germain, the twenty-seven people wounded in the Montreal Stock Exchange bombing of February 1969, and, lastly, Pierre Laporte.

Robert Côté was on duty the night that Wilfrid O'Neil died. He and another young constable were inspecting the taverns, restaurants and night clubs of Pointe-Saint-Charles to ensure that the proprietors were adhering to the liquor licensing regulations. They returned to their detachment shortly after midnight and immediately learned that there had been another bombing and that a night watchman had been killed.

Radio stations were broadcasting bulletins and the other officers were discussing this latest incident. Amid the back and forth, Maurice Plante, a middle-aged lieutenant, said, "If I were younger I'd apply to join the new bomb squad the department is setting up."

"What bomb squad, lieutenant?" Côté asked.

"Ah, you young guys," Plante replied. "You're all the same. You don't read the memos on the bulletin board. It's a good thing there's a lieutenant here to read them for you. Come here. I'll show you."

The memo stated that training was scheduled to begin on April 29 at the base of the Canadian Ordnance Corps at Sainte-Thérèse, a suburban community some twenty-five kilometres north of Montreal. Detective Sergeant Léo Plouffe would be the head of the new squad. Plouffe was, among other things, the MPD's sole bomb disposal expert.

He was a big, rotund man with a personality to match. Plouffe, a native Montrealer, had joined the police department in 1946 shortly after earning a bachelor of science degree from the Université de Montréal, and by the early 1960s was well known to his fellow citizens. His picture had appeared frequently in the city's newspapers—on page one as often as not. Readers had seen him in the spring of 1963 inspecting the FLQ bomb placed at the foot of the communications tower on Mount Royal, examining the damage to the staff locker room in the basement of the National Revenue building and surveying the carnage in the alley behind the Canadian Army Recruiting Centre.

Bombings were rare in Montreal in the 1950s and early 1960s, and they were usually mob related. But Plouffe found other things to keep himself busy. He was an innovator who applied the emerging science of forensics to crime scene investigations. He had studied forensic medicine, ballistics, hematology, toxicology and bacteriology at the FBI Academy in Quantico, Virginia, and received further instruction from doctors at the Royal Victoria Hospital in Montreal and from scientists at a provincial laboratory on St-Hubert Street.

In 1952, Plouffe convinced the department to create what came to be called the Mobile Laboratory. The mobile lab was a GMC delivery van equipped with the department's first hand-held walkie-talkies, a three-thousand-watt Briggs and Stratton generator, several 110-volt spotlights, two large reflector screens like those used by photographers to light a shoot, and a vacuum cleaner to collect traces of plaster, paint, hair and other matter that could be used as evidence. The lab also carried two sub-machine guns, two 12-gauge shotguns, a .32-calibre Winchester rifle, and a tear-gas kit for flushing out hostage takers. The kit included a 37-millimetre gas gun, gas grenades, gas masks and bulletproof vests.

On May 10, 1963, Plouffe took on a new role as head of the Mobile Emergency Unit, the original name for the bomb squad. He took charge of Robert Côté and several other young officers who had completed their training in bomb disposal at the army base at Sainte-Thérèse, and he needed the extra hands. The FLQ had ratcheted things up in the month of May.

Editorial writers, politicians and labour leaders all denounced the bombings. So too did the president of the RIN. "Not only do we dissociate ourselves completely from these acts, we condemn them," Guy Pouliot said after the first outburst of FLQ violence in early March 1963. "In the two years our movement has existed we have always advocated democratic change and that is the only way to achieve independence."

Blue-collar Montrealers were equally appalled, to judge from a rough sampling of opinion that appeared in the weekly newspaper *Le Petit Journal*. The paper sent a reporter into the street to pose a question: What do you think of the acts of sabotage of the FLQ? The paper published the answers on Sunday, April 21:

"They're a bunch of sick individuals," said truck driver Conrad Barrette.

"They've got no brains and no plan," said taxi driver Conrad Boulanger. "If I were the police and I caught them I'd hang them by the feet from a lamp post without a trial."

Boiler repairman Yvanhoe Houle said, "I'm fifty-three years old and I've never seen anything like it in Canada. It makes me think of the Ku Klux Klan."

The editors were equally perplexed. "Who are they?" the paper asked. "What do they want? When it happens elsewhere—across the sea, near some presidential palace in Latin America, or in the bush of one of the new African states or in the jungles of Malaysia you can tell yourself that Canada is a land of perpetual peace. Bombs, Molotov cocktails and threatening phone calls are not for us." They were the stuff of coups, rebellions and revolutions. None of these had made an unwelcome appearance in the streets of Montreal, but revolutionary violence had, and the perpetrators pressed on.

They planted two bombs on May 3, a Friday, one under the front steps of the Royal Canadian Legion Hall in Saint-Jean-sur-Richelieu, a small town some thirty kilometres south of Montreal. It blew at 1:05 a.m., after members, guests and staff had left for the night. A second bomb was discovered in mid-afternoon of that same day, in the four-teenth-floor washroom of the Provident Building at 507 Place d'Armes, across the square from Notre-Dame Basilica. The target was Solbec Copper Mines, which was embroiled in a labour dispute with its mostly French-Canadian workers. Plouffe was called in to dismantle the device. He ordered the floor evacuated and then went to work. He found the wire between the detonator and the timing device and snipped it at 3:28 p.m.—two minutes before the bomb was set to blow. Afterward, he met the reporters waiting in the lobby and calmly told them, "It was a real live one." A fellow officer guarding the entrances to the four-teenth floor added, "All of us sweated like men in Hell."

Bombs exploded outside military establishments on May 10 and 13. The first was planted in a narrow alley behind the armoury of the Royal Highland Regiment, also known as the Black Watch. This unshakeable structure, with its walls of stone and brick, was located on the east side of Bleury Street, a block or so south of Sherbrooke. Night watchman Ward Thompson completed a round of the exterior at 12:45 a.m., and one minute later he heard a mighty blast. It was audible at the port more than a kilometre south, and it immediately attracted a large crowd. Plouffe arrived and pushed through to inspect the damage. The armoury was unscathed, save for a few broken windows, but the explosion had ripped a three-foot hole in the building opposite and cracked the foundation from front to back.

The attack of May 13 occurred in the dead of night but was, by comparison, a feeble effort. The target was a Royal Canadian Air Force (RCAF) building at 2585 Bates Road in Côte-des-Neiges. By day, one hundred civilians worked there, a mix of aircraft designers, engineers and quality control specialists. Commissionaire Harry Hewson was alone in the building when the bomb exploded, blowing a small hole in one wall.

The authors of these acts had learned an essential lesson about the use of terror. Government institutions and private corporations were not easily intimidated. The bombers would need to hit a softer target. It was time to give the people a taste of the FLQ's brand of revolutionary violence.

They struck on the eve of the Victoria Day weekend, the holiday that honoured a long-dead British monarch and reminded the bombers that they lived in a country dominated by British traditions and values. Their target was Westmount—an exclusive enclave for affluent and wealthy English Montrealers, a place sometimes said to be more British than Britain, and a symbol of English-Canadian financial might and economic domination of Quebec.

Westmount oozed privilege. It stood on the southwestern slope of a mountain, which was adjoined to but smaller than Mount Royal. The splendidly treed, well-tended streets and avenues of Westmount were bathed in sunlight from spring through fall, and shielded from the full force of winter winds by the crest of the mountain. This suburban community, with its small-town charm, arose in the late nineteenth and early twentieth centuries when Montreal was the unrivalled financial and corporate capital of Canada. The city's financiers and corporate chieftains worked by day on rue Saint-Jacques, known in English as St. James Street, and many resided in Westmount. Their homes—the two- and three-storey terraces in Lower Westmount, the semi-detached houses in the heart of the community and the mansions of the upper reaches—lined avenues with staunchly English names: Clarke, Kitchener and Redfern, among others, on the east side of Westmount, where it abutted the municipal limit of the City of Montreal, and Mount Stephen, Strathcona, Lansdowne and Victoria on the west.

In the early morning hours of Friday, May 17, 1963, self-proclaimed patriots of the FLQ prowled Westmount's streets, surreptitiously planting bombs in mailboxes. The bombs were small, crude, improvised explosive devices. Each consisted of three one-half-pound sticks of dynamite, a small battery and a detonator wired to a timer. In each case, the timer was a Dax pocket watch, commonly known as a dollar watch. The first exploded at 2:58 a.m. at the corner of Ste. Catherine Street and Lewis Avenue in Lower Westmount. Four others blew over the next twenty minutes.

So began Westmount's Black Friday, as it came to be known. The chief of police immediately called the city manager, who alerted Colonel Chipman H. Drury, a World War II veteran and the city's forty-five-year-old mayor. Drury set up a command post at police headquarters. He called in the entire seventy-member force and ordered the officers to inspect all eighty-five mailboxes within the municipality. They found six more bombs, although one had been planted just inside the Montreal city limits. Drury also summoned the army's Royal Canadian Engineers, whose armoury was located on Hillside Avenue in Westmount. Some of their personnel were trained explosives and ordnance disposal technicians, and Sergeant-Major Walter Leja was one of them. Leja was a forty-two-year-old Polish immigrant who had grown up in Pointe-Saint-Charles. He had served in World War II and afterward had remained in the armed forces. His physical prowess had earned him the nickname Rocky.

Leja went to work at 10:45 a.m. He disabled one bomb, then another and then moved on to a third at the corner of Westmount and Lansdowne Avenues. Garth Pritchard, a *Gazette* photographer, stood a mere sixty feet from the mailbox while two hundred onlookers watched from behind police barricades a safe distance away. "Sgt-Mjr Leja just strode up and looked into the box," Pritchard later wrote. "It was as though he did it every day." Leja reached for the bomb and then, as Pritchard recounted: "There was a great bang and a piece of the mailbox went flying over my head. There were clouds of black and white smoke."

When the smoke cleared, Leja was lying in the street some twenty feet from the mailbox. His left hand had been blown off. He was bleeding profusely. Police officers applied a tourniquet to halt the blood flow and a doctor emerged from the crowd, but there was nothing he could do. Leja lay there fifteen minutes before an ambulance arrived. He never stirred or uttered a sound. Horrified onlookers—as well as the police—assumed he was dead, or so near death that he couldn't possibly survive. An army chaplain delivered the news to Leja's wife Sophie at the downtown office where she worked. He escorted her home, and she spent three hours discussing funeral arrangements with relatives. Late that afternoon, she received a call from St. Mary's Hospital. Her husband was on the operating table fighting for his life. "Thank God," she exclaimed and fell to her knees. "Thank God!"

Meanwhile, Westmount authorities were still dealing with the mailbox bombs. The mayor and the chief of police decided that the last three should be detonated on site, and they turned to Herman Friede, an employee of Atlas Construction Co. Ltd. Friede was a German immigrant who had dismantled more than two hundred Allied bombs during the war. At each site, he placed two sticks of dynamite next to the bomb. He attached detonating wire and unravelled the wire to a distance of about one hundred feet and connected it to a plunger. An officer with a loudspeaker shouted, "Take cover!" and Friede depressed the plunger. The work went on all afternoon and into the evening. A convoy of police cars, fire trucks, ambulances and army vehicles moved from site to site. Streets were closed. Traffic was rerouted. The last bomb was detonated at 7:30 p.m. and, as one witnessed recalled, pieces of the mailbox landed on a lawn 150 yards away.

By day's end, things were slowly returning to normal in Westmount, and attention turned to the condition of Sergeant-Major Leja. He had spent five hours on the operating table. Surgeons had amputated his left arm below the elbow and operated on his chest and face to repair shattered bones. Throughout the day, the hospital issued bulletins. He was "still fighting" at 3:40 p.m., but "slipping" at 4:15. A surgeon spoke at 4:35 and said, "We don't know whether he'll make it." At 6 p.m. it was "No change." At 11:35 p.m., "He might make it, he might not."

Leja remained unconscious for over three weeks and was permanently disabled. The right side of his body was paralyzed and he could not hear or speak. *La Presse* reported on July 16, 1965, that Leja had been moved to the veteran's hospital in Sainte-Anne-de-Bellevue, a suburb at the far west end of the island, after a two-year stay at St. Mary's Hospital. He spent the better part of three decades at the veteran's hospital and died there in 1993.

The bombings of the spring of 1963 had set nerves on edge in Montreal. Government officials ordered heightened surveillance around federal buildings. Montreal's police director, J. Adrien Robert, had dozens of officers pursuing the FLQ. The department stepped up street patrols, but these measures scarcely reassured Montrealers. The city was rife with rumours about who was behind the attacks. Some blamed Algerian immigrants who had fought in that North African country's long, barbarous, atrocity-filled war to overthrow their French colonial rulers. Others said it was communists trained in Cuba. Conspiracy theorists suspected English Canadians masquerading as separatists to discredit the independence movement.

Jittery Montrealers flooded police headquarters with accounts of suspicious packages, and members of the newly formed bomb squad responded to each report by racing to the scene. Others phoned in false bomb threats, one of which led to the evacuation of the city's central post office on the day of the Westmount bombings.

The mailbox bombs had done more than any previous attack to instill fear. As Alan Edmonds of the *Toronto Star*'s Montreal bureau observed, they made people wonder, "What's next? The luggage locker at the bus station? The waste basket at the rail terminal? The unattended suitcase in the post office? The paper towel box in the washroom? In this city, you find that somewhere in the recesses of your mind is the small fear that it could happen."

Having instilled fear, the bombers grew bolder. They planned to blow up a bridge that spanned the Ottawa River between Hull and the nation's capital. The explosion was to occur on the holiday Monday meant to celebrate Queen Victoria's birthday. Three members of the movement drove to Hull late on Sunday night, but were stopped near the bridge by two inquisitive police officers. This chance encounter spooked the bombers and they returned to Montreal and chose another target—the armoury of the 2nd Technical Regiment of the Royal Canadian Electrical and Mechanical Engineers.

The armoury was located at 1055 St-Grégoire Street in the largely French-Canadian district of Plateau-Mont-Royal. The squat, imposing, two-storey structure occupied an entire city block. An eight-foot fence protected the perimeter of the armoury on three sides, but the west side was open. Four cars belonging to employees of the nearby J.J. Joubert dairy were parked there. The bomb, with its seventy-five sticks of dynamite, was placed beneath one of the vehicles. It exploded at 9 a.m. Shock waves destroyed the autos, blew open a crater four feet wide by two feet deep, tore doors off their hinges in the armoury, bent and twisted the heavy metal grates over the windows, hurled chunks of masonry fifty yards, hurled a tire one hundred and fifty yards, severing power lines in the process, and shook homes for five hundred yards around.

A couple identified only as Mr. and Mrs. Larivée told reporters they were sitting in the kitchen of their house on St-Grégoire Street, some 250 feet from the blast. "Suddenly a flower pot flew off the window sill and just missed my husband's head," said Mrs. Larivée. "I was thrown to the floor." Mr. Larivée added, "I felt as if I was in an old-fashioned barn dance. I was spun around and I heard the crash of a window breaking."

The bombers had been on the loose for three months. They had challenged the capabilities and credibility of the authorities. Police director Robert told the *Star*'s Alan Edmonds that he had been working ten to fourteen hours a day since the bombings began and was getting by on coffee and smoked meat sandwiches. "I have had scores of men on special detail working only on trying to track down the terrorists," he said. But terrorism was new to them and the perpetrators were criminals of a different sort. They were not part of the city's underworld. They did not have criminal records and the police had no informants among them.

However, something had to be done. Robert summoned police chiefs from suburban communities on the island and beyond to a conference on Saturday, May 18. Twenty-four attended. Together they commanded six thousand officers and they promised a coordinated effort to keep their citizens safe and stamp out the FLQ. On the holiday Monday, Premier Jean Lesage held a ninety-minute emergency meeting of his Cabinet in Quebec City. That evening, he delivered a province-wide TV address and announced a fifty-thousand-dollar reward, on top of the ten thousand dollars already offered by the city for information leading to the arrest of those responsible.

In a matter of days, money did for the police what hours and hours and week after week of investigative spadework had failed to do. Someone came forward and started to talk.

---

1.   Dorchester Boulevard was later renamed René-Lévesque Boulevard.

Two

THE FLQ UNMASKED

THE FIRST PUBLIC HINT OF A BREAK in the case occurred on May 28, a Tuesday, when Georges-Émile Lapalme stood in the Legislative Assembly and delivered a brief statement. Lapalme was the attorney general in Jean Lesage's Liberal government. The previous day, he had received a visit from someone whom he described as "a serious person." This individual had revealed information pertaining to the FLQ that he had obtained from an informant and Lapalme had passed on everything to the police.

The first arrests occurred on the evening of Saturday, June 1, followed by more on the Monday, Tuesday and Wednesday. When the police were done, fourteen young men and one woman were in custody. The city's newspapers announced each roundup of suspects in big, bold, triumphant front-page headlines, and police director Robert told a packed news conference that the FLQ had been broken.

But events quickly took an unexpected turn. The police had been roundly criticized as inept in April and May because they had been unable to stop the bombings. Now they were chided for being unnecessarily harsh and authoritarian.

Some of the suspects were locked up in windowless fifth-floor cells at police headquarters at 750 Bonsecours Street in Old Montreal. Others were held at stations around the city. Days passed and no names were released. No charges were laid. None of the suspects were arraigned before a magistrate. Some were denied access to legal counsel, and those who had lawyers were allowed to meet with them only in the presence of a police officer.

Defence lawyers cried foul. Newspapers ran scathing editorials. "The accused is innocent until proven guilty," *The Globe and Mail* declared in its lead editorial of June 5, which *Le Devoir* translated and ran on page one. "This may make police work more difficult than the Gestapo found it, but it makes justice more reliable. It is not possible to preserve democracy and rule of law by using the tools of authoritarianism." Gérard Pelletier of *La Presse* was even harsher. "Where are we living then," he asked rhetorically, "in a totalitarian country or a liberal democracy? . . . With contempt for the law, Montreal officers, under direct order from Chief Robert, have conducted themselves like they were living in the U.S.S.R. or Franco's Spain."

The authorities had chosen to start the legal proceedings against the suspects by holding a coroner's inquest into the death of Wilfrid O'Neil. The detainees were being held as "material witnesses" under warrants issued by coroner Marcel Trahan. The Quebec Coroners Act gave the authorities open-ended powers to arrest and detain. It stipulated that "The coroner, before or during an inquest, has the full power to order the detention, with or without warrant, of every person or of every witness of whom he could have need and who, in the opinion of the coroner, could neglect or refuse to attend the inquest."

The inquest opened Monday, June 10, under a heavy police presence. Cruisers were parked around the building. Officers stood guard at the entrances while others carefully screened the one hundred journalists and one hundred members of the public eager for a first glimpse of the terrorists.

When the coroner had taken his place and the five men of the jury had taken their seats, police brought in the suspects and murmurs rippled through the galleries. Almost everyone was struck by their youthfulness. Most were in their late teens or early twenties and were legally still juveniles since they had not attained the age of majority—then twenty-one. The first witness provided a comical account of his brief stint as a terrorist. Alain Brouillard was short, slight and boyish-looking. He was an eighteen-year-old science student at the Université de Montréal and had turned himself in, accompanied by his father. Brouillard testified that he joined the FLQ at the behest of his childhood friend Raymond Villeneuve, one of the founders. He met Villeneuve and his co-founders, Georges Schoeters and Gabriel Hudon, one evening in late February at a restaurant called the St. Denis Bar-B-Q, named for the street on which it was located. They handed him a questionnaire and he provided his name, address and marital status and answered several questions. Did he own firearms? Did he have a hideout? Was he a fascist, a socialist or a communist? Was he ready to die for the cause? They reviewed his responses, interviewed him and he was in. Brouillard participated in the Molotov cocktail attacks on the armouries on March 8. He also stored twenty-five to thirty sticks of dynamite in his locker at the university until they were required for bomb-making, and that was the extent of his involvement.

Things took a darker turn when Yves Labonté was in the stand. He was the first to testify directly about the bombing that killed Wilfrid O'Neil. He was eighteen and worked as a wholesale grocery messenger boy and remained unflustered while being grilled by Crown attorney Guy Desjardins. Labonté testified that Gabriel Hudon had assembled the bomb in the kitchen of Raymond Villeneuve's apartment. Villeneuve had instructed him to place it at the foot of the Macdonald Monument, which stood in a small park then known as Dominion Square, one block south of Ste-Catherine Street and within a stone's throw of the Sun Life building and the Windsor Hotel. Labonté and an accomplice, Jacques Giroux, arrived at the square lugging the bomb in what he described as a "blue flight bag." There were too many people around, so Giroux suggested they try another location. That led them to the Canadian Army Recruiting Centre. They set the bomb to explode at 10 p.m. and went to a sandwich shop on Metcalfe Street, two blocks away, to await the blast. It failed to occur at the designated time, so they went home. Desjardins asked him why he had done what he did and Labonté replied, "For kicks."

Desjardins, taken aback, asked again, "Are you sure it wasn't for the FLQ, for separatism . . . independence or anything like that?"

"No," Labonté said. "Just for kicks." Then he made another jarring admission. After the bombing, Villeneuve had told him, "It's not all that serious. It was only an Englishman. It would have been much more serious if it had been a French Canadian."

The Crown called Jacques Giroux, an unemployed photographer. Giroux was the first of five witnesses who either refused outright to testify or would not co-operate fully. Trahan got around the problem by allowing police officers to read statements the suspects had given investigators, though he refused to allow defence lawyers to cross-examine witnesses for the Crown. Giroux's statement corroborated Labonté's account of the April 20 bombing. He told police he went home before the time the blast occurred. He slept in on Sunday morning and got up just in time to attend 11:30 Mass. "Coming out of the church," he said, "I picked up a newspaper and read that a man had been killed in the explosion."

Villeneuve and Hudon also refused to testify, but their statements provided the court with an account of why they had formed the FLQ, why the violence had escalated quickly and how they were able to obtain so much dynamite. Villeneuve was just nineteen, but he was tall and athletically built, and looked and behaved beyond his years. He had attended the École secondaire Saint-Stanislas and had been such a promising student that one of his teachers, a Brother Gabriel, had provided a character reference. "I commend him for his good behaviour, his seriousness and his general attitude," he had written.

Villeneuve had failed chemistry in his final year and was ineligible to go on to college without retaking the course, and so was working part time in a bakery. But he was no average youth trying to sort out his life. He was full of ideas for changing Quebec and he believed that the best way to do it was through revolutionary action. He became a member of the RIN and its underground offshoot, the Réseau de résistance, a group formed to commit minor acts of sabotage such as painting slogans on federal buildings and stealing Canadian flags.

Hudon had recently turned twenty-one and was therefore legally an adult. He had quit school in grade eleven and had worked as a delivery boy and cashier while attending a technical school in the evenings to train as a draftsman. He had been working as a designer for an aircraft parts manufacturer for two years. He had also been a member of the RIN and the Réseau de résistance, but had almost immediately become disillusioned with both. He told police that members of the Réseau de résistance "couldn't do much more than paint." As for the RIN, "I kept thinking they were a bunch of wet hens and kept telling the guys that Quebec independence would only be achieved through violence."

The bombings had begun after the two youths and their collaborators discovered how easy it was to obtain dynamite. The city was building two subway lines, and construction companies could not bore through the solid rock subsurface. They had to blast. The excavations for the future Metro were poorly lit, poorly fenced and poorly guarded, usually by a lone and elderly night watchman. Furthermore, the province's decades-old regulations for the storage and handling of dynamite were extraordinarily lax. The material was generally kept in fire-engine-red boxes marked—in large, white letters—EXPLOSIFS.

On one occasion, they had lowered a ten-year-old boy into an excavation to steal explosives. Villeneuve admitted that he had stolen some too. He had helped assemble the bomb that killed O'Neil and had also placed the bomb in the fourteenth-floor washroom of the Provident Building, adjacent to the head office of Solbec Copper Mines. Hudon acknowledged the theft of dynamite from a construction site. He had come across four cases and took two of them containing 323 sticks and placed them in a bag, then hailed a taxi to make his getaway.

Hudon and Villenueve had met a fellow traveller in separatist circles who was equally restless and eager to take a more radical path to independence. He was older, worldly by comparison and had been inspired by Fidel Castro and the Cuban Revolution. His name was Georges Schoeters. He was thirty-three, a native of Antwerp, Belgium, and the illegitimate son of a Flemish mother and a Balkan diplomat. He never met his father and seldom saw his mother, who had become the mistress of a wealthy man and travelled frequently, and young Georges spent part of his youth in an orphanage. He had been a messenger for the Belgian resistance during World War II, claimed to have spent two years in a Gestapo internment camp, and after the war lived for a time in a community of Christian brothers.

In mid-1951, Schoeters left Belgium. He sailed from Rotterdam, landed in New York and almost immediately left for Montreal. There, he boarded with a large, French-speaking family and for the first time experienced a real home. He took a number of odd jobs, moved to Vancouver for a year to learn English, returned to Montreal, decided to become an electrician and spent a year learning the trade. Then he changed direction. He enrolled at the Université de Montréal, studied sociology and economics, became a Canadian citizen and, on December 7, 1957, he married. He completed his degree in the spring of 1959 and, coincidentally, his life took another turn.

On April 26, Fidel Castro visited Montreal. Hundreds of Montrealers greeted him at the airport, Mayor Sarto Fournier presented him with the keys to the city and reporters eagerly interviewed him. That evening, Castro addressed an audience of admiring students at the Université de Montréal and concluded his speech by extending an invitation to visit Cuba. Schoeters was among the crowd. He was also among a delegation of agronomy students who visited the Caribbean island that summer at the invitation of the National Institute for Agrarian Reform, the body charged with turning large private landholdings into state-owned collectives. The students met leading figures in the new government and toured agricultural co-operatives.

Schoeters paid a second visit to Cuba in 1960, again as a guest of a state agency. He returned deeply impressed and was inevitably attracted to the emerging movement for Quebec independence, but soon migrated to the radical fringes. There, he encountered Villeneuve and Hudon and together the three of them formed the FLQ.

A reporter covering the coroner's inquest described Schoeters as a "nervous, pudgy little man with thick-rimmed glasses," adding that he was wearing a dark-blue shirt and a grey sports coat and clearly hadn't shaved in several days. And, upon stepping into the witness box, Schoeters told the Crown attorney, "I'm weak, upset and dirty. I've been in a cell for eight days and I haven't been permitted to wash."

Schoeters proved to be a slightly more co-operative witness than his youthful collaborators. Desjardins asked about the objectives of the FLQ. "It was formed for the purpose of stimulating action to achieve the independence of Quebec," Schoeters replied. "We saw it as best achieved by extraordinary actions."

"Was there someone in the organization who specialized in making the bombs?" Desjardins asked.

"Ah, yes," Schoeters replied. "There was obviously someone who knew how to make them and I saw some of them being made. I had three of them in my house for three days."

He also acknowledged storing three hundred sticks of dynamite in his home, which prompted Desjardins to ask, "In which part of the house did you store the dynamite?"

Schoeters: "In the living room."

Desjardins: "Do you live in a big house?"

Schoeters: "I believe it's called a three-and-a-half-room."

Desjardins: "You kept dynamite in the living room? Don't you have two children?"

Schoeters: "Please don't refer to my children. They were quite safe. There was a lot of dynamite but no detonator caps."

Desjardins: "What was the function of Hudon in the FLQ operations? Was it Hudon who made the bombs in your presence?"

Schoeters: "I don't wish to reply."

Trahan interjected: "You are obliged to reply."

At this, Schoeters became defiant. He stood, grabbed the microphone and said, "In the name of the FLQ and Quebec's independence, I regret that I am unable to testify any further."

Vigorous applause erupted in the galleries. Police officers immediately removed the demonstrators, and Trahan turned to Schoeters and said, "I declare you in contempt and sentence you to one month in jail."

Trahan had already sentenced Villeneuve, Hudon and Giroux to a month, and he imposed the same penalty on a fifth reluctant witness, Richard Bizier, an eighteen-year-old elevator operator at the Queen Elizabeth Hotel.

Bizier had initially been co-operative. He told Crown attorney Jean Bienvenue that one day in early April he, Villeneuve and Hudon had gone to the summit of Mount Royal to look for potential targets. The communications tower caught the attention of his companions, but Bizier testified he was surprised to learn later, through the newspapers, that police had discovered two bombs at the base.

"I never thought they'd do anything to the tower," he told Bienvenue. "French Canadians are tied very closely to their televisions. I was sure they wouldn't touch a thing like that."

Bienvenue asked if he knew where they had obtained the dynamite. Defence lawyer Raymond Daoust then sprang to his feet and said, "You don't have to answer that if you don't want to."

Trahan and Daoust then had a sharp exchange. Things became more heated when another defence lawyer, Guy Guérin, addressed the coroner. Bienvenue interrupted and asked Trahan to order them both out, assisted by the police if necessary. Daoust was incensed: "I can't believe that a representative of the Attorney General's office, a lawyer, would have sought assistance by police to have a fellow lawyer ejected from a courtroom." At that, he gathered his papers and left, accompanied by Guérin.

Bizier refused to answer any more questions without his lawyer present, and Trahan cited him for contempt, at which point Bienvenue rose and said, "The Crown does not wish to establish a record for the number of persons cited for contempt of court at an inquest. We consider enough evidence has been provided members of the jury so that they can render a verdict." Trahan agreed and declared, "This inquest is over."

It was 4:20 p.m., Wednesday, June 12. The number of suspects had now grown to twenty-one since police had made six more arrests while the inquest was in progress. The one woman among them was Jeanne Schoeters, who had been a reluctant participant in some of her husband's activities. The five-man jury deliberated for thirty-five minutes. Upon returning, the foreman told Trahan, "There is one dissenting vote. Ours is a majority verdict. We hold all twenty-one persons named criminally responsible for the O'Neil death."

The inquest did little to advance the cause of justice. Nine defence lawyers had applied to the Quebec Superior Court for an injunction to halt the proceedings, and they listed thirty-three grounds to support their position. The hearing produced another unintended consequence. It generated sympathy and support for the suspects. Eighty-four writers, comedians, painters, actors and filmmakers signed and sent a petition to Attorney General Lapalme condemning "certain odious and manifestly unjustifiable actions on the part of the police and others in authority."

And hours after the jury delivered its verdict, 350 people packed a hall in Montreal and enthusiastically greeted a rousing speech by Pierre Bourgault, a fiery orator, a leading member of the RIN and the editor of the organization's newspaper, *l'Indepéndance*. "Today, there are children in prison," Bourgault said. "Several were members of RIN. We know it. We accept it and we will defend them." He argued that others shared responsibility for FLQ violence: French Canadians who had complacently accepted domination and exploitation; the Lesage Liberals, who had aroused nationalist fervour during the election campaign of 1960 but had done nothing in government to fulfill the public aspirations; and those in the independence movement. "We haven't done enough and the proof is that some young people, some children have lost confidence in us," Bourgault bellowed. "We haven't worked hard enough for independence." Members of the audience repeatedly interrupted him with applause and shouts of approval, and on the way out they contributed $450 toward a defence fund for the suspects. And the legal proceedings were about to begin in earnest.

The suspects were back in court forty-eight hours after the inquest ended—this time to be arraigned on charges ranging from theft to murder. Their numbers had been pared back to seventeen since Crown prosecutors had found no grounds to proceed against four of those detained. Judge Émile Trottier opened the hearing at 5 p.m. on June 14. Two clerks of the court read the charges. It took them two hours and forty minutes. The Crown had laid 165 charges—ninety of them against four individuals—Georges Schoeters, Gabriel Hudon, Raymond Villeneuve and Jacques Giroux, all of whom, along with Yves Labonté, were charged with non-capital murder in the death of Wilfrid O'Neil.

Several of the accused applied for bail, notably Jeanne Schoeters, who had been held since early June. She was charged with being a party to the May 13 bombing at the RCAF Technical Services Unit on Bates Road, a ten-minute walk from the tiny apartment she shared with her husband and their two children, a preschooler and an infant of seven months. She told Judge Trottier that her parents were looking after the youngsters, and also said that she had tried on many occasions to discourage her husband from participating in terrorist activities. Trottier initially denied her request for bail, but agreed to release her on July 5 after an artist named John H. Spendlove posted bail of ten thousand dollars. Spendlove lived on Dorchester Boulevard in Westmount, and his home had been damaged slightly in the mailbox bombings.

The others remained in custody to await the start of the preliminary hearings, which began immediately and lasted until mid-August, due in part to the conduct of some of the accused. Schoeters, Hudon, Villeneuve and Giroux all refused to testify about the bombing that led to the death of Wilfrid O'Neil, while three of the five suspects in the Westmount mailbox bombings—Denis Lamoureux, Mario Bachand and François Gagnon—also refused to co-operate.

Giroux was the first hostile witness to take the stand. Crown prosecutor Gabriel Lapointe asked, "Does FLQ mean anything to you?"

Giroux replied, "My political principles forbid me to testify here."

Trottier told him, "Your political principles do not constitute any reason in law for interfering with the course of justice."

"They do form a reason for me," he replied.

Trottier read the section of the Canada Evidence Act that made it an offence to refuse to answer questions.

"Just the same," Giroux said, "I refuse to testify because of my political principles."

"Did someone give you that fine phrase which has no validity here?" Trottier said.

"It's valid for me and I refuse to testify," Giroux said.

Hudon proved to be the most defiant. When they arrested him, police found fifty sticks of dynamite and parts for two bombs concealed in a shed behind the family home. Crown prosecutor Lapointe called Hudon as a witness three times. Each time, he refused to testify, at one point protesting, "I would answer all the questions if I were considered a political prisoner, but here I am treated like a common criminal."

Lapointe later showed him a statement he had given to police and signed. The prosecutor asked him to confirm his signature.

"I refuse to look at it and if you leave it in front of me I'll tear it up," Hudon said.

"Tear it up," Lapointe said. The tall, well-dressed young man slowly and methodically tore it up. "Did you tear it up because you were ashamed of it?" Lapointe asked.

"No," Hudon replied, "because you were bothering me with your questions about it."

Lapointe asked about the structure of the FLQ. Hudon replied, "If you want to amuse yourself, keep asking questions. I'll refuse to answer them."

Judge Trottier was perplexed by François Gagnon's refusal to testify. Gagnon was implicated in the Westmount mailbox bombings. He was nineteen, a student and the son of a prominent Outremont lawyer who later became a judge. "You surprise me," Trottier told Gagnon. "You who have been so close to the law since the day you were born."

"I don't think it's right for me to testify . . . to betray my comrades," he said.

Two of Gagnon's comrades did testify. Gilles Pruneau was nineteen, a clerk and a student. He said that Denis Lamoureux, a twenty-year-old student at a classical college, had planned the Westmount operation. Pruneau met Lamoureux after night classes on May 14 and Lamoureux provided him with forty sticks of dynamite, Dax pocket watches, detonators and other materials. Pruneau testified that he rented a room at the Diplomat Motel in the city's east end. There, he assembled five bombs on the evening of May 14 and five more the following night, although he admitted he had no expertise in bomb-making and relied on what he had learned in grade seven science about electrical circuits.

Each bomb consisted of three one-half-pound sticks of dynamite, a detonating device, a battery and a pocket watch. Pruneau explained that he began by securing the dynamite with tape, then attached a detonator to the dynamite. He fastened one end of a wire to the detonator and the other to one of the terminals of a battery. Next, he removed the plastic face from the pocket watch and pierced a tiny hole in it. He snipped off the minute hand, then replaced the face—ensuring that the hole was aligned with the hour at which the explosion was to occur. Then he took a second wire, attached one end to the battery and inserted the other end into the face of the clock. When the hour hand touched the wire, the circuit was complete. A jolt of electricity would hit the detonator and cause an explosion.

Pruneau and Lamoureux had arranged to meet on Sherbrooke Street

East on the evening of the bombings. Lamoureux and three other young men arrived in a small European car driven by Gagnon, who had borrowed it from his father. Pruneau handed Lamoureux five bombs, each concealed in a small, unaddressed package, but there was no room for him in the vehicle. Instead, he took a bus to Westmount and walked through the community, depositing the bombs in designated mailboxes.

"How did you put the bombs in the mailboxes?" a lawyer representing Lamoureux asked. "Did you have a key?"

"No," Pruneau replied. "I just dropped them in through the regular opening."

"Did you not think they might explode immediately?" the lawyer asked.

"I thought of that minor problem," said Pruneau. "I put cardboard between the parts of the bombs and around the bombs to avoid the risk of an immediate explosion."

Pierre Schneider was the second participant who was willing to testify. He was eighteen and a messenger boy at Radio-Canada. Schneider, Gagnon and Lamoureux had worked for the RIN, mainly plastering small placards, emblazoned with separatist slogans, on store windows, bus stops and telephone poles. They had joined the Réseau de résistance and had painted similar slogans on monuments in Montreal honouring English-speaking politicians and military figures. Then they set out on a more radical course.

Crown Attorney Jacques Bellemare asked, "What was the immediate result you were looking for when you placed bombs in mailboxes?"

"To make lots of noise," Schneider replied.

Despite the distractions, Judge Trottier heard enough evidence to order all of the accused to stand trial. He also released several of them on bail, and one—Richard Bizier—promptly fled. He turned up on the French islands of Saint-Pierre and Miquelon in the Gulf of St. Lawrence and declared that he was seeking political asylum.

Bizier had no legitimate claim and was promptly sent back to Montreal. On Monday, October 7, he appeared before Mr. Justice Maurice Cousineau of the Court of Queen's Bench. Eleven other FLQ defendants were also in court that day, although the Crown withdrew the charges against one of them. The proceedings against the others concluded quickly. The Crown had agreed to reduce or withdraw some of the charges and the defendants had agreed in advance to plead guilty to those left standing. The defendants were called one by one. A clerk of the court read the indictments then asked, "How do you plead?" In each case, the response was "Guilty," though that wasn't the end of it for some.

Several defendants read the same prepared speech: "As a member of the FLQ, I do not recognize the foreign law under which I am accused. However, my lawyers advised me that the law applies in this case. I acknowledge the facts mentioned in the indictment. It is true that I committed these acts, but I committed them because I believe and still believe that this is the only approach that can free the people of Quebec from the colonial domination and the yoke that weighs upon them."

Hudon and Villeneuve were sentenced to twelve years each on charges of manslaughter in the death of Wilfrid O'Neil. Jacques Giroux received six years and Yves Labonté four for their roles in that tragic incident. The Crown withdrew the charge of murder against Georges Schoeters, but he pleaded guilty to five other charges and got ten years. Two of the Westmount bombers were also sentenced, Denis Lamoureux to four years and François Gagnon three. Bizier received six months for his part in the bombing of the RCAF building, which caused $544 damage, and Jeanne Schoeters was handed a suspended sentence.

Four defendants—Gilles Pruneau, Mario Bachand, Pierre Schneider and Roger Tétrault—were not in court that day. They had been granted bail but had fled, and one distraught mother publicly urged her son to return. Muriel Tétrault showed up in the newsroom of the *Gazette* with an impassioned, handwritten note to her son and told a reporter, "I don't know whatever possessed Roger and his friends to fail to show up in court. It's all so much unlike Roger to do a thing like that. I can't explain it even to myself."

Tétrault's whereabouts soon became known. He was arrested in Boston on Thursday, October 10, along with Bachand and Schneider. Tétrault had US$640 on him. His companions had between two and three thousand French francs and said they were headed for Mexico. Bachand and Schneider agreed to return to Montreal. Tétrault applied for political asylum, which delayed his return by several weeks. He was eventually sentenced to four years for his part in the spring bombing campaign. Bachand received the same sentence. Schneider got three years.

Pruneau, meanwhile, escaped to Paris and stayed there for many years. The others served their sentences, or portions of them, and were released one by one in the coming months and years. Villeneuve was paroled on September 14, 1967, so he could attend the École des hautes études commerciales at the Université de Montréal. Hudon was granted parole three months later, in December 1967.

Prison changed for the better some of the young men involved in the first wave of FLQ terrorism. Others, when released, took up where they had left off. In 1969, Hudon and his younger brother Robert formed a so-called fundraising operation—two cells that robbed banks to come up with the money to finance the FLQ. He led the group that scouted out locations while Robert and several others carried out the robberies. They were responsible for nineteen hold-ups in Montreal and a dozen outside the city that netted in total about twenty-five thousand dollars. The Hudon brothers and two accomplices were arrested in late May. Police did not have enough evidence to link Gabriel Hudon directly to the robberies, but he was convicted of car theft. He was sentenced to five years on that charge and was ordered to finish serving his twelve-year sentence for manslaughter.

As for Villeneuve, he eventually abandoned his studies, joined the RIN and, with Pierre Bourgault's blessing, became president of the organization's youth wing. He left for Cuba in late 1968, stayed there for eighteen months, then moved to France and from there to Algeria. Villeneuve lived abroad until 1984. He joined the Parti Québécois after returning and worked on the party's election campaigns, but he quit after the 1995 referendum on sovereignty and formed the Mouvement de libération nationale de Québec. As leader, he commanded a youthful following and espoused radical views that bordered on hate crime. At one rally, he threatened to use commandos to attack his opponents, namely anglophones who argued that Quebec could be partitioned after a positive vote on sovereignty. During an appearance on a French-language morning talk show, he singled out—by name—a McGill University law professor and the founder of the anglophone rights Equality Party and said, "It can happen to them—bombs, but perhaps there are also simpler means, like Molotov cocktails."

As for Schoeters, he was released from prison in December 1967 on the condition that he leave Canada, and he was advised that he would be compelled to complete his sentence if he returned. Canadian authorities put him on a plane to Belgium on Christmas Day. Schoeters's wife had had their marriage annulled while he was in prison and he hadn't had a chance to say goodbye to his children. By February 1968, he had left Belgium for Switzerland. He applied for political asylum there, but was turned down and ordered to leave the country. His next stop was Paris, where he was granted a three-month visa but not allowed to work. Schoeters then moved on to Stockholm, where he worked for a time in the post office. He died there in March 1994, having had one brief and not very successful reunion with his daughter.

Three

INSIDE THE MOVEMENT

BY THE END OF OCTOBER 1963, Georges Schoeters, Raymond Villeneuve and Gabriel Hudon were serving their sentences in federal penitentiaries, but by then three things had happened to ensure that the movement they founded would survive. Another wave of terror had begun. Two accounts of the FLQ had been published. And the first typewritten, crudely produced issue of *La Cognée*—a journal created to promote independence through revolutionary action—had been printed and circulated to a select audience of like-minded readers.

The second wave of terror began at about 1:45 a.m. on August 22, 1963, when a bomb exploded on the 1.5-kilometre-long railway bridge that crossed the St. Lawrence from Lasalle to the Mohawk community of Kahnawake. The blast occurred atop a two-hundred-foot tower. The explosion had ripped into the huge engine and lift mechanism that raised a section of the bridge spanning the shipping channel on the St. Lawrence Seaway. The bombers had hoped to shut down the Seaway—a vital commercial artery—at one of the busiest times of the shipping season. They would have succeeded had the span been at rest at bridge level when the bomb exploded. At that moment, a grain carrier was travelling upriver and the span was raised and it would remain there several weeks until repairs were complete. Vehicle traffic was disrupted, but ships could come and go.

Over the next few days, there were four arson attacks, one at the armoury of the Régiment de Maisonneuve on Craig Street, a second at the Fusiliers Mont Royal on Pine Avenue, another at a Royal Canadian Legion Hall in Laval West and a fourth at a CN property on Île Bigras. Then, on September 26, a Thursday, five young men robbed the Royal Bank at 5301 Sherbrooke Street West. One drove the getaway car. One served as lookout. Three others entered the branch, at least one of them brandishing a gun. They placed two bombs at the front door and fired a warning shot. They demanded money, the terrified tellers complied immediately and the bandits fled in a blue Plymouth Valiant.

Police stopped the car on Maplewood Avenue in Outremont, on the north side of Mount Royal, about five kilometres from the scene of the crime. There were by then only two occupants, a passenger named Claude Soulières and the driver Jules Duchastel. The loot—$6,929— was still in the car. Soulières and Duchastel, both twenty, came from opposite ends of the social spectrum. Soulières had quit school at age fifteen. He had worked mostly as a labourer and lived in the poorer east end of the city. Duchastel lived in Outremont, a leafy enclave of spacious, comfortable homes for affluent and wealthy francophones, and he was studying philosophy at the Jesuit College of Sainte-Marie.

During a court appearance, Duchastel's lawyer described him as "a young man from a good family . . . studying at a fine school." The presiding judge, Roger Ouimet, needed no introduction. "I have been a friend of your family for a long time," Ouimet told Duchastel. "It is an honourable family and I will continue to be their friend. I was a very close friend of your father. I articled as a student in the law office of your great-uncles. My son knows you since you went to school together. How painful it is to realize the dangers to which today's youth are exposed. They are led into acts of violence by unscrupulous people with a grudge against authority, who defy the law and who have no regard for what is good in our society." Then he sentenced Duchastel, as well as his accomplice, to two years in prison.

Meanwhile, as this case was unfolding, the first accounts of the movement were being published. *La Véritable Histoire du FLQ* was an insider's view. The writer, Claude Savoie, was an aspiring journalist and a former classmate of the Westmount bombers Denis Lamoureux, Pierre Schneider and François Gagnon. He had frequented their circles in the spring of 1963 and was detained briefly in the police roundup of early June. According to Savoie, the founders and their ardent followers believed that "the Canadian confederation had annihilated the Quebec people, their language, their traditions, their culture and their economy." The goal of the first wave of terror was to awaken the populace. Bombs were the chosen means and they were meant to be the spark that unleashed a revolution. The revolution would lead to independence and independence would transform Quebec politically, economically and socially and would, in addition, "destroy the foreign presence among us."

Bernard Smith was the author of a second, slender volume, entitled *Les Résistants du FLQ*. Smith was a teacher. He lived in Hull and was a founding member of the RIN. Smith disapproved of terror and violence, but he shared the aspirations of the young people who resorted to it, and understood their frustrations. "One can put one's mind at ease by saying that the terrorists are a bunch of crazies," Smith wrote. "But it remains no less true that intelligent and generous young men—like some members of the first wave of the FLQ—will opt for this way if other ways seem closed. And don't tell them: You will have your turn . . . in twenty years!! A true emancipation of the French-Canadian nation is the only solution to the problem of terrorism."

There was no immediate prospect of that happening. Therefore, the struggle had to continue and it would be waged with guns, bombs and words. Guns stolen in brazen robberies of military armouries. Bombs aimed at an array of perceived enemies. And words that appeared in the pages of the FLQ's journal *La Cognée*.

The word *cognée* means axe, specifically one used to fell trees. The journal's name was taken from the following lines, which appeared in

Les Insolences du Frère Untel, a series of essays published in August 1960 that attacked Quebec's education system, the degradation of the French language and the subservience of French-speaking Quebeckers: "The axe! We must work with the axe! This is no time for being subtle."[1]

Sixty-four issues of *La Cognée* appeared between October 1963 and January 1967. Initially the journal was a monthly, but beginning in March 1964 it was published on the fifteen and thirtieth of each month. It usually ran to eight pages, and was produced clandestinely and printed on mimeograph machines. Three individuals wrote most of the copy and published the journal, under the pseudonyms Paul Lemoyne, Paul-André Gauthier and Louis Nadeau. They launched the inaugural issue with a summons to battle. "We will look for the Hudons, the Villeneuves, the Schoeters, the Gagnons and others," they wrote. "The great struggle will call on all partisans." Their enemies were "the colonial overlords in Ottawa and their lackeys in Quebec" and they promised, "We will sweep them away with revolutionary action."

That first edition ended with a series of rousing declarations: "*La Cognée* will teach patriots to fear no more, to proclaim their thirst for justice and liberty. *La Cognée* will strike the enemy where they hide— behind the screens and phantoms of biculturalism and federalism. On the day of independence, the entire people will acclaim the patriots who have liberated their homeland."

The triumvirate behind *La Cognée* detested federalism and consistently denounced it in all its manifestations. They described a federal–provincial conference held in the fall of 1963 as "a meeting of the seigneur and his vassals" and concluded that such gatherings were nothing more than "a parody of democracy." A federal defence contract that went to a British firm instead of a Quebec company was "a new betrayal" and proved yet again that "the humiliation of our leaders is inevitable."

Quebeckers, urban and rural, were the poor cousins of Confederation. In an article entitled "The Bare Minimum," Nadeau argued that the standard of living of the average Quebecker was 28 percent lower than that of Canadians in Ontario and 50 percent below the American average. Farmers were even worse off. They earned, on average, $1,550 annually or about $30 a week. To supplement their farm income, many worked in the winter as loggers for private, foreign companies.

Worse still were the enemies within. They fell into two categories—the Quebec bourgeoisie who had profited by aligning themselves with English commercial interests, and the collaborators in the media and the universities who believed that Quebec and Canada could be reconciled.

There was, in the minds of the young men behind *La Cognée*, only one conclusion. "We are prisoners living in the shackles of confederation and can never exercise our rights . . . ," they wrote. "That is why we are taking up arms. Only revolutionary action will permit us to effect the complete transformation necessary for the full flowering of the Quebec nation."

The creators of *La Cognée* dispensed practical advice for making a revolution. One article suggested that clusters of three to ten individuals, comprising trusted friends or companions, form cells to engage in revolutionary activity. Secrecy was of the utmost importance. Members of a cell must be kept informed day by day, and even hour by hour, of any imminent action.

La Cognée was loaded with inflammatory rhetoric, yet the authors also preached caution. Quebec was in a pre-revolutionary phase. Quebeckers were only just awakening to their long history as an exploited and colonized people. They weren't ready to reject the status quo and embrace liberation. The movement wasn't strong enough to mount an insurrection.

The *La Cognée* network recommended agitation and propaganda and, only occasionally, spectacular actions. Lemoyne argued that the movement needed a central committee to organize and direct the work of the cells. "The pre-revolutionary phase is the most delicate and difficult," he wrote. "Before engaging in open struggle, it is necessary to assemble systematically a revolutionary machine. It leads us to condemn, formally, adventurism and romanticism."

That may have been sound advice, but by the time it was printed—on April 15, 1964—a new group calling itself the Armée de libération du

Québec (ALQ) had staged several spectacular actions over the previous six months.

Paul Boulianne came face to face with heavily armed members of the ALQ shortly before 8 a.m. on Thursday, January 30, 1964. Boulianne was sixty years old and was the night watchman at the armoury of the Fusiliers Mont Royal at the corner of Pine Avenue and Henri Julien Street. He had just finished another night's work and had retired to the basement to have a coffee and a cigar and await the arrival of the trades-men and day labourers employed at the armoury. After lighting his cigar and taking a sip of coffee, he heard footsteps and someone calling him by name from the top of the stairs. "When I came up from the cellar," he later told reporters, "I saw them standing above me with guns pointing at me. They tied me up and put me back in the cellar."

Then the tradesmen and day labourers began arriving. There were eight all told and each received a similar welcome. "I got there about eight o'clock," Roger Perrault recalled. "As I approached the door some-one opened it and shoved a sawed-off rifle into my ribs and told me to get inside. I thought it was a joke. At that moment another young man stuck a gun into my left side. I realized they weren't fooling." They hus-tled Perrault to the basement, where they bound his hands, blindfolded him and left him with the others. These gun-toting intruders were after weapons and ammunition. They broke open cabinets and loaded everything into a red panel van parked inside the armoury, and they worked quickly. The whole operation took less than thirty minutes.

The men in the basement spent an hour freeing themselves and immediately called the police, but they hardly assisted the investigation. All agreed that the perpetrators spoke very good French, and therefore were likely well educated, and that they were polite. They estimated that there were fifteen participants, but otherwise provided conflicting accounts of the robbery. Furthermore, no one in the neighbourhood had observed anything suspicious or unusual. "It was a real good job," one investigator commented. "To go into an armoury with fifteen people and drive out with a load of weapons and not be noticed by anyone . . . it's just amazing . . . almost unbelievable."

The thieves had made off with enough firepower to equip an infantry company, according to one officer, and the haul included:

- fifty-nine Belgian FN semi-automatic rifles, the standard NATO infantry weapon
- thirty 9-millimetre Sten machine guns, only five with breech blocks, meaning that they could be fired
- four .303-calibre Bren machine guns, three with breech blocks
- four field mortars, though no mortar bombs
- three bazookas, or shoulder-mounted rocket launchers, minus the rockets
- two Browning machine guns
- eleven walkie talkies
- 2,344 .303-calibre bullets, 1,922 7.6-millimetre bullets for the FN rifles, and 13,000 .22-calibre bullets.

Within minutes of the robbery, anonymous callers phoned the newspapers, as well as the radio and TV stations, and attributed the heist to the Comité révolutionnaire du Québec. Otherwise, this new group of terrorists remained silent. They issued no communiqués and made no declarations to explain their motives.

The police reconstituted the Combined Anti-Terror Squad (CATS), which had been formed to deal with the first wave of FLQ violence in the spring of 1963, and Montreal police director J. Adrien Robert promised that some seventy officers from his department, the SQ and the RCMP would spare no effort to arrest the bandits. The Department of National Defence sent troops from the Royal 27th Regiment in Valcartier to guard Montreal's armouries, and the minister of defence, Paul Hellyer, set up a special commission to investigate all aspects of security related to national defence property and establishments across the country.

Three weeks passed and CATS made no arrests. Then the ALQ struck again, this time on Thursday, February 20, just hours before the defence department's special commission on military security submitted its report to the minister.

Octave Heppel, World War II veteran and, at age sixty-two, a custodian on the cusp of retirement, came face to face with a gun-wielding gang from the ALQ at 7:50 a.m. on that cold, snowbound Thursday.

Heppel worked at the armoury of the 62nd Field Regiment, Royal Canadian Artillery, in Shawinigan, a small industrial town 130 kilometres northeast of Montreal. He was the first to arrive on the day of the raid. "I let myself in by the front door and locked it behind me as I usually do," Heppel later recounted. "There didn't seem to be anything wrong and I went into the cloakroom to hang up my jacket. When I came out I saw a revolver pointed at my head. I noticed at least five young men . . . and all were armed." They asked where the firing pins were kept. He said he didn't know. Then they marched him at gunpoint down to the basement and into the washroom. They bound his hands behind his back and tied them securely to the exposed pipes that formed part of the plumbing. One young man removed Heppel's glasses. Another blindfolded him.

Two officers of the regiment arrived separately, shortly after 9 a.m., and the bandits ordered one, then the other, to the basement and bound and blindfolded them, and then they went on a rampage. They defaced portraits of the Queen, smashed telephones, broke locks on the doors, emptied desk drawers and filing cabinets, and loaded weapons onto a truck parked behind the armoury. They stole thirty-three Belgian FN 7.62-millimetre semi-automatic rifles and three 9-millimetre pistols, though the firing pins had been removed. They grabbed walkie-talkies and a Gestetner printing machine and they painted "ALQ" in large, black letters in three different places.

The police concluded that the gang had entered the building between 3:00 and 3:30 a.m. by breaking a window and unlatching a door. Major-General Frank Fleury, commander of the Canadian Army's Quebec region, ordered a court of inquiry to investigate the robbery, and the following day Defence Minister Hellyer rose in the House of Commons and announced new security measures at all seventy-five armouries in Quebec, as well as those in Ontario and New Brunswick that were close to the Quebec border. Hellyer ordered the removal of all portable arms and instructed the department to post at least one guard twenty-four hours a day at all reserve establishments. Each day for the next week, Hellyer had to defend the measures in the House during Question Period. He had to endure opposition barbs and ridicule. However, the heightened security worked. The raids on the armouries stopped.

But the various police investigations were stalled. The ALQ was still on the loose and would continue to operate until early April, following a bank robbery in Mont-Rolland, a tiny community in the Laurentians, eighty kilometres north of Montreal.

The robbery occurred at the Banque Canadienne Nationale. Five men burst in wearing white hoods and wielding revolvers and sub-machine guns. They fled with five thousand dollars and the bank called the SQ. The police set up several roadblocks, and the officers posted on a back road between Mont-Rolland and Rawdon stopped a white, late-model Pontiac. There were three occupants. The officers searched the car, the driver and his two male passengers and found one small object that aroused suspicion—a device used to clean machine guns.[2]

They took the men to the Saint-Jérôme detachment to question them, and one of them—the youngest—confessed. He and his accomplices were from Montreal. They had stolen the Pontiac the previous day. They belonged to the ALQ and they had been robbing banks to rent apartments in the city and hideouts in the country, to buy and operate vehicles and to cover personal expenses since these aspiring young revolutionaries either were students or unemployed or held low-paying jobs at the margins of the economy.

The Saint-Jérôme detachment immediately called in the criminal investigation bureau of the MPD. Detectives came north to question the suspects, and then brought them back to the city and turned them over to CATS detectives. René Dion, the youngest suspect, was seventeen and a plumber's apprentice, and Jean Lasalle was the twenty-two-year-old son of an Outremont doctor. The leader of the gang was twenty-six-year-old Jean Gagnon, whose name alone was enough to disclose another of the gang's secrets. He was the older brother of François Gagnon, who was serving a three-year sentence in St-Vincent-de-Paul Penitentiary for his part in the Westmount mailbox bombings, and the family connection revealed the ALQ as a successor to the FLQ.

One of the three suspects had in his possession a receipt for the rental of a garage at the rear of a residential property on De La Roche Street. Detectives searched the building and discovered most of the weapons, military equipment and accessories stolen from the Shawinigan armoury.

On April 13, four days after the Mont-Rolland robbery, police arrested a fourth suspect, nineteen-year-old Claude Perron, and issued warrants for two others—André Wattier, twenty-three, and Robert Hudon, twenty, an electrician's helper and the second member of the gang with a familial connection to the FLQ. He was the younger brother of Gabriel Hudon, co-founder of the revolutionary terrorist front. Wattier and Hudon had gone into hiding. A police surveillance team spent several days watching an apartment the pair had rented, but the wanted men never appeared.

Police nabbed Wattier on May 4 at a house in Saint-Hyacinthe, a small town on the south shore of the St. Lawrence some forty-five kilometres east of Montreal. Shortly before ten o'clock the following morning, they closed in on Hudon as he sat behind the wheel of his truck at the corner of Sherbrooke and Hutchison Streets. The wanted man smiled, meekly raised his hands and surrendered. Then he led police to a garage behind a home at 5814 8th Avenue in Rosemont, where he and his accomplices had hidden ten homemade bombs and most of the weapons stolen in the raid on the Fusiliers Mont Royal armoury.

The police were triumphant. J. Adrien Robert told reporters that the ALQ had "been crushed by our combined anti-terror squad." Attorney General René Hamel announced Hudon's arrest in the Legislative Assembly, and the Liberal benches erupted in applause when he described the ALQ as "the most important band of terrorist agitators which ever operated in the province."

Eight members of the gang appeared in court for the first time on Thursday, May 8. They were all clean shaven and well dressed. Most wore shirts, ties and jackets. They looked every bit like serious young men, but behaved otherwise. "Six took their court appearance in a flippant manner," the *Gazette* reported. "They smiled, nodded to friends and chatted with each other as clerk A.J. Cousineau read the charges." They faced a total of forty-eight charges arising from the armoury raids and three bank robberies that had netted the gang a total of $33,400.

Preliminary hearings began one week later, and again the defendants were in a jovial mood. Their demeanours changed as the preliminary hearings progressed and the solidarity of the gang cracked. René Dion had been held in a separate detention centre because of his young age and had agreed to become a Crown witness. He testified for a day and acknowledged his misdeeds. He had stolen a taxi and two other automobiles, which were used in bank robberies.

Dion told the court that he, Robert Hudon and Claude Perron had rented an apartment in January at 1457 Aylwin Street in Montreal's east end. It served as the gang's headquarters and it was there that they planned their operations. Dion testified that on January 30 he, Jean Gagnon and Claude Perron had entered the Fusiliers Mont Royal armoury first, seized the night watchman and the employees at gunpoint and tied them up. Hudon then drove the red truck into the armoury, accompanied by André Wattier and Jean Lasalle, and they, in his words, "smashed down doors and loaded the arms and ammunition into the truck." The youth fingered Wattier and Lasalle as the principal organizers of the Shawinigan armoury raid.

A second member of the gang, Maurice Leduc, also turned Crown witness. Hudon, a friend of three years, had recruited him, and he admitted participating in one of the robberies, but said he had done so unwittingly. According to his testimony, Wattier had given him the keys to a blue truck and instructed him to wait at the corner of Davidson and Notre-Dame Streets. He sat for two hours until Wattier, Hudon, Gagnon and Dion arrived on foot, each carrying a bag stuffed with cash and cheques, and then drove them to the garage on De La Roche Street, but he only learned what had happened when he heard reports of the robbery on the radio.

Leduc and Dion were amply rewarded for their co-operation. They were convicted but received suspended sentences. Perron and Pierre Nadon were sent to prison for four years, while the leaders of the ALQ—Hudon, Wattier, Gagnon and Lasalle—were sentenced to eight-year terms.

The demise of the ALQ was a devastating defeat for the movement, and the authors of *La Cognée* admitted as much. "The blows that the Armée de libération du Québec has absorbed and the difficulties it has encountered have weakened the revolutionary movement," Paul Lemoyne wrote. "To deny it would be infantile.

"One thing is certain," he continued, "the counter-revolutionary forces—far from dampening our spirits—have only strengthened our determination to wage our struggle for liberation to the end."

The movement had suffered other setbacks in the spring of 1964. CATS officers raided an apartment on St-Denis Street in late March. They seized nine sticks of dynamite, detonators and copies of *La Cognée*. They arrested three Université de Montréal students, and the April 15 edition of *La Cognée* noted that more "soldiers had fallen into the hands of the enemy."

On April 21, the day that Queen Elizabeth turned thirty-eight, police foiled an attempt to blow up the bronze statue of Queen Victoria that stood in front of Royal Victoria College, a McGill University student residence on Sherbrooke Street. A passerby spotted a dark-coloured canvas bag at the foot of the edifice and called police. Constables Robert Côté and James Hill of the bomb squad arrived first. Hill opened the bag, immediately realized it was a bomb and dismantled it.

Police broke up a newly formed cell during a series of raids conducted on May 2 and 3. They searched a cottage in Saint-Damase, near Saint-Hyacinthe, uncovered 135 sticks of dynamite and 35 detonators, as well as separatist literature and a duplicating machine, and arrested five men. *La Cognée* reported on May 15 that twenty-four members of the FLQ or affiliated groups were behind bars, and by the end of that month others had been arrested.

The FLQ had hit a low point just as the independence movement was gaining credibility. *The New York Times* had taken note, Prime Minister Lester B. Pearson had addressed the issue, a committee of the Quebec Legislative Assembly was examining the feasibility and ramifications of secession, and René Lévesque, a leading minister in the Lesage cabinet, caused a stir when he broke with the premier and the party over Quebec's place in Confederation.

The *Times* story ran to four thousand words and began on page one of its editions of February 24, 1964. "After three years of what has become known as the Quiet Revolution under Jean Lesage, the temper of French Canadian nationalism has hardened perceptibly," correspondent Tania Long wrote. "Quebec's secession from the Canadian confederation is no longer viewed as a remote contingency. It is seen as a possibility if the province's demands for more autonomy are not met." Politicians, pundits and educators were debating the pros and cons of separation, Long added, though the public was far from sold on the idea. She cited a *Maclean's*/CBC poll which revealed that 43 percent of Quebeckers wanted to remain in Canada. Twenty-three percent were undecided. Twenty-one percent knew nothing about the issue, while 13 percent supported independence, and that small separatist minority was splintered and unstable.

Pearson denounced the separatists in sharp, unequivocal terms on April 21 when he addressed a Canadian Labour Congress convention. "To a degree far greater than their numbers warrant," he said, "and in part because of the publicity they receive, they are making too much progress in this evil, destructive design. In Quebec, they cry 'separate.' In other parts of the land, they cry 'go.' It is for us to rouse the great and moderate majority for Canada: This shall not be."

Premier Lesage had told the *Times* that "separation would be a disaster for Quebec." Nevertheless, the constitutional affairs committee of the Legislative Assembly held public hearings on the question in mid-May. The committee asked fourteen economists, constitutional lawyers and other experts to assess the political, economic, social and cultural repercussions of such a move. They also invited seventeen individuals and associations to make submissions, and all were told to avoid using the term *separation*—with its negative connotations—and to use *independence* instead.

Studies, submissions and recommendations would do for some, but not for René Lévesque, the minister of mines and natural resources. He had said on several occasions that his allegiance lay with Quebec, not Canada, and that he was a Quebecker, not a Canadian. On May 9, he went much further. He told some four hundred students at Collège Sainte-Marie that the Pearson government's brand of co-operative federalism "would only make a greater mess of something that is already somewhat of a mess." The solution, Lévesque said, was something called "*état associé*." Quebec would become an autonomous state operating in association with Canada. This would have to be negotiated, he said, and then he made two incendiary statements. It would be negotiated "without guns and without dynamite—if possible." And: "If they refuse to grant this to Quebec, we must separate."

Lévesque's comments infuriated the premier, lit up the editorial pages of the province's newspapers and undoubtedly inspired the largest demonstrations for separation since the start of the Quiet Revolution. They occurred on May 18—La Fête de la Reine in Quebec, Victoria Day in the rest of Canada. Youthful demonstrators—most of them students—marched in the streets of Quebec City, Trois-Rivières, Drummondville, Chambly and Saint-Hyacinthe, and there were three events in Montreal.

The FLQ, meanwhile, hovered precariously at the margins of the independence movement. This badly listing fragment may have sunk from sight were it not for the *La Cognée* group. They were there, as noted in the May 31, 1964, issue, to guide the FLQ through "the highs and the lows of our fight, our victories and our defeats, the periods of calm and the periods of intensity . . ." And they made a bold prediction: "Each time one of ours is imprisoned, ten others will come forward to take his place."

---

1. *Les Insolences du Frère Untel* was written by Brother Jean-Paul Desbiens. He was a member of the Marist Brothers of the Schools, a Roman Catholic lay teaching order, and his superiors insisted that the book be published anonymously. It sold 120,000 copies, shattering all Quebec publishing records, and it was later published in English as *The Impertinences of Brother Anonymous*. The *Gazette* once described the book as "a powerful handful of yeast in the growing ferment in French Canada."

2. At the time, a device commonly used to clean the barrel of machine guns was known as a "pull-through." It was a length of cord with a three- to four-inch-long brass cylinder at one end and a loop at the other end. The user inserted a piece of flannel soaked in oil into the loop and then dropped the brass cylinder into the barrel of the gun. He or she then pulled the device through the trapdoor at the breech and the oil-soaked flannel removed any contaminants in the barrel.

Four

THE GENERAL AND HIS MEN

SURE ENOUGH, OTHERS DID COME forward. They formed a new army that self-destructed in one brief spasm of spectacular violence—an ill-conceived gun store robbery that left two men dead and five charged with murder, two of whom would be condemned to hang.

Such things were bound to happen, as the FLQ was not in any sense a conventional organization. There was no central authority, no governing body, no charter or constitution and no rules or bylaws to determine who could be a member. It was a clandestine, revolutionary movement with many participants as well as multiple cells, fronts and groups. They shared a common goal—Quebec independence—but differed on how to achieve it. The *La Cognée* group could advise, though no one was obliged to listen and all were free to criticize.

Issues 13 through 17 of *La Cognée*, published between June 15 and August 15, 1964, contained much advice. The pseudonymous writers argued that organization must precede action. The movement needed a province-wide network of cells within colleges and universities, neighbourhoods and communities, factories and businesses. These cells would agitate for separation and distribute separatist propaganda through all ranks of Quebec society. "We will then have a powerful party, well structured and indestructible," they declared. And they pleaded with their readers to get on with the job. "Here is the first task asked of all militants," they wrote. "It is clear, precise, necessary and urgent. It is necessary this fall, which is to say by October, that each militant will have created a new cell."

Militant activists read and circulated *La Cognée* in the cafés, common rooms and dingy rented quarters where they gathered to discuss the movement and plot their next moves, and many did not like what they were reading. They accused the writers of *"attentisme,"* a wait-and-see approach that could only appeal to timid, uncertain souls. The criticism became so widespread that the *La Cognée* group felt compelled to respond. "Several impatient militants want to swing into action," Paul Lemoyne wrote in the issue of July 15, 1964. "They criticize our desire to prepare with realism for direct action. These people are demonstrating a lack of realism and a spirit of adventurism. One doesn't move to direct action for the principle of the thing."

Lemoyne's veiled criticism was aimed at the recently formed Armée révolutionnaire du Québec. The ARQ had set up a base camp in the bush outside the village of Saint-Boniface-de-Shawinigan in the Mauricie region, about 160 kilometres northeast of Montreal. The camp was little more than a few tents and a hunting cabin, and the army had but twelve recruits. However, their leader commanded respect and exuded confidence, and his subordinates referred to him as "The General."

His name was François Schirm, and he was a worldly, battle-tested veteran of the French Foreign Legion. Schirm (pronounced "scheerm") was thirty-two. He was born in Budapest and christened Ferenc. He was the only child of a carpenter and his devoutly religious wife, and the family enjoyed a secure, comfortable middle-class life until the advent of World War II.

The family fled to Austria in 1944 ahead of the advancing Red Army, and young Ferenc became known as Franz. The Schirms returned to Hungary after the war only to uproot again in 1947 before the Soviet-backed Communist authorities had completely sealed the borders. They settled in Bavaria, in West Germany. The younger Schirm once again changed his given name from Ferenc to Franz and quit school to take up his father's trade.

In 1950, at age eighteen, he left Germany and joined the French Foreign Legion, despite his mother's anguished pleas and his father's vigorous objections. Schirm spent six years in the Legion. He changed his given name to François, fought in Vietnam and Algeria and was promoted to sergeant. He led men in battle, but was appalled by the brutality he witnessed on all sides. He saw no possibility of a French victory in either colonial war and secretly sympathized with the Vietnamese and Algerian insurgents who were fighting for their independence.

While he was in the Legion, Schirm corresponded with a medical secretary of Hungarian descent who lived in Montreal. They exchanged letters and photos, and in 1957 he travelled to Montreal to meet her. They married the following year and their daughter was born not long after. The marriage quickly went bad and Schirm fared little better in the workforce. He held a number of jobs—bricklayer, glazier, security guard and night watchman—but stuck with none.

Schirm felt he had been humiliated and exploited by his mostly English bosses and was attracted to Quebec's independence movement, though he knew little of the province's history or its politics. He joined the RIN, migrated to the radical fringes and met a number of activists connected to the FLQ. The bombing campaign of the spring of 1963 seemed to him the start of a revolution and he was for it. He and two former members of the Canadian armed forces founded the ARQ in June 1964, and the following month they set up their base camp at Saint-Boniface-de-Shawinigan.

The *La Cognée* group took a very dim view of this new army and its recruits. "These hotheads," they declared, "are not revolutionaries. They are opportunists, who hope to pull chestnuts out of the fire. Unfortunately, they risk seeing the chestnuts explode in their hands and finding themselves on the margins of the revolution."

Years later, after his death sentence had been commuted to life and he was inmate No. 4247 at St-Vincent-de-Paul Penitentiary, Schirm would tell a visiting psychiatrist named Gustave Morf that he had seen the vast, sparsely populated forests north of Montreal as ideal country for guerrilla warfare. He described it as "the perfect bushland for partisans. Nobody could hunt out the revolutionaries."

Schirm led his recruits north to Saint-Boniface-de-Shawinigan to train for action. They would participate in urban protests and demonstrations and use the country as a base for an insurgency campaign. Schirm began teaching them how to handle and use firearms, and warned that they should be prepared for armed conflict with police. But his embryonic army was short of food, supplies, money and, above all, guns.

Nevertheless, Schirm pressed on. He decided to solve the army's weapons problem with one bold stroke. They would rob a gun shop, and he chose the target—the International Firearms Co. Ltd., the largest weapons and ammunition retailer in Quebec at the time. It was located at 1011 Bleury Street in the downtown core, and a sign spanning the front of the store announced in English only that it sold shotguns, pistols, rifles, ammunition and accessories—all at the lowest prices in Canada.

Schirm planned the operation, chose the participants and assigned each a role, though none, himself included, had ever staged a holdup. Edmond Guénette, age twenty, was the youngest member of the gang and the most ideologically committed. He had left school at sixteen and worked as a microfilm photographer at Northern Electric, but he had been deeply perturbed by the poverty he saw in some of Montreal's French-speaking neighbourhoods. He quit his job in June 1964 to become a full-time FLQ activist.

Cyriaque Delisle, age twenty-seven, and Marcel Tardif, twenty-two, shared an apartment at 2565 Davidson Street with another member of Schirm's army, and both had served in Canada's armed forces. Delisle had difficulty mastering English, had no prospect of advancing and left the forces embittered by the experience. Tardif was discharged from the Royal Canadian Navy in August 1963 after a bout of depression, and he had been stung by the anti-French prejudice of his fellow sailors.

Gilles Brunet, age twenty-nine, was the fifth member of the gang. He was the most reluctant, and understandably so. He was married and the father of three boys and two girls. He had had great difficulties in school and had quit at age sixteen, having advanced no further than grade six. He was, however, happily married and supported his large family through menial, low-paying jobs. But he grew to resent his English bosses and the English workers who always seemed to hold the better positions. That resentment had driven him to become involved with the militant activists of the FLQ, and he had been captivated by Schirm and his stories about the French Foreign Legion and life in wartime Europe.

On the afternoon of the robbery, Saturday, August 29, 1964, the gang gathered at the Davidson Street apartment. A car thief had supplied them with a late-model Pontiac. Brunet tried to back out at the last minute, and Delisle agreed to participate only if he could drive the getaway car. They piled into the vehicle, stopped at a tavern and consumed a round or two of beer to steady their nerves, and arrived at the Bleury Street store a few minutes before closing time.

Schirm and Guénette entered through the front door. Delisle drove to the rear of the store with the others. Schirm asked the sales clerk for an M1 rifle—a compact, semi-automatic American military weapon and a favourite among police officers as well as underworld figures. The clerk handed it to Schirm, who stepped back, inspected the weapon, and said it cost too much. Then he nudged Guénette, who pulled from his jacket a semi-automatic rifle with fifteen cartridges in the clip. Schirm reached for a clip concealed in his pocket and inserted it and pointed the now loaded M1 at the clerk's chest and said, "We don't want any money, just rifles and ammunition."

At that moment, Leslie McWilliams, the fifty-eight-year-old vice-president of International Firearms, walked into the showroom. He saw the rifles pointed at the employee but didn't realize what was happening. "Don't be crazy!" he shouted, "Don't do that!" Guénette wheeled and fired. The shot hit McWilliams point blank in the abdomen and knocked him over. He lay on the floor bleeding profusely, mortally wounded, unable to speak.

Brunet then entered, bearing an unloaded pistol, and went upstairs and brought the secretary down to prevent her from calling the police. Schirm and Guénette began rounding up the employees. There were about ten in the store, and they herded them, including company president William Sucher, past the dying man and into a back room. "Please don't harm us," Sucher said. "I have five children and everything here you can have. Here is my billfold." Schirm told him to put it away. He and Guénette stood guard while Brunet and Tardif began hauling weapons and ammunition out to the car.

However, one employee had slipped out the front door unnoticed and hailed two constables who had been called to the area to investigate a burglary that turned out to be a false alarm. One of the officers hopped into the cruiser and radioed for assistance. Then the officer and his partner drove to the rear of International Firearms. There, they saw Brunet and Tardif exiting the back door, each with an arm full of weapons, and ordered the pair to drop them and lie face down on the ground. Then Schirm stepped out the door and fired at the officers. They fired back and he retreated and fled out the front door with Guénette.

The two officers entered the shop and spotted a man coming up from the basement with a rifle in hand. It was Alfred Pinisch, who was thirty-seven, a father of two, a gunsmith and an expert marksman. "Stop right there!" one of the officers shouted. Pinisch kept coming, but said, truthfully, "Oh no, I'm an employee. I work here." Too late. An officer fired and killed him instantly.

Meanwhile, Schirm had fled down the street, with rifle in hand and police in pursuit with guns drawn. They cornered him in a shed in a laneway. He opened fire and they fired back. Schirm's weapon jammed and he threw it away and came out with his hands raised. He had been hit in the thigh and blood spilled from the wound.

Guénette commandeered a taxi driven by a young man named Jean Guy Doré, who later testified about the wild ride that ensued. The fugitive aimed his rifle at Doré's back and said, "Drive or I'll shoot." They went up and down a dozen streets. Guénette ordered Doré to cross the Jacques Cartier Bridge to the south shore. Doré refused, then asked Guénette, "Why do you want to do such things as you're doing now?"

"It's too late to think about these things now," Guénette replied. "You don't know how it feels to kill a man."

Doré finally dropped him off at Bélanger Street and 7th Avenue in Rosemont, several kilometres north of the bridge. Guénette remained free for three days and was ultimately arrested at the Saint-Boniface-de-Shawinigan base camp along with six others, who were each charged with conspiracy to commit armed robbery.

The International Firearms robbery shocked Montrealers. Newspapers and other news media condemned the perpetrators and the movement that had inspired them. Their revolutionary brethren quickly responded. On September 1, the *La Cognée* group sent an FLQ communiqué to all the city's French-language newspapers, though only *Le Devoir* published it.

"We are not bandits or murderers as the police deceptively accuse us of being," the anonymous authors declared. "We are men who love our country and who want its people to be freed."

> Leslie McWilliams became a victim of his stupidity. At the beginning of the attack, the chief commando presented himself as a member of the revolutionary movement. The man should have been wise enough not to interfere, but, on the contrary, as a good Anglo-Saxon, he opposed the action of the commando. The latter cut him down as a collaborator. Let that be a lesson to others!
>
> As to Alfred Pinisch, everybody knows that he was felled by police bullets.
>
> Moreover, each of the partisans carried with him an authorization, identifying him by name and occupation and revealing

his affiliation with the revolutionary movement. We demand that they be treated by Canadian justice as prisoners of war, in conformity with Articles 3 and 4 of the Geneva Convention and with Articles 1 and 2 of the regulations of The Hague.

The conspiracy charges against those arrested at the Saint-Boniface-de-Shawinigan base camp came to nothing, but those directly involved in the International Firearms calamity were charged with capital, or premeditated, murder, which carried the death sentence, though juries could recommend mercy.

Gilles Brunet and Marcel Tardif pleaded guilty to non-capital murder early in the new year. Tardif, who had made a full confession shortly after his arrest, was sentenced to twenty years in prison, while Brunet, who was ashamed of his role in the robbery and expressed deep remorse, was sentenced to life in prison. Cyriaque Delisle, who had not entered the store, later received a life sentence.

François Schirm and Edmond Guénette went on trial in late May 1965. A court-appointed lawyer defended Guénette, while Schirm represented himself. The trial lasted five days. Guénette remained quiet and respectful throughout, unlike his co-accused. Schirm was brazen and defiant when he addressed the court. He applauded Delisle, who refused to testify due to his political convictions, but denounced Brunet as a traitor for providing a full account of the robbery.

The jury deliberated for forty-five minutes before finding both men guilty, and another ten before recommending against mercy. On the morning of May 21, Mr. Justice André Sabourin of the Court of Queen's Bench, attired in a black robe, black tricorn hat and black gloves, looked down at the two convicted men and passed sentence. He addressed Guénette first: "The sentence now pronounced against you, Edmond Guénette, is that you be returned to the prison of the district whence you came and that, on Friday, October 22 of this year, within the precincts of the prison where you are held, you will be hanged by the neck till death ensues. May God have mercy on your soul."

Then Judge Sabourin turned to Schirm and said, "You have had your turn. Now it is mine. You were allowed to conduct your own defence and spoke with arrogance of men and institutions. Your smile mocked what we hold most sacred. You have had no pity for men, women or children and now you are getting what justice holds for you. You will be hanged by the neck on October 22." Schirm flashed a V sign to the sparse audience in the gallery, shouted, *"Vive le Québec libre!"* and was led away with the other condemned prisoner.

The death sentences were never carried out. Both men appealed and the executions were postponed again and again while the appeals were heard, first by a Quebec court and later by the Supreme Court of Canada, which ultimately granted each man a new trial. Schirm and Guénette were convicted a second time, though by then the death sentence had been abolished and they were sentenced to life in prison. Guénette served eleven years, Schirm fourteen. Canadian authorities offered to grant Schirm his liberty in 1974 if he would agree to be deported. He refused and spent another four years in prison before being released on day parole on July 24, 1978. Schirm was unrepentant to the end and often said, "As a revolutionary, I was prepared to sacrifice my life and am still prepared to do so for the liberation of the people of Quebec."

Five

___

ONE TROUBLED SUMMER

THE SCHIRM GANG'S DISASTROUS GUN SHOP RAID and its awful consequences cast a chill over the movement. Other young men seized by a fervent desire to remake Quebec through revolutionary action stayed on the sidelines rather than coming forward to lead further spectacular assaults on the established order.

The fall of 1964 and the first few months of 1965 were so quiet, save for a few isolated incidents (detailed below), that one might well have imagined that the revolutionary fervour had been extinguished altogether, but this was not so. *La Cognée* continued to appear twice a month. It remained the work of a few pseudonymous writers—Paul Lemoyne, Louis Nadeau, P.-A. Gauthier, Georges Simard and Maurice Martel—but Lemoyne was by far the most prolific. He and his associates peppered the pages of their journal with revolutionary slogans, invariably in capital letters and punctuated with exclamation marks:

THE LIBERAL PARTY IS DYING!
DEATH TO PARASITES!
DEATH TO TRAITORS!
LONG LIVE A FREE QUEBEC!
LONG LIVE THE REVOLUTION!

The *La Cognée* group demeaned those on whom they looked with disfavour and denounced those whom they deemed to be enemies. They dismissed electoral politics as a fraud and a sham, and they mocked the RIN, which was preparing to run candidates in the 1966 general election. "The RIN will be unable to break the jaws of the gangsters in their first election," they wrote, finishing the piece with one of their all-caps slogans: "THE MEMBERS OF RIN ARE INCONSEQUENTIAL! THEIR SERIOUS MILITANTS ARE JOINING US!"[1]

The *La Cognée* group despised Jean Lesage and his Liberals, who would—as it happened—be defeated by Daniel Johnson's Union Nationale in 1966. They routinely labelled them collaborators and traitors, or crooks, hyenas and rats. They had a special loathing for Claude Wagner, the tall, handsome, no-nonsense former Sessions Court judge who served successively as Lesage's solicitor general, attorney general and minister of justice. He was, in their words, a "convinced federalist" and a "stinking dog."

There was, however, more to the *La Cognée* group than street-corner demagoguery. In almost every issue, they ran a news-in-brief feature entitled *"La Révolution En Marche."* There, they reported on signs of momentum in the independence movement—usually student groups that had come out in favour—and they documented actions by their supporters against perceived enemies of the Quebec people. On October 31, they reported that "The automobile of federal Conservative MP Léon Balcer has been burned by a commando operation. We will not hesitate to strike all Quebeckers who betray their nation." Two weeks later, they noted that "The transmission tower of radio station CFCF has been knocked down. An operational commando unit has replied to the continual attacks of this English station against the patriotic movements."

An issue early in the new year carried the following item: "A commando set fire (20/1/65) to the lumber yard of L.G. Power Sawmills Ltd., property of Lorne Power, president of the Régie des Alcools du Québec. The lumber yard is in Giffard, near Quebec."[2] In the April 1 issue, *La Cognée* reported that "Several cases of dynamite and detonators disappeared from an Expo construction site in Caughnawaga. Our stocks are increasing continually."

Earlier in 1965, a new feature entitled *"Technique de Sabotage"* appeared, and the first instalment contained detailed descriptions, along with crude, hand-drawn illustrations, of three different methods of blowing up a railway track. The second instalment of *"Technique de Sabotage"* contained instructions, along with illustrations, for constructing a simple hand grenade that could be hurled at police during large, unruly street demonstrations or protests.

The final instalment appeared in the issue of April 15, 1965, and explained the components of detonators and how they worked. "Detonators are devices containing a very sensitive explosive, susceptible to detonating under the effect of flames, a wick or an electric current," the article stated. "The last type is used most frequently because it is the simplest to manipulate. Detonators are placed directly on the dynamite in order to cause the explosion."

> They consist of copper metal tubes containing a small amount of mercury fulminate and an inflammatory charge. When you pass an electrical current through this charge, the heat causes the mercury fulminate to explode, which in turn causes the dynamite to explode.
>
> Detonators MUST must [sic] be handled with caution, being particularly sensitive to shock, and must be stored separate from other explosives to prevent serious accidents.
>
> In order to ignite a detonator, you connect the two wires attached to it to the terminals of a source of electricity and, if the source of electricity is strong enough, you can ignite several detonators at once, thereby increasing the impact of the explosion.

The *La Cognée* group could preach or instruct, but others had to act, and in the spring of 1965, others were ready to do so. Dock workers, truckers and garbage collectors were on strike. Students protested American escalation of the war in Vietnam or demanded independence for Quebec. Small left-wing fringe groups—the Parti Socialiste, the Caucus de gauche (Caucus of the Left) and Ligue socialiste ouvrière (Socialist Workers' League) to name a few—encouraged the unrest.

La Fête de la Reine—Victoria Day—unleashed it. Bombs exploded. A political demonstration very nearly turned into a full-fledged riot. Police officers were injured, and dozens of people, mostly young, were arrested.

The first bomb exploded at or about 1 a.m. on the holiday Monday. Two officers on patrol spotted a suspicious-looking brown bag lying on the sidewalk at 635 Dorchester Boulevard, head office of the Prudential Assurance Co. Ltd. They inspected and found dynamite, halted traffic on the six-lane thoroughfare, and called Léo Plouffe. Plouffe and his men had already responded to six other calls that night—all false alarms. They were just pulling up to 635 Dorchester when the dynamite detonated. "Had we called Plouffe a minute earlier it would have exploded as he approached it," an officer at the scene told reporters. "He was there before the dust settled."

Plouffe was next dispatched to the armoury of the Fusiliers Mont Royal—another false alarm—and then to the central post office on Peel Street, where an employee on the fourth floor had found a package that raised suspicions. Plouffe inspected and found two sticks of dynamite and a timing device. He spent the rest of the night handling calls that came to nothing. Hundreds of his colleagues spent most of the afternoon and all evening attempting to control violent mobs of protesters. The disturbances began at La Fontaine Park on Sherbrooke Street in the east end, where members of the St. Jean Baptiste Society gathered for a ceremony before the monument honouring the French-Canadian hero Dollard des Ormeaux.[3]

The president of the society, lawyer Yvon Groulx, roused his followers with a provocative late-afternoon speech. Quebec, he said, should be a unilingual French province. The Legislative Assembly possessed the constitutional authority to pass a language law and should do so "as a firm expression of our will to comport ourselves like a proud nation," and he envisioned the day when "all of Quebec will fly the colours of the fleur-de-lys, the distinctive symbol of Quebec and the French Canadian nation."

The gathering remained peaceful until a crowd of sixty or so placard-bearing, slogan-shouting separatists arrived, led by the ex-boxer Reggie Chartrand and fifteen of his followers who called themselves the Chevaliers de l'indépendance, or Knights of Independence. They were street-level agitators. They specialized in disrupting public events and inciting picket line violence, and disturbances quickly erupted when they arrived. Police moved in and arrested Chartrand and several of his Knights. They dispersed the rest and restored order, but only momentarily.

Fresh crowds arrived and continued to do so into the evening. Police later estimated that two thousand to three thousand young people gathered in the park, and the next day's *Gazette* reported that "The demonstrations erupted into reckless, leaderless hooliganism in several parts of the city's east end. Hundreds of youths ran wild along Ste. Catherine, Amherst, Dorchester and several streets around La Fontaine Park." They smashed large plate-glass windows at the French-language radio station CJMS, the Dupuis Frères department store and several other French-Canadian-owned businesses. Between five hundred and six hundred police officers attempted to control the situation. Mobs of young people attacked police vehicles, hurled Molotov cocktails and, at one point, mounted an assault on Station No. 16 at the northwest corner of La Fontaine Park.

The following morning, Justice Minister Claude Wagner stood in the Legislative Assembly and declared: "I've had enough of these absurdities." Then he provided an inventory of the holiday Monday havoc and destruction. The bomb at the Prudential Building had caused fifteen thousand dollars' damage and shattered windows twelve storeys above the street. A second explosion, on Île Sainte-Hélène—where Expo 67 would be held—destroyed a bulldozer. Property damage—mainly broken windows—totalled about ten thousand dollars. Eight police vehicles and a departmental ambulance were heavily damaged. Thirteen officers were injured and sent to hospital, two of them with serious injuries, after being struck by Molotov cocktails. Trees and shrubs in La Fontaine Park were destroyed and a police kiosk burned. Just over 200 people were arrested and 131 were charged.

"I have been expecting such incidents for some time," Wagner said. "The relative calm that has prevailed for some time was only superficial. Beneath the calm, the cauldron was boiling."

And it continued to boil well into the summer.

Militants launched three attacks on CN freight trains in the month of June. The first occurred near the tiny south shore community of Saint-Apollinaire. The attackers pelted the train with Molotov cocktails. Two other CN trains were derailed, one near the village of Saint-Damien-de-Buckland, about forty-five kilometres east of Quebec City, and the second in the South Shore Montreal suburb of Saint-Lambert.

The motive for the derailments was economic, according to *La Cognée*. One train was coming from New Brunswick with a cargo of potatoes "destined to flood the Quebec market while our farmers can't sell theirs," a short news item stated, while the other was carrying Ontario produce. "The FLQ has acted with patriotism," the journal concluded. "The Quebec economy will eventually profit from these accidents."

FLQ militants struck again a few minutes after midnight on July 1—the start of the Dominion Day national holiday. A powerful bomb containing five to ten sticks of dynamite exploded outside Westmount City Hall. The device had been placed against a wall and caused only minor damage to the building. But residents of nearby homes and apartment buildings bore the brunt of the blast when their windows shattered without warning.

Police, meanwhile, braced for major street demonstrations. According to a report that appeared in *La Presse*, separatist groups had distributed two hundred thousand copies of an anonymous tract during the St. Jean Baptiste Day holiday, calling on Quebeckers of all stripes to join them in a vast Dominion Day protest. Several thousand young people heeded their call—far fewer than the tens of thousands hoped for—and police maintained control. Over five hundred officers were on duty during the afternoon and evening. *La Presse* reported that they were well organized and highly mobile, and that they occupied strategic intersections. They kept rowdiness and property damage to a minimum, but nevertheless arrested 105 people.

The following day, a bomb destroyed the transmission tower of the English-language radio station CKTS in Sherbrooke, and investigators found the letters "FLQ" painted on a nearby structure.

By then, some militants had embarked on a new initiative. They were reviving the FLQ's military wing. The *La Cognée* group was behind the project, and so were several members of François Schirm's ARQ who had not taken part in the disastrous gun shop raid. They rented a camp on the shores of Lake Macaza, a long, narrow, L-shaped body of water in the Laurentians, which they assumed to be isolated enough for training insurgents.

It was located about 110 kilometres northwest of Montreal, a few kilometres from the village of La Macaza and, more importantly, RCAF Station La Macaza. This military installation was a product of the Cold War. It was built at a cost of five million dollars in the early 1960s, under the auspices of the North American Aerospace Defence Command, NORAD for short. Twenty-eight Bomarc surface-to-air missiles were housed there in underground silos. The missiles, which weighed eight tonnes each and travelled at twice the speed of sound, carried either conventional or nuclear warheads and were designed to track and shoot down Soviet or other enemy aircraft. Their presence on Quebec soil had attracted anti-war protesters from Montreal and elsewhere. They were an equally tempting target for terrorists in training. An armed assault, however ineffective, would earn the attackers and their cause national, and even international, attention.

They wanted no attention when they arrived at Lake Macaza but were noticed from the outset. There were large gatherings at the camp on weekends. Most of the outsiders were young men from Montreal, and they were, to all appearances, well educated. The majority were gone by Monday morning, but some stayed behind and their behaviour struck the neighbours as odd. A farmer's son later told a journalist that he had had a chance encounter with the insurgents, but instead of offering a friendly greeting, they had darted into the woods and disappeared. Cottagers reported seeing several men cross a road in the manner of infantrymen at war—one at a time, with companions providing cover from the shoulders.

The curious newcomers had formed a seven-man squad. Four of its members came from Montreal and three from Alma, a small town in the Saguenay–Lac-Saint-Jean region northeast of Quebec City. The two contingents had never met before arriving at Lake Macaza, and the men from the Saguenay later confessed that they had responded to a coded message instructing them to report to the camp.

The leader was Daniel Bélec, age twenty-one, a medical student at the Université de Montréal. Serge Boudreau, twenty-three, his second-in-command according to newspaper reports, was alternately described as a bookstore clerk or an unemployed librarian. Jean-Guy Lefebvre was twenty-six, a truck driver and a father of three. Claude Nadeau, twenty-two, was a student, and he and Lefebvre had been arrested a year earlier when police raided the ARQ camp at Saint-Boniface-de-Shawinigan. The volunteers from the Saguenay were André Lessard, Bertrand Simard and Réjean Tremblay. They were all in their early twenties. Lessard was a student, Simard an apprentice electrician and Tremblay a surveyor.

None of the seven had any experience with firearms or matters military, but they were very well equipped. They had been supplied with high-powered rifles and 2,500 rounds of ammunition, and each insurgent's kit included top-notch, olive-green knapsacks; hammocks with mosquito netting; good sleeping bags; identical jeans, shirts and green rubber hunting boots; pick-axes for digging trenches; fishing gear; rations; compasses; guides to surviving in the woods; separatist song sheets; notebooks with sketches and instructions for committing acts of sabotage; and government-produced topographic maps of the Laurentians. In addition, they had a medical kit that included bandages, disinfectants, syringes, tourniquets and other materials for treating minor wounds and injuries.

The youthful newcomers to Lake Macaza did nothing to frighten the neighbours until Thursday, July 16. That evening, a cottager named Marion Niemec encountered three young men in the bush, and she later told *La Presse* that they were "armed to the teeth." She had no phone, but managed to hail a passing boater and fellow cottager and told the woman to call police. Another local resident recounted that she had glimpsed seven men, with packs on their backs and arms at their sides. They were marching toward the La Macaza military base and she too immediately called police.

The nearest detachment was at Labelle, ten kilometres to the south-east. Two constables were on duty—Ronald Noël and Onile Bourdon. Noël, twenty-one and married, had a child and had been a police officer for eighteen months. Bourdon, twenty, was a raw recruit and had started six weeks earlier. They received the calls at about 6 p.m., finished their dinner and left for Lake Macaza.

Neighbours pointed out the camp where the armed men had been sighted. It was three hundred feet off the road. Noël and Bourdon followed a trail to a clearing in the woods and encountered six men, all clad in identical attire, all armed with .303 rifles and all wearing ammunition belts full of cartridges. "I immediately realized we were in a dangerous situation," Noël later told *Le Petit Journal*.

He asked them what they were doing. "We're camping," one of the men replied. "We're students."

"You have rifles, but no hunting permits," Noël said. "I have to take your names and seize your weapons and ammunition. You can reclaim them after paying a small fine. I am a game warden as well as a police officer and I am obliged to do that."

Noël collected some of the arms and munitions and started down the trail when an explosion occurred and he dove for cover. There was a seventh man at the camp. He had hidden in the bush and fired at Noël. The bullet grazed the officer and struck one of the shooter's companions.

Noël scrambled for several yards on all fours, then got up and ran to the cruiser to call for support, but he could not make contact with the detachment because of the surrounding mountains. He locked the cruiser and crawled back to the camp and found three of the men looking after their wounded companion.

"He had a wound in the back of his neck," Noël recalled. "He was screaming with pain. There was blood everywhere. It was dreadful.

"I threw them my first aid kit and said, 'Look after him.' Then I went to a neighbouring house to call for help. Two hours later, I heard a shot in the woods. I thought they'd killed Bourdon."

In fact, Bourdon had been abducted. Three of the men at the camp had overpowered him. One held a rifle to Bourdon's back. A second pressed a knife to his throat and said, "Don't move or make a sound." Another seized the officer's service revolver. They pulled his hands behind his back and handcuffed him, then marched him off at gunpoint. Twenty-four hours later, Bourdon escaped. He walked out of the woods, still handcuffed, though his hands were now cuffed at the front, and he approached a startled farmer who was peeling potatoes on his back porch.

His captors had trudged with him through the woods until about 11 p.m. on Thursday. They stopped for the night at the foot of a mountain, but nobody slept much. The men had fled in a panic and left all their supplies behind, and Bourdon later told a journalist that "the mosquitoes were so thick you could grab them by the handful." At daybreak, they set off again. A thick fog had settled over the area, but they kept moving all morning and all afternoon. They had nothing to eat and paused only two or three times to drink from streams they crossed. At about 5 p.m., they stopped for the night. They left Bourdon untended and went off to cut pine branches to sleep on, and he fled. He had managed to retain a sense of his location and was able to find a road and then the farm, which was about five miles from the camp.

The provincial police had mounted a huge search for Bourdon and his abductors. Some fifty officers were involved. They used tracking dogs and a helicopter and dozens of local volunteers, but the fugitives eluded the dragnet. They turned up Monday afternoon on the Cache Lake Road, which ran around the perimeter of a small body of water of the same name. It was about five kilometres east of Lake Macaza. An elderly cottager spotted them and called police. Noël was one of the three officers who responded and he was in no mood to treat them gently.

They drove past the three men, stopped and got out. Noël was armed with a .30-30 hunting rifle and he fired a shot that hit the dirt road behind the fugitives and off to the side. "That made them jump," he later told *Le Petit Journal*. "We ordered them to lay down, searched them, then made them crawl to the cruiser with guns at the back of their heads."

With that, the La Macaza gang was broken and all seven members were in custody, including the wounded man, Bertrand Simard, who was treated and moved to a provincial police detention centre. They were charged with a number of offences, including abduction, conspiracy to abduct, forcible confinement of a police officer, illegal possession of firearms and assault. All were convicted of one offence or another and all but one went to jail. Bélec, their leader, was sentenced to four years. Lefebvre, Lessard and Nadeau, the three who abducted Bourdon, received two and a half years each. Tremblay got two years, Simard six months and Boudreau earned a suspended sentence.

---

1. RIN candidates contested 73 of 108 ridings in 1966. They received 129,045 votes, or 5.55 percent of the total cast, but failed to elect a single member. A second separatist party, the Ralliement national, ran 90 candidates, earned 74,670 votes (3.2 percent of the total), but were shut out.

2. At the time of the arson, employees of the Régie des Alcools du Québec, provincial liquor control board, were on strike. There had been several boisterous demonstrations in Montreal in support of the workers, including one led by Reggie Chartrand and his Knights of Independence.

3. Dollard des Ormeaux and fifteen followers died in May 1660 at the Battle of Long Sault on the Ottawa River. Historians have long debated the nature of this fight with the Iroquois. In the early, heroic versions, des Ormeaux, his men and forty-four Indian allies held off a force of three hundred Iroquois warriors for several days, prevented an attack on the fort of Ville-Marie, as Montreal was then known, and saved the tiny colony from sure destruction.

Six

MORE BOMBS, MORE CASUALTIES

THE FORTY-THIRD ISSUE OF *La Cognée*, dated Wednesday, September 15, 1965, carried a brief item announcing that there had been "changes in the leadership of the FLQ and the editorial staff of its newspaper." The journal said nothing about who was leaving or who was taking over; nor could it, since everyone associated with the publication used pseudonyms to conceal their identities. And for good reason: they were, in many issues, counselling their followers to commit violent crimes.

For the next several months, *La Cognée* remained more or less the same shrill, crudely produced journal that it had always been. But the work of a new contributor, writing under the pseudonym Mathieu Hébert, was the clearest signal of a change. Hébert made his debut in the issue of October 1 and was introduced to readers as "a convinced revolutionary" who had hesitated to align himself with the movement due to its weaknesses, and he bluntly described them in an article entitled "Does the FLQ Exist?"

"For all practical purposes," he wrote, "the FLQ is a vague collection of tiny, more or less active groups, whose members are all known to the police and to each other. Only *La Cognée* carries on, although we cannot claim that it is really contributing at the moment to the theoretical and practical education of revolutionary cadres.

"At the level of action, there seems to be a tendency to act on a day-to-day basis, whenever the occasion arises, using bombs or Molotov cocktails, organizing demonstrations or other political events, rather than pursuing an overall strategy, based on an in-depth analysis of the balance of forces in Quebec, North America and the world, and not just with the aim of making noise, but of overthrowing the established order and setting up a government of and for the people.

"The struggle we have undertaken is not an adventure," Hébert advised. "It is a genuine war, subject to the scientific laws of warfare. Amateurism can only lead us to defeat. . . ."

He elaborated on his ideas in a piece that appeared on December 15 under the heading "What Does the FLQ Mean by Armed Struggle?" In his view, there could be no more individual terrorism or hastily improvised sabotage. Instead, the movement had to form small, disciplined, clandestine units to wage guerrilla warfare. It made no difference whether such units were operating in an underdeveloped, agricultural country or an industrialized and urbanized one like Quebec. The goals were the same. First: "Weaken the colonial infrastructure, its system of communications, its economy, its government, its infrastructure." Second: "Disrupt the forces of repression [army, police], divide them, demoralize them." Then: "Gain the support of the population, win its confidence, demonstrate that you are a force which it can count on to replace the established order and effectively liberate it."

The first issue of the new year—1966—promised action. The formation of a new army for the liberation of Quebec. "The ALQ will be our strike force," the journal announced. "Without doubt this will be an historic year for Quebec in its fight for independence and sovereignty." The FLQ needed recruits for its new army—though not many since it would be a small, disciplined force of dedicated revolutionaries—and it needed to broaden its base beyond those already committed. It would do that through *La Cognée*. Henceforth, there would be four editions, each aimed at a different audience. The national edition was reserved for known militants who were not necessarily active in the movement but were prepared to lend financial, intellectual or other forms of support. The others would serve as organs of agitation and propaganda and would be aimed at union members, high school students and their university counterparts.

The high school edition urged its young readers to reject authority and get behind the movement for independence, but did not counsel them to engage in illegal acts. The university edition was another matter. Volume one, number one denounced the province's institutions of higher learning as "the biggest prostitutes of the regime and, at the same time, its saddest victims." They were mere instruments of the rich and powerful and were dependent on their largesse for survival.

The journal went beyond denunciations and issued a call to arms: "Above all, *La Cognée* urges you to engage you in concerted action, strikes, violent demonstrations, and, if necessary, bombs." And the last line in the issue read: "IT IS TIME TO MELT YOUR PENS AND TURN THEM INTO PLASTIC BOMBS."

The big promises and strident statements generated expectations among those eager to act. But January came and went, February too, and all remained quiet; and by March, discontent had surfaced. Supporters and sympathizers complained that the FLQ was all talk and no action. The criticism had to be addressed and was—in the April 1 issue of *La Cognée*.

"The FLQ, the bombs, the fireworks, that was wonderful," a pseudonymous contributor named André Jacques wrote. "That shook Quebec, that gave us the impression that we were on our way. We believed that something was finally going to happen. Today the FLQ is no more than a *feuille de chou* [literally, a leaf of cabbage] that appears every two weeks.

"One hears these defeatist remarks now and then. Others have them on the tips of their tongues. No more bombs, no more FLQ, they think. But their impressions are utterly unjustified."

Militants had come together. They had formed a central committee and an action group, and they were preparing to unleash another wave of revolutionary violence. It would be brief but calamitous. The members of this new gang would commit armed robberies. They would steal weapons, ammunition and dynamite. They would establish a base camp in the Laurentians. They would use bombs to terrorize perceived enemies, and their bombs—five within the city of Montreal—would kill an older woman approaching retirement and a teenager who was barely old enough to drive.

The first bombing occurred on May 5 at the H.B. LaGrenade Shoe Company, a small, family-owned manufacturer located in a four-storey building at the corner of Rachel Street and d'Iberville, a busy east-end intersection. Henri LaGrenade and his five sons ran the company, and they had been embroiled in a labour dispute for over a year. In the spring of 1965, the Confédération des syndicats nationaux (CSN)—the provincial federation of labour—had organized the company's hourly workforce. But the LaGrenades, who paid the women ninety cents an hour and the men $1.05, maintained they could not boost wages and improve benefits and compete against low-cost foreign manufacturers. They refused to bargain and the CSN called a strike.

It began on April 25, 1965. Some sixty-four employees set up pickets while twenty others remained on the job. The LaGrenades hired replacement workers and a long stalemate began. The CSN organized noisy demonstrations in front of the plant and provided strike pay, but the strikers began to drift away to other jobs, and by the one-year mark only twenty-three remained. That's when the FLQ decided to deliver a blunt message to an employer who was seen to be exploiting its workers. The action group staged the attack over the lunch hour. A tall, slender youth, who appeared to be a messenger boy, entered the front door of the building. He handed a LaGrenade shoebox to the first person he met, saying it was a return from an unhappy customer and that the customer would call later to explain. Then he left abruptly.

A few minutes later, a powerful explosion occurred. Three people were seriously injured: André LaGrenade, age fifty-seven; Henri B. LaGrenade Jr., the fifty-one-year-old vice-president of the company and the recipient of the package; and Mrs. Viateur Sirois, an employee, who was twenty-three and eight months pregnant and was blinded by the blast. Thérèse Morin, who had returned a few minutes early from lunch, died instantly. She was sixty-four and was Henri LaGrenade's secretary, and had worked for the company for forty years. "Her battered body was found in the middle of the office," the next day's *Gazette* reported, "among twisted steel filing cabinets, shattered typewriters and fallen plaster."

Constables Réal Faust and Jean-Louis Negant were the first to arrive and Faust told journalists, "People were running in and out of the building, apparently in shock, while others cradled the injured in their arms." Léo Plouffe and Robert Côté of the bomb squad arrived next, followed by two homicide detectives, Marcel Allard and Julien Giguère. Plouffe and Côté spent more than three hours combing through the wreckage and blood-splattered debris. The blast had torn doors off hinges, ripped tiles from the floor and blown out all the windows. But they found what they were looking for—fragments of a Westclox Silver Bell alarm clock and a nine-volt Ray-O-Vac battery that had served as the bomb's timer and electrical charge and could be used as evidence in criminal proceedings against the perpetrators.

Allard and Giguère questioned several strikers but turned up nothing, and the investigation stalled there. Five other Quebec footwear manufacturers offered a $2,500 reward for information leading to arrests and condemned the attack. However, the province's labour leaders remained silent, and they said nothing when a bomb exploded later in May outside a Dominion Textile plant in Drummondville, another Quebec company with labour troubles. Some five thousand workers were on strike there and at plants in Sherbrooke, Magog and Montmorency, and had been for several weeks with negotiations going nowhere. No one was injured in the Drummondville bombing and the Montreal newspapers ignored the incident, but the bombers' next move made the front pages.

It occurred on Friday, June 3, two days before a provincial election. Jean Lesage and his Liberals were in trouble. Two separatist parties—the RIN and the Ralliement national—were siphoning Liberal votes, and Daniel Johnson had erased memories of the Maurice Duplessis regime and revived the Union Nationale with a campaign built around a bold slogan: *"Égalité ou Indépendance"* [Equality or Independence].

The Liberals held a last-minute rally at Paul-Sauvé Arena in Montreal to energize their supporters. A crowd of six thousand filled nearly every seat as well as the chairs placed on the arena floor. Lesage and his Montreal-area ministers—Claude Wagner and René Lévesque among others—made a grand entrance. Lévesque was in the midst of a typically passionate speech when a bomb exploded in the men's washroom, about three hundred feet from the stage. Lévesque continued to speak and the crowd remained fixed on him, but most of the press corp dashed down the corridor to where the explosion had occurred. It had damaged the interior of the washroom—nothing more. Plouffe arrived a few minutes later, surveyed the damage and the tattered remains of the bomb, and dismissed it as nothing more than "a big homemade firecracker."

The police made no arrests in any of the bombings and no one claimed responsibility—publicly at any rate—until mid-June when a statement appeared in *La Cognée* under the heading "We are at the root of the attack against LaGrenade!" The statement read: "The political bureau of the FLQ considers that the moment has come to give a few explanations concerning the action of May 5 against the reactionary management of the LaGrenade company. . . . Following the approving silence of the leading unions, the positive neutrality of certain newspapers and the mercantile gesture of the managers of five shoe companies, the population of Quebec has understood that right is on the side of the strikers and that the LaGrenade family is first and foremost responsible for the accident which happened that day. . . .

"The FLQ wishes to make it clear that the operation of May 5 was carried out under the direct suggestion of its leaders who want to assume paternity and responsibility for the action, despite the fact that their militants were not directly involved. We therefore advise the powers concerned—industrialists and police—that any action against its author will be considered an action against the FLQ. We publicly assure the author of the action of our solidarity and our protection."

The attack on the LaGrenade family firm marked a decisive turn in the terror of the 1960s. Initially, the movement had primarily attacked symbols of federalism or Anglo domination. Henceforth, Quebec-owned or Quebec-based companies would be prime targets.

The final bombing of 1966 occurred behind a Dominion Textile plant in Saint-Henri, one of the city's poorest neighbourhoods, shortly before 10:30 p.m. on Thursday, July 14. The four-storey structure backed onto the Lachine Canal. There were some 250 employees in the building when the blast occurred, and one of them, René Tremblay, was first on the scene. "We saw nothing but a cloud of dust and debris scattered everywhere," Tremblay told a reporter from the *Gazette*. George Bone, chief of security at the adjacent Stelco plant, added, "I was doing my rounds when I heard a stunning explosion. I rushed to the scene and found several persons gathered around a car. There was smoke coming from its front end and the men were looking at a badly mutilated body."

The blast attracted a crowd of onlookers, but workers from the plant kept them at a distance until Léo Plouffe and fellow officers arrived. Plouffe noted that there was a blue 1958 four-door Plymouth Savoy parked very close to the building. It had been abandoned and the licence plates removed. The explosion had demolished the car's front end and shorn off the left fender. The ground was strewn with broken glass and pieces of twisted metal.

"There was a body in front of the vehicle," Plouffe wrote in his incident report. "It was that of a slender young man or an adolescent with long hair and brown eyes. His arms and his right leg were completely severed and his left leg was almost severed.

"The body of the victim was found 29 feet in front of the vehicle and portions of his limbs were discovered on the banks of the canal, 89 feet from the body."

Plouffe concluded that the youth had either been leaning over or kneeling to place the bomb between the car and the wall when it exploded.

The dead youth was Jean Corbo. He was sixteen. He lived in the Town of Mount Royal, an affluent, largely English-speaking suburb, and attended Collège Ville-Marie. His funeral was held at 10 a.m. on Tuesday, July 19, at the Church of Notre-Dame-de-la-Défense. His father, Nicolo Corbo, a notary and a Quebecker of Italian descent, and his mother, Mignonne Côté, invited only family, friends of their son Jean and his older brother Claude, and the parents of the friends. And Nicolo Corbo spoke publicly about the tragedy only once and only briefly, saying, "He was a servant of the high priests of separatist terrorism . . . and the naive instrument of adult conspirators."

The police likewise believed that the Dominion Textile bombing was the work of separatists who had chosen terrorism as a means of achieving political goals. They also suspected that terrorists were behind the bombing that took the life of Thérèse Morin. But two and half months had passed since the LaGrenade attack, and the homicide detectives in charge of the investigation—Julien Giguère and Marcel Allard—had made no arrests.

"I came back from vacation and learned that there had been another bombing," Giguère recalled in an interview many years later. "Sometime in August, a lieutenant came to me and said: Julien, what's new with LaGrenade?

"I said: Nothing new, sir.

"He said: If you have nothing new, you have carte blanche to work on it full time. You do whatever it takes, but you have to do something. We worked like hell on it."

Then they got a lucky break. On August 27, police arrested three people who had attempted an armed robbery at a movie theatre on Jean Talon Boulevard: Claude Simard, a nineteen-year-old nurse; Rhéal Mathieu, also nineteen and a lab technician; and Gérard Laquerre, a twenty-four-year-old Université de Montréal social science student.

"We were suspicious about Mathieu," Giguère recalled. And for good reason: Mathieu had been part of a gang of youths who had participated in a number of violent demonstrations at La Fontaine Park. Police had attempted to arrest him at one of these disturbances, but he fought back vigorously and, as a result, spent two weeks in jail. Other members of his circle drifted into petty crime, but Mathieu joined an FLQ gang in 1964 at age seventeen. He was deemed to be too young to take part in the group's criminal activities—these being the theft of arms and dynamite. But he was an enthusiastic participant in their street protests, and at one of them was charged with burning the new Canadian flag.

"Mathieu was being held at Bordeaux Jail in Montreal North so we went to Bordeaux and brought him downtown to headquarters and talked to him for a whole night," says Giguère. "We questioned him from 8 p.m. till 8 a.m. and we got the whole story." By mid-September, the police had arrested fifteen people on the basis of Mathieu's confession and they had seized firearms and five cases of dynamite. Legal proceedings began immediately. First, there were coroner's inquests— one into the death of Thérèse Morin and a second into the death of Jean Corbo—and then there were preliminary hearings. Most of the suspects testified, and they revealed the startling scope of their activities. By the end of the month, the Crown had charged nine individuals with forty-nine offences—including non-capital murder, manslaughter, armed robbery, conspiracy to commit armed robbery, and break, enter and theft.

Serge Demers was one of the key witnesses. He was soft spoken, according to one newspaper report, and always wore a shirt, tie and jacket. Demers was twenty-one years old and driven by deep resentments that had arisen from personal experience. His father had been a staunch unionist and was employed for fifteen years as a maintenance man at a factory until he organized his fellow workers. The company fired him and later dismissed the rest of its maintenance crew and contracted out the work. The elder Demers became a self-employed contractor who installed vinyl siding. But he died of a heart attack at age fifty-one and the son attributed his father's premature death to the stress and bitterness caused by his dismissal.

Demers found an outlet for his own anger and resentment by joining the FLQ. He began by distributing leaflets and copies of *La Cognée*, but quickly advanced. He had not only assembled the bombs used in the spring and summer of 1966 but was the leader of the movement's action group and a member of its central committee.

Demers and others testified that the central committee was formed in October 1965 and that two men were behind it—Charles Gagnon, a former lecturer in politics and economics at the Université de Montréal, and Pierre Vallières, an ex-reporter at *La Presse* who had posed as Mathieu Hébert in *La Cognée*. Vallières and Gagnon recruited new members over the winter, and they looked for young men who were willing to engage in violence. They presided over the deliberations of the central committee, which had seven members, and coordinated and directed the operations of the action group.

Demers disclosed that on the evening of April 3, he, Mathieu and two other men had borrowed Gagnon's car and driven to South Stukely in the Eastern Townships. Around midnight, they arrived at an unguarded quarry operated by Waterloo Marble Works and stole four cases of dynamite, a large supply of detonators and two .22-calibre rifles. On April 15, members of the action group broke into Collège Mont-Saint-Louis, then located at the corner of Sherbrooke and Sanguinet Streets in the east end, and stole twenty-one rifles (all of them .22-calibre), several thousand rounds of ammunition and assorted military equipment.

Their next move was an armed robbery committed at midnight on May 1. Rhéal Mathieu, Claude Simard and a third man, Robert Lévesque, confronted the twenty-four-year-old manager of the Cinéma Elysée, Serge Doyon, as he was locking up. They were armed with sawed-off .22-calibre rifles and ordered him into his car. Piling in behind him, one of the three said, "Drive slowly and don't go through any red lights. This is no time to be stopped and given a traffic ticket." They directed Doyon to a laneway off Mount Royal Avenue, told him to get out and drove off with his briefcase, which contained the weekend's receipts—some $2,265.

Demers testified that the central committee had met twice that spring and that Vallières and Gagnon had attended both meetings. The first was held over the Easter weekend at his mother's home in the South Shore community of Saint-Philippe-de-Laprairie. They discussed recruitment and the LaGrenade strike, which had become a lost cause for the labour movement. They feared that other employers would also refuse to negotiate until union locals withered and died. "When the question of LaGrenade arose," Demers said, "there was agreement among the members of the central committee that something must be done about this strike and it was a question of planting a bomb." The second meeting was held at the start of May. This time the committee made detailed plans and Demers carried them out—with the help of a seventeen-year-old student named Gaétan Desrosiers, who testified that he had agreed to participate after being told he would be delivering "a harmless, little bomb."

On the day of the attack, Demers drove his motorcycle to Desrosiers's school at the lunch hour. The bomb was in a shoebox and the box strapped to the seat behind him. He picked up his young accomplice at the front door and they rode to a park two blocks west of the factory. The bomb contained one and a half sticks of dynamite. Demers set the timing device, closed the shoebox and handed it to the youth, who set off at a brisk pace. Afterward, they stopped at a street-corner phone booth. Demers called the shoe company and warned a male employee that a bomb would explode in eight minutes. Then he dropped off Desrosiers at school and returned to his construction job at the Expo 67 site.

Members of the group also acknowledged responsibility for a bombing that caused minor damage to the bronze Dollard des Ormeaux monument in La Fontaine Park on May 22 and the explosion at the Drummondville Dominion Textile plant, which caused five thousand dollars' damage. Demers was behind those attacks as well as the bombing at the Liberal election rally, which was meant to sabotage the event. He testified that he assembled two small crude bombs of dynamite packed into cigarette packages. Accomplices placed them in separate washrooms. Each had a fuse, which was to be lit by a cigarette butt wedged into a book of matches, but only one went off.

Demers and another witness, twenty-one-year-old Marcel Faulkner, testified that the central committee discussed the unresolved Dominion Textiles strikes during a meeting in early June at the group's camp near Saint-Alphonse-Rodriguez, about ninety kilometres north of Montreal. "The committee studied the question a long time and came to the conclusion that planting a bomb was all we could do for the strikers," Faulkner told the court. "We acted in support of the strikers and secondly to demonstrate to the company that the workers would not let themselves be beaten."

This time, though, they decided to hit the Saint-Henri plant even though the workers there were not on strike. Neither Faulkner nor Demers explained how they recruited Corbo. But both testified that he was eager to participate and had inspected the site and had met with Demers to plan the attack. On the night in question, Demers picked up the youth in a small truck in front of the Montreal Forum and drove him to the plant. He handed him a travel bag containing the bomb. They shook hands and agreed to meet afterward at a nearby restaurant. Demers was waiting for Corbo when he heard sirens and saw fire trucks and police cars racing toward Dominion Textiles. "I immediately thought an accident had occurred and started to drive home," Demers said. "Then I heard on the radio that someone had died in an explosion at St. Henri." At that, he changed plans and picked up Gérard Laquerre. They drove to the camp at Saint-Alphonse-Rodriguez and met several members of the central committee and decided that night to cease their activities.

To their credit, none of the young men arrested in the police sweep of September 1966 attempted to evade the justice system. One by one, they pleaded guilty to multiple offences, sparing the families of the victims long, arduous, complex trials. By mid-1967 most had been sentenced and sent to prison. Rhéal Mathieu was convicted of thirteen offences and given nine years, six months.[1] Serge Demers received eight years, ten months for his thirteen convictions. Marcel Faulkner and Gérard Laquerre were each sentenced to six years, eight months. Claude Simard got five years, ten months, and fellow accused André Lavoie, three years, six months. Gaétan Desrosiers, the juvenile, got off lightly.[2] He was charged with murder and pleaded guilty in Social Welfare Court, but was released on the condition that he live with an uncle—a lieutenant on the MPD.

The leaders of the gang—Pierre Vallières and Charles Gagnon—chose a different path. They fled.

---

1. Rhéal Mathieu was arrested in October 2000 after attempting to firebomb three Second Cup coffee shops in Montreal as a protest against the company's English name. Mathieu spent seven months in custody. On July 6, 2001, he was sentenced to one month in jail for attempted fire bombings and six months for possession of weapons. He was fifty-four years old.

2. Desrosiers made headlines in November 1996, when Elizabeth Thompson, then of the *Gazette*, disclosed that he held a position with the Quebec government that was equivalent to assistant deputy minister and was earning $91,300 a year. Thompson reported that Desrosiers was a long-time Parti Québécois activist who worked as an aide to PQ education minister Camille Laurin from 1980 to 1984. He served as executive director of two different organizations aimed at revitalizing Montreal's economically depressed east end before becoming chief of staff to Mayor Jean Doré in 1993. In November 1994, newly elected premier Jacques Parizeau named him associate secretary to the Cabinet's Comité special d'initiative et d'action pour le Grand Montréal.

Seven

THE FUGITIVES

HIS CELL MEASURED FIVE FEET BY SEVEN and he shared it with another inmate. At some point, the administrators of this place—the Manhattan House of Detention for Men, commonly known as The Tombs—had doubled the capacity by adding a second bunk to each cell. The bunks were three feet wide, leaving a scant, two-foot margin to accommodate the amenities—a toilet, a sink, a table and a chair—and the daily coming and going of two inmates. This jail was beyond crowded. There were some two thousand men crammed into a facility designed for just over nine hundred, but then Charles Gagnon was accustomed to living in close quarters.

Gagnon had grown up in Bic, near Rimouski, on the south shore, where the St. Lawrence meets the sea, and he was the youngest of fourteen children in a farm family. He and three brothers shared a bedroom with two beds, and the beds nearly filled the room. They slept on straw mattresses and the straw was changed at least once a year, usually after the grain had been harvested and threshed and winter was about to set in. There were two store-bought mattresses in the Gagnon home—one in the parents' bedroom, the other in the room reserved for guests—but the children were never allowed to sleep there, though that didn't bother young Charles. Newly replenished straw mattresses were stiff and prickly at first, but they smelled fresh and they soon became soft and cozy as a nest, but they did not hold the heat and Charles and his brothers shook and shivered on cold winter nights.

Gagnon landed in The Tombs at the end of September 1966, along with Pierre Vallières. Both had fled when the arrests began, and for three weeks or more the Montreal police had no idea where the fugitives were. They found out when the French- and English-language newspapers announced on their front pages that the missing men had turned up at United Nations headquarters in New York.

They had appeared in the UN press gallery on Tuesday, September 27, and introduced themselves to a room full of international journalists as emissaries of a new liberation movement—the FLQ—and they had distributed a communiqué. Their goal was to take Quebec out of Canada and to make it an independent, socialist republic. Furthermore, they had begun a hunger strike to protest the treatment of fellow members who were in jail or prison. And they were prepared to starve themselves until the governments of Canada and Quebec recognized the inmates as political prisoners rather than common criminals.

The Montreal police had by then issued warrants for the arrests of Vallières and Gagnon on charges of non-capital murder in connection with the death of Thérèse Morin, and they asked the New York Police Department to apprehend them. That happened on September 28. At around 10 a.m. that day, the fugitives returned to the UN, this time bearing signs in French and English declaring that they were FLQ hunger strikers. They had just begun picketing when law enforcement agents moved in from all directions.

A Montreal police spokesperson assured reporters that officers would be sent to New York to bring back Vallières and Gagnon. But they refused to return voluntarily, and the MPD launched extradition proceedings. Meanwhile, the escapades of the Vallières-Gagnon gang, as it came to be known, had caused another meltdown in the movement. The publication of *La Cognée* had been suspended from mid-June to mid-September, and when it resumed, with issue No. 61, the entire first page was given over to a message to the Corbo family. "Now that the newspapers, television and radio have ended their gluttonous sensation-alism over the death of your son," it began, ". . . we dare to ask your forgiveness. . . . Because believe us, it is not the pontiffs of separatism who have killed him, but the parasites of the working world and those responsible for our degradation. . . . Your son died in combat at age sixteen, the age in which others dream of adventure and embrace everything in life. . . . Like you, we regret it. We regret all the Jean Corbos of the world. We offer you our most humble and most sincere sympathy."

In issue No. 62, dated October 16, 1966, the *La Cognée* editors attempted to distance themselves from the fugitives and their acolytes. "No, the FLQ is not communist," they wrote, "contrary to the image which Vallières and Gagnon have given it through their writings and declarations. . . . It is necessary to emphasize that there was not even a hint of collaboration between us and the Vallières-Gagnon gang."

But even as the battered rump of the FLQ abandoned Vallières and Gagnon, others rallied to their side. On October 28, *Le Devoir* published a lengthy letter signed by sixteen Université de Montréal faculty. "We declare our solidarity with the hunger strike undertaken by Pierre Vallières and Charles Gagnon," they wrote. "We are fighting for the liberation of the workers of Quebec and, moreover, we are struggling against all forms of exploitation of man by man and we are trying to promote a more just and fraternal society through socialism.

"If Pierre Vallières and Charles Gagnon believed it was necessary to use VIOLENCE in organizing a new FLQ terrorist cell, they knew what they were doing. One can contest the realism and effectiveness of this method of action . . . just as one can contest the realism of decent people who believe the world to be peaceful when it is really based on violence done daily to the weakest."

The authors asked all others who shared their ideas to sign a petition at the office of the university's student newspaper. Some sixty people did so, and the following month several of those supporters formed the Comité d'aide au groupe Vallières-Gagnon. The committee maintained that Vallières and Gagnon were innocent, and its members stuck with the two defendants throughout the lengthy criminal proceedings against them, which began on January 17, 1967, after they were flown back under police guard and made their first appearance in a Montreal courtroom.

Pierre Vallières and Charles Gagnon were children of la Grande Noirceur. The Great Darkness. The Quebec of Maurice Duplessis and his Union Nationale government. The old church-dominated, priest-ridden Quebec. An era tainted by cronyism and corruption and mutually beneficial collusion between church and state. Vallières and Gagnon saw in their own families everything that was deplorable about that tradition-bound society and its docile populace.

Vallières was born in 1938, Gagnon in 1939. Vallières was the oldest of three boys, the son of a blue-collar labourer who worked for years at the CPR's vast, dirty and fume-filled Angus Shops in the city's east end, where a workforce of thousands manufactured and repaired locomotives and rail cars. Gagnon was one of ten boys and four girls, the offspring of a farm couple who worked the land together in the summer but lived apart in the winter while the elder Gagnon was off working as a lumberjack. The family farm was located on a concession road 2.5 kilometres from the St. Lawrence, on land well above the great river, and the young Gagnon could gaze upon its broad waters and dream of a different life—one far removed from the rocky soil and dilapidated barns, sheds and dwellings in the district. Vallières spent most of his youth in the drab and disorderly suburb of Ville Jacques-Cartier, which sprang up on the south shore opposite Montreal in the mid-1940s before municipal authorities had paved the streets, laid out sewers or installed sidewalks.

Vallières and Gagnon were both educated by religious authorities. Both were bright and read voraciously, but Gagnon was the better student. For seven years, he attended a tiny local school. He always stood first in his class, and in September 1952, at age thirteen, he was admitted to the seminary at Rimouski, a rarity for the son of a farmer. He spent eight years there, being taught by stern and demanding priests, and he gradually grew restless and discontented. He found the town dull and stifling, and he made few friends. Most of his classmates were the sons of doctors, lawyers or notaries, and he had little in common with them.

By the time he had completed his studies, he no longer fit in at home either. "My father rejoiced in my academic success," Gagnon later wrote in an autobiographical essay, "but he knew that we were drifting apart. My air of the emancipated young student, my new comportment, my taste for reading, my clean clothes, all that made me a member of the *'gens instruits*,' the educated people, whom he detested because he knew very well their tendency to profit from the uneducated."

Gagnon received his baccalaureate in the spring of 1960. That fall, he enrolled in the Faculty of Arts at the Université de Montréal to pursue a master's degree, then known as a *licence en lettres*. He was dazzled by the size and pace of the city. Everyone seemed wealthy to this newcomer from the country, especially the residents of Côte-des-Neiges and Outremont, the predominantly French-Canadian neighbourhoods around the university. Gagnon spent two years earning his degree, but by the time he had completed it, in the spring of 1962, he was again restless and discontented. He saw Quebec as "a country where one suffocated, a country where liberty did not exist, a country that was culturally oppressive."

Europe, he imagined, would be different. He accompanied a group of fellow students to Amsterdam and then Paris. He hoped to find liberated citizens and enlightened societies and he had vague plans to settle in the French capital. Instead, he returned to Montreal four months later a changed man. "I discovered that I was Québécois, that I was very attached to my country, that I missed my compatriots. . . ."

Gagnon was broke, a little desperate and took a job teaching French at a seminary in Valleyfield, a small town in southwestern Quebec, near the Ontario border. It was all too reminiscent of Rimouski, and he quit in June 1963 and returned to the Université de Montréal as a student and part-time lecturer in politics and economics. He was accustomed to the city and he had acquired an appetite for political activism. Dabbling in student journalism, he also became a founding member of l'Action sociale étudiant, a student social action group.

Volunteering with the Chantiers de Saint-Henri, a lay charitable organization that distributed food, clothing and household goods to residents of low-income neighbourhoods, was for Gagnon a radicalizing experience. He saw two worlds mere kilometres apart. He saw comfort and affluence in Outremont and Côte-des-Neiges on the north face of Mount Royal. But when he descended the mountain and went to Saint-Henri, down by the river, he saw poverty and hardship amid rundown, overcrowded row houses and tenements.

Gagnon made a crucial, life-altering decision in 1964. He rejected student activism, which he now saw as nothing more than earnest, well-meaning young people immersed in endless discussions. He concluded that the Chantiers de Saint-Henri would never change the world. He wanted no part of the RIN, which was, in his opinion, too centrist. He dismissed the Quiet Revolution as the work of politicians who were prepared to compromise with Ottawa, appease Washington and accept Anglo-Saxon capitalism and he opted instead for a revolution that would lead to a total transformation of Quebec society and he found a kindred spirit in Pierre Vallières.

Vallières was an angry young man who had tried his hand at many things and stuck to none. He had grown up in a three-room wood-frame house that was clad in red Insulbrick and was set too close to the unpaved street, which was dusty on hot summer days and a muddy mess when it rained. He had loved his father, but pitied him.

The elder Vallières had been put to work at fourteen when his own father was disabled by illness, and he had spent the last twenty years of his life working at the Angus Shops, and then at age fifty-three he had died of cancer. Whatever drive and dreams he had once possessed had been sucked out of him and Pierre Vallières blamed his mother for that. She was consumed by anxieties. In her mind, one never knew when unemployment or illness or some other calamity might deprive them of everything they had. She scrubbed and cleaned their little home—which grew over time as her husband added to it—with obsessive fervour and she managed household expenses with equal diligence. Vallières resented her caution and prudence and was at war with her for most of his youth.

Vallières thought little better of his teachers. He had attended three schools, the first run by nuns, the second by Christian brothers, the third by Franciscans. These teachers were, with rare exceptions, poorly educated but steeped in Church doctrine and charged with ensuring that the next generation absorbed and adhered to the faith. He regarded them as imbeciles or ignoramuses and behaved accordingly, and he quit school twice, the second time for good.

Vallières took a job as a clerk at the Ville Jacques-Cartier branch of the Banque Provinciale du Canada, but quit after a few months. He lasted two years at his next stop—L.G. Beaubien and Co., the country's largest French-Canadian-owned brokerage house, which was located on St. James Street in Montreal's financial district. Vallières processed dividend payments. It was dull, undemanding work, but he had no interest in advancing. He saw the stock market as the corrupt heart of capitalism, which delivered dividends to rich individuals and profits to powerful corporations.

Vallières read widely and deeply from the onset of adolescence—novelists, philosophers and theologians, French, German and Russian—and he read with even greater gusto and abandon when he was clerking at Beaubien. He had a good salary and there was a bookstore nearby named Beauchemin's, and on Friday afternoons, when it was payday, he would stock up, sometimes divesting himself of half his pay. It was there that he met Gaston Miron, the poet. Miron was the sales manager. That was his job, the work he did to pay the rent and to prop up his precarious publishing enterprise, Les Éditions de l'Hexagone.

Vallières befriended Miron and the two of them dined often at a restaurant on St-Denis Street, near Saint-Louis Square and Miron's home.

They talked for hours, discussing the evils of colonialism and oppression and the paths to liberation, and Miron introduced Vallières to poetry. Miron published emerging Quebec poets. He brought out two or three volumes a year, but he never published himself, though he had by then written "La marche à l'amour," which would become his most famous and oft-cited work, and he would recite it to Vallières, who listened like a dazed and star-struck teenager.

Vallières was writing in those days and he wrote with the same frenzied vigour as he read, shutting himself in his room for the evening, pen in hand, stacks of drafts and papers before him, and he would stick with it well into the night, long after the rest of the house was asleep. Miron advised him to slow down, take some time away from it all, but the advice went unheeded. Vallières wrote a novel and submitted it to a publisher. The publisher rejected it and he destroyed it. He wrote a second and destroyed it too. He had nearly completed a third and decided it was worthless, and one day in the spring of 1958, just after he had turned twenty, he heard a garbage truck on the street and he raced outside, manuscript in hand, and tossed it onto the heap of refuse at the rear of the vehicle.

Vallières quit the brokerage in the fall of 1958. He had dreamed about God. He felt called and he joined the Franciscans, spending a year as a novitiate and another at the order's monastery and school of philosophy in Quebec City, and for a time he experienced a joy he had never known. Peace and tranquility swept away the rage that had tormented him throughout adolescence, but his newfound sense of harmony didn't last. He came to despise the monastic life. It required blind obedience, belief without understanding and complete surrender to the will of God, and none of it was for him. The old rage returned. He felt like smashing everything in sight—statues, alms boxes, holy water basins—and he knew it was time to leave.

Vallières re-emerged into secular society in 1960, on the eve of the Quiet Revolution. He took a job as a sales clerk at the Université de Montréal bookstore and wrote occasional articles for the political journal *Cité libre*. But he soon ran afoul of the editors, Pierre Trudeau and Gérard Pelletier. They were preparing an issue in 1962 devoted to the pros and cons of Quebec separatism. When Vallières submitted a piece that was overtly sympathetic, they spiked it and he severed the relationship. He quit his job at the bookstore, endured a jobless winter and then took a job as a construction worker.

Then he changed direction again. The new Quebec emerging from the Quiet Revolution seemed hardly different from the old, insufferable Quebec of his childhood, and in September 1962 Vallières sailed for France. He imagined he would find a society enlightened by its great thinkers, its revolutionary past and its magnificent architecture, but he was disappointed. Paris appeared drab and the populace disillusioned after a long, vicious, losing war with Algeria, the former French colony in North Africa. He picked grapes in Burgundy, spent a workless winter in Paris, and day after day he wandered the streets lonely and depressed. Surviving on the charity of French Canadians living in Paris, he met leftist intellectuals and French communists who proved to be dull, uninspiring bureaucrats rather than revolutionaries. In a low moment, he nearly threw himself into the Seine. Instead, he wrote his mother, asked for money and booked passage home.

Vallières arrived in Montreal in March 1963 with little or no idea what he would do next. Pelletier solved his problem. He offered Vallières a job writing on world affairs for *La Presse* and suggested he also write for *Cité libre*. Six months later, Pelletier made him deputy editor, a decision he quickly regretted. Vallières recruited writers who were ardent nationalists, outright separatists or committed socialists, and in February 1964 he wrote and published a long article arguing for "a separatism wholly secular and anti-religious, a totalitarian socialism installed by violence, with the inevitable civil war provoked by the systematic agitation of a revolutionary party." Pelletier and the editorial board were appalled and they informed him that he had to adhere to the magazine's principles or resign. He resigned, and most of the writers he had recruited quit as well.

Vallières had by then embraced the thinking that would lead—albeit circuitously—to the campaign of terror in 1966. He had read Karl Marx and he was struck by a central notion in Marx's philosophical writings: Ideas must be linked to action. Knowledge had to produce practical results. He read Lenin, Mao Tse-tung, Che Guevara and other leading twentieth-century revolutionaries, and decided he needed to act. He had two clear goals: independence and revolution. Independence for Quebec and a socialist revolution for Quebec society. The overthrow of the capitalist economy and the creation of a new order run by workers for workers.

In October 1964, Vallières and Gagnon held a press conference to announce that they were launching a journal called *Révolution québécoise* to promote their agenda, and in early 1965 Vallières quit *La Presse* to work on it full time. The venture quickly failed, but Vallières turned his revolutionary fervour in a new direction. He, Gagnon and their *Révolution québécoise* team joined forces with Parti Pris, founded in 1963 to fight for independence, socialism and secularism, and they formed the Mouvement de libération populaire (MLP). This new movement hoped to win over the unions, the labour federations and the workers of Quebec. They marched on picket lines to show their solidarity with striking workers, organized anti–Vietnam war demonstrations in front of the U.S. consulate in downtown Montreal, and incited the crowds of young people who gathered in La Fontaine Park to protest on Victoria Day and Dominion Day.

But none of this was enough for the angry, restless Vallières and the like-minded Gagnon, and they opted for the FLQ and clandestine action. They wrote for *La Cognée*, Vallières under the pseudonym Mathieu Hébert, Gagnon as André Jacques. And in the fall of 1965 and winter of 1966 they recruited the young men who would carry out armed robberies, thefts, burglaries and bombings to advance their revolutionary goals.

———

Gagnon wrote letters while he was imprisoned in The Tombs, some to an older brother Georges and one long, churlish missive that was addressed to his father, Jules. The latter was published in a journal called *Jeune Québec*. The elder Gagnon was a proud and ambitious man who had had only a few years schooling, who had worked from dawn till dusk on the farm every summer and then done the same every winter in the lumber camps, who had still owed money on his land when he sold it in 1952 (having farmed it for thirty-five years), and who in 1966 was retired and living on a modest pension.

Gagnon described his father as a typical Quebecker of his generation, one of the "little guys" who was repeatedly hoodwinked by the politicians and their promises. "You believed Duplessis was a man of the people," Gagnon wrote. "I do not understand that at all. You knew you were being robbed. You cursed, yes you cursed—against taxes, against the bosses, against the mayor, the notary, the dentist, the manager of the co-op and, at the worst of times, likely the priest." Quebec was run by politicians who were beholden to big business, he told his father. They did nothing to bring industry or good jobs to depressed regions, or to improve the lot of farmers or the wages of the workers in the lumber camps. Instead, they bought them off with false promises at election time or with the prospect of a minor patronage position. "You see, father, there are not ten solutions. There are not even two. The little guys must organize themselves to run their affairs together. They must take power and rid themselves of those who exploit them. This will not happen through elections. It will take a revolution. Yes, a revolution."

Vallières wrote as well while incarcerated in The Tombs and fighting extradition, though he didn't write letters. Instead, he wrote a book—one of the most inflammatory polemics ever written in Canada. It was part memoir (the story of his family, his childhood and his peripatetic career), part history of the French, rural, Catholic and downtrodden people of Quebec, and part revolutionary manifesto. It was written, he declared in the opening pages, to "bear witness to the determination of the workers of Quebec to put an end to three centuries of exploitation, of injustice borne in silence, of sacrifice accepted in vain, of insecurity endured with resignation.

"This book," he continued, "bears witness precisely to the efforts, the trials and errors we must be willing to go through in order to free ourselves from all the balls and chains that capitalist society attached to our feet as soon as we were born, chains which are so deeply embedded in our flesh that it is impossible to shake them off completely." The people of Quebec, Vallières argued—the farmers and the workers as opposed to the clergy and the professionals (the lawyers, notaries, doctors, journalists and French-Canadian businessmen who formed the petty bourgeoisie)—were no better than exploited, second-class citizens in their own homeland. "Have they not been, ever since the establishment of New France in the seventeenth century, the servants of the imperialists, the white niggers of America?" he asked "Were they not *imported* like the American blacks to serve as cheap labour in the New World? After three centuries, their condition remains the same. They still constitute a reservoir of cheap labour whom the capitalists are completely free to put to work or reduce to unemployment, as it suits their interests, whom they are completely free to underpay, mistreat and trample underfoot. . . ."

The Quiet Revolution had done nothing, in Vallières opinion, to improve the lives of ordinary Quebeckers. They needed to rise collectively, he wrote, and launch "a total revolution, which will not only overthrow the capitalist state but at the same time abolish everything that has for centuries perverted and poisoned social relations, life in society: private ownership of the means of production and exchange, the accumulation and concentration of capital in the hands of a few. . . ."

Independence would do nothing either if the French-Canadian business class and the ravenous capitalists of English Canada and the United States retained control of the Quebec economy. "Political independence is only a myth (a luxury we can do without, bled white as we are!)," he wrote, "except on condition that it is preceded by the expropriation of foreign capital (American and other) and the nationalization of natural resources, banks and other enterprises that belong to foreign capital; the modification in depth of the monetary, financial, commercial and customs relations that enslave us to the United States; and a social transformation that can lead to the disappearance of the parasitic classes (the English-speaking and French-speaking petty bourgeoisie of Quebec) which are tied to imperialism and profit from the sale of Quebec to foreigners. Those are the prerequisites of true independence." It would require revolutionary violence, and by that he meant "the organized and conscious violence of a people, a class, a national or multinational collectivity that has chosen to confront, combat and overcome the violence—it too organized and conscious—of the established Order that is crushing it."

Vallières produced his manuscript in less than four months while he was cooped up in a cell. He wrote standing up and used the upper bunk as a writing surface. He wrote in pencil because pens were not allowed in The Tombs, and he told his jailers that he was writing notes to his lawyer, who took bits and pieces of the manuscript with him after each visit. Vallières's book—*Nègres blancs d'Amérique* or *White Niggers of America*—ran to some 524 pages and was published on March 15, 1968, while Vallières was on trial for the murder of Thérèse Morin.

The trial began on February 28 and ended on April 4. The Crown's principal witness was Serge Demers, the bomb maker in the gang. Demers had implicated Vallières in the LaGrenade bombing on four occasions, first when he was arrested and later when he testified at preliminary hearings or trials of his accomplices. Each time, he told his interrogators that Vallières had been present at meetings when the LaGrenade strike was discussed. He swore that Vallières had proposed the attack on the factory and had helped plan it. Then, at the Vallières trial, he completely rejected his previous testimony. Demers told the court that the detectives had fabricated parts of his statement and that another Crown attorney had told him he was compelled to stand by the statement when he testified. A second member of the gang, Marcel Faulkner, who had been called as a Crown witness, also denied that Vallières played any part in the attack.

With these reversals, the Crown had no direct evidence linking Vallières to the bombing and, mid-trial, was compelled to reduce the charge from murder to manslaughter. To make this stick, prosecutors produced hundreds of pages of Vallières's prose, most of it loaded with revolutionary rhetoric that read as though forged in fire. The prosecution hoped to prove that Vallières had incited his followers and was therefore responsible for their violent attacks. The Crown's case was weak, but the defendant's conduct hardly endeared him to the presiding judge, Yves Leduc, or the twelve men of the jury. Vallières defended himself, and he was constantly bouncing out of his chair, raising objections, all to no avail.

The jurors deliberated less than four hours before returning with a verdict: guilty as charged. Justice Leduc asked Vallières if he had anything to say. "Mr. Chairman," he said, "the only thing I have to say is that I am not at all guilty of the crime with which I am reproached and for which I am convicted today. I have to say that the jury here was deliberately led into error. I have to say that today is the conclusion of a political trial, a conclusion which does indeed have its logic. I have to say that perhaps the interests of a particular class were defended, were very well represented before this court through this trial. I have to say that this court, in fact, is a court tailor-made to get the man it wanted to get." Then Justice Leduc said, "In view of your clearly belligerent attitudes, I sentence you to imprisonment in perpetuity."

Vallières appealed the verdict and the Quebec Court of Appeal overturned it. The justices of the higher court wrote that Vallières had been convicted largely on the basis of his political writings and criticized the prosecution for appealing to "passion or prejudice or fear." Vallières was convicted a second time and sentenced to thirty months, a decision that was also overturned. As for Gagnon, he was acquitted on the charge of murder, but was convicted for conspiring to commit an armed robbery and handed a two-year sentence, which was struck down on appeal.

Vallières and Gagnon repeatedly applied for bail and were repeatedly turned down, which enhanced their status among FLQ militants as well as moderate separatists and prominent members of the Quebec arts community all of whom rallied to their cause. In May 1968, shortly after Vallières's initial conviction, two leaders of the Comité d'aide au groupe Vallières-Gagnon, the singer Pauline Julien and one-time CBC journalist Jacques Larue-Langlois, organized an evening of solidarity called Poèmes et Chansons de la Résistance. A standing room crowd packed Gesù Hall in Montreal. Nearly fifty of Quebec's leading musicians and writers, including rock and roller Robert Charlebois, actor Jean Duceppe and poet Gaston Miron, participated, and similar benefits were held in Hull, Sherbrooke, Trois-Rivières and Quebec City.

Meanwhile, the two inmates continued to wield considerable influence from Bordeaux Prison. *White Niggers* became a sacred text for militants and was widely read beyond such narrow circles. And Vallières urged a more radical measure to spring himself and Gagnon. In late June 1968, he wrote to Larue-Langlois, stating, "If you really want to get us out of here before independence comes, you'll have to take drastic steps and organize a spectacular operation: a political kidnapping—two influential members of the Quebec government or the Trudeau government, or maybe two judges, who would only be released in return for our freedom. . . . It would only take half a dozen serious guys, two guns, a camp or isolated farm and somebody to issue communiqués. That's all—plus a lot of secrecy and nerve."[1]

Even after all that, the two diehard revolutionaries, and convicted terrorists, were still sitting in prison in early 1970, by which time the Comité d'aide au groupe Vallières-Gagnon had been transformed into the Mouvement pour la défense des prisonniers politiques du Québec in order to agitate for their release. Gagnon was freed on bail in late

February, and Vallières in May—both unrepentant and unreformed and ready to rejoin the ranks of the militants who believed that violence was the only path to independence.

---

1. Police discovered the letter while conducting raids in October 1970 under the provisions of the War Measures Act and charged Vallières with three counts of counselling kidnapping. He pleaded guilty to the charges in September 1972.

Eight

"VIVE LE QUÉBEC LIBRE!"

IN THE 365 DAYS THAT constituted Canada's centennial, only three bombs exploded in the city of Montreal and the surrounding suburbs. The first blast occurred at 12:40 a.m. on January 1, 1967, destroying a mailbox in the financial district, the second on February 12, demolishing another mailbox. The third detonated on October 16 outside a 7 Up bottling plant in the Town of Mount Royal, where a labour dispute had turned ugly after some of the workers went on strike and management hired replacements.

The relative lull in separatist-inspired terrorism was a good thing. Canadians in virtually every city, town, village and hamlet from coast to coast to coast were celebrating one hundred years of Confederation, and the epicentre of it all occurred in Montreal—host city of the Universal and International Exhibition called Expo 67.

The exhibition was the biggest, grandest, most ambitious event in the nation's history, and was held on two islands in the St. Lawrence—Île Sainte-Hélène, a natural feature, and Île Notre-Dame, an artificially created one. Twenty-eight million tons of rock and rubble—most of it removed from beneath the city of Montreal during the creation of its subway system—was dumped into the river to enlarge Île Sainte-Hélène, to create Île Notre-Dame and to serve as the base for 850 buildings and pavilions.

One hundred and twenty nations were represented and the 183-day fair attracted 50,306,648 paying visitors—a total second only to that of the Paris exhibition of 1900 and nearly double the number the site was designed to handle. In addition, there were five million unpaid admissions, those being employees, performers, journalists, special guests and official visitors. The special guests included Ed Sullivan, Bing Crosby, Marlene Dietrich and Thelonius Monk, while the truly astonishing list of official visitors included a prince and princess—Rainier III of Monaco and his radiant wife Grace Kelly; an emperor—Haile Selassie of Ethiopia; a former First Lady—Jackie Kennedy; two monarchs—our own Elizabeth II and Thailand's King Bhumibol Adulyadej; and two presidents, Lyndon B. Johnson of the United States, who came and went without causing a ripple, and Charles de Gaulle of France, who detonated a diplomatic bomb that caused outrage in Ottawa and delirium in Quebec separatist circles.

De Gaulle sailed from France aboard the navy cruiser *Colbert* and arrived in Quebec City on the morning of Sunday, July 23. Governor General Roland Michener and Quebec premier Daniel Johnson and some two thousand beaming, cheering Quebeckers welcomed de Gaulle, and, later that day, an adoring and much larger crowd jubilantly greeted the French president on the steps of City Hall and sang "La Marseillaise," the national anthem of France, with him.

The next morning, de Gaulle left Quebec City for Montreal in a black limousine, amid an eight-kilometre-long motorcade that followed the historic Chemin du Roy, or King's Road, built originally by the French regime in the early eighteenth century to link the capital with Montreal. The Quebec government adorned the 300-kilometre route with the flags of France and Quebec and scheduled brief stops in Donnacona, Sainte-Anne-de-la-Pérade, Trois-Rivières, Louiseville, Berthier and Repentigny. The government had distributed tens of thousands of small, hand-held flags, and at each stop de Gaulle emerged from his limo, spoke briefly and gazed upon thousands of Quebeckers waving France's *Tricolore* flag and Quebec's *Fleurdelisé*.

The government had predicted that a million Quebeckers would greet the seventy-six-year-old French president, but Quebec's French-language newspapers put the crowds at half a million while their English-language counterparts considered one hundred thousand a generous estimate. It made no difference to de Gaulle. The rapturous reception at every stop reminded him of the liberation of France from Nazi occupation and his triumphal arrival in Paris on August 25, 1944. It touched the old man so deeply that he spoke from the heart, and everything he said lifted the spirits of Quebec separatists.

De Gaulle's motorcade took ten hours to reach Montreal. "By the end of the journey," the *Gazette* reported, "the general was slowing down and beginning to look haggard, his normally clear and powerful voice began to grow hoarse from thundering into the dead microphones at the last two stops." De Gaulle and his entourage, which included a press corps of 350, arrived at City Hall at about 8 p.m., half an hour late. A big crowd awaited the French president—at least three thousand according to the English-language newspapers, more like fifteen or twenty thousand according to the French press. When the presidential motorcade pulled up, dozens of placard-bearing, flag-waving separatists began chanting *"Québec libre! Québec libre!"* while the rest of the crowd unleashed a deafening ovation and hundreds of police officers attempted to maintain control.

De Gaulle was scheduled to make a brief appearance on the red-carpeted steps leading to the front doors of City Hall. He was to stand facing the crowd—shoulder to shoulder with Premier Johnson and Mayor Jean Drapeau—while the Montreal Firemen's Band played the national anthems of France and Canada. Then he would attend an official reception. But his emotions got the better of him. He sang "La Marseillaise" and the crowd sang with him. He stood in silence while the band played "O Canada" and the booing, hissing and heckling nearly drowned out the music. He, Johnson and Drapeau turned to enter City Hall and a thunderous chant arose—"We want de Gaulle! We want de Gaulle! To the balcony! To the balcony!"

De Gaulle soon appeared on the balcony above the entrance and a new chant arose—"Speech! Speech!" There was no microphone because he hadn't been scheduled to speak, but a Radio-Canada technician quickly produced one and connected it, and de Gaulle delivered more than anyone expected. "In the name of France, I salute you," he said. "I salute you with all my heart. Here and along the route I have found an atmosphere the same as that of the Liberation. All along the route, I witnessed an immense epoch of development, of progress and liberation. Some day you will be able to help France. All of France sees you today."

And then the diplomatic bomb: "*Vive Montréal! Vive le Québec! Vive le Québec libre!*"

The federal government had ignored all of de Gaulle's other provocative statements, which amounted to meddling in the country's internal affairs, but it could not ignore this. The Cabinet met twice the next afternoon to decide on a response. At 6 p.m., the Prime Minister's Office issued a statement and by then the office had received 936 telegrams, as well as hundreds of phone calls, from Canadians appalled by the French president's comments. Prime Minister Pearson's statement accused de Gaulle of encouraging the tiny separatist minority that wanted to tear Canada apart and went on to say, "The people of Canada are free. Every province of Canada is free. Canadians do not need to be liberated. Indeed, many thousands of Canadians gave their lives in two world wars in the liberation of France and other European countries. Canada will continue to remain unified and will reject any effort to destroy her unity."

De Gaulle was miffed, but would not be silenced. During a luncheon hosted by Montreal mayor Jean Drapeau, he again encouraged Quebec's separatists. "You must become masters of your own destiny," he said. "You must not stop, you must not pause even for a moment. You must go straight ahead on the road to your destiny." Then he cancelled a scheduled visit to Ottawa and flew home from Montreal-Dorval International Airport.

Separatists were jubilant. RIN leader Pierre Bourgault told an interviewer, "For the first time in 200 years someone has come to our own land to tell us in French what he thinks. He is the first man who is a winner to come and say to us: don't give up." Less than a week later, Liberal deputy François Aquin declared his separatist sympathies and quit the Liberal caucus to sit as an independent. And René Lévesque, still a Liberal deputy but an ardent nationalist, told the weekly paper *La Patrie*, "It is undeniable that de Gaulle's visit gave a lot of vigour to the thinking of independentists."

That fall, Lévesque added fresh momentum and jolted the established political order when he became the first major public figure to support independence. On September 18, 1967, less than a month before a provincial Liberal policy convention, Lévesque released a six-thousand-word manifesto, later published as a booklet entitled *Option Québec*. It began with the following emotional appeal to his fellow Quebeckers:

> We are Québécois. What that means first and foremost . . . is that we are attached to this one corner of the earth where we can be completely ourselves: this Quebec, the only place where we have the unmistakable feeling that "here we can be really at home."
>
> Being ourselves is essentially a matter of keeping and developing a personality that has survived for three and a half centuries.
>
> At the core of this personality is the fact that we speak French.

The Canadian confederation, he argued, in which two nations attempted to function within a single political framework, was finished. Quebec had to take control over certain essential elements of statehood—citizenship, immigration, international relations, social security and welfare, among others—if it were to develop and progress. But these two nations need not sever their ties completely. Given that a newly independent Quebec would remain wedged between the remnants of Canada, an economic union would be practical and inevitable.

Lévesque's concept—sovereignty-association—was anathema to most of his caucus colleagues, the party leadership and the membership. It was put to a vote at the Liberal policy convention in October in Quebec City. Lévesque asked for a secret ballot, but the matter was settled by a show of hands. Of the 1,500 delegates in attendance, only four supported him, according to newspaper reports. But before the vote was called, Lévesque and a small band of supporters had left the convention and the party and bet their futures on a separate and independent Quebec.

De Gaulle's visit and Lévesque's dramatic exit from the Liberal Party reinvigorated the entire separatist movement—including the FLQ and others on the radical fringe. There had been no violent crimes or terrorist acts throughout the spring and summer of 1967, and even the voice of the FLQ had gone silent. The sixty-seventh issue of *La Cognée* had appeared in April 1967 and publication had then ceased.

However, in November a new FLQ journal appeared. Called *La Victoire*, it was more professional in look than *La Cognée*, and more militant and menacing in tone. The inaugural issue declared that the FLQ would lead the Quebec people "in their struggle for social, economic and political independence" and provided detailed, well-illustrated instructions on how to make bombs and Molotov cocktails. There was advice on the weapons of choice and number one on the list was the compact, lightweight .30-calibre M1 rifle, a firearm favoured by both police and mobsters. "Let us take all the time we need to get ready," *La Victoire* advised. "And when we strike, the blows will be so powerful that the enemy will not soon recover."

The next wave of unrest and violence was slow to build, but washed over Montreal in 1968. There were street protests and disturbances, one of the worst of Montreal's many riots and more bombings. The trouble began on the evening of February 27, outside the 7 Up plant in the affluent and suburban Town of Mount Royal.

The beverage company's 106 drivers and sales representatives had walked off the job on June 15, 1967. They had voted to join the International Union of Brewery and Soft Drink Workers in the summer of

1964. The Canadian Labour Relations Board had certified the union, but for three years the company had refused to negotiate and defied or appealed all orders to commence bargaining. Instead it hired replacement workers and put its fleet of seventy-five trucks back on the road.

The labour movement had organized several demonstrations that were small and relatively peaceful. The protest on the chilly evening of February 27 was large and violent. At least 2,500 people participated— representatives from the province's largest labour federation, unionized workers from other plants and a large contingent from the RIN. They assembled on the eastern boundary of the town and then marched to the 7 Up plant, led by a truck equipped with a loudspeaker and bearing two Quebec flags. The marchers chanted "Re-vo-lu-tion! Re-vo-lu-tion!" and "Down with the scabs!" They stopped briefly at the plant and unleashed their fury. Hurling objects of all sorts, including Molotov cocktails, they nearly set the place on fire.

Then they marched fifteen blocks to the town hall, smashing dozens of windows, setting utility boxes on fire and tearing down street signs. They also battered two police cruisers and a radio station news car. At the town hall, the mob met the municipal police force and 150 members of the SQ riot squad and, after a tense standoff, turned and began marching back toward the 7 Up plant. The demonstration lasted two and a half hours. Five people were arrested and several dozen were injured. And the first bomb scare of the year occurred when a letter carrier discovered an explosive device in a mailbox and a local officer dismantled it while a crowd of newspaper photographers watched attentively from a safe distance.

The first indication of an FLQ resurgence occurred in early May when the SQ reported that two cases of dynamite—fifty sticks all told—had been stolen from the Dominion Lime quarry in Saint-Bruno-de-Montarville and the perpetrators had written on a wall: *"Merci. FLQ."* Then the chief of police for the Town of Mount Royal announced that one of his officers had dismantled a bomb outside the 7 Up plant. But these events were overshadowed by Montreal's St. Jean Baptiste Day riot of Monday, June 24, 1968, and by Prime Minister Pierre Trudeau's courageous defiance of a separatist-inspired mob.

The St. Jean Baptiste Day parade was the major event of the holiday as always. One newspaper told its readers to expect "a dazzling display of color" amid the twenty-six floats and the usual mix of majorettes, marching bands and happy-go-lucky, flag-waving youngsters. It would begin at the Maisonneuve Shopping Centre in the east-end suburb of Ville d'Anjou and would proceed west for ten kilometres, largely along Sherbrooke Street, before terminating at the downtown Château Champlain hotel. Upwards of half a million Montrealers were expected to line the route while an equal number of Quebeckers watched on TV.

Prior to the parade, newspapers speculated whether Trudeau would be among the dignitaries on the reviewing stand that was being erected in front of the Municipal Library, on the south side of Sherbrooke Street, opposite La Fontaine Park. Trudeau had won the Liberal leadership on April 6 that year. He had immediately succeeded Lester B. Pearson as prime minister, and a few days later he had called a general election for June 25—the day after the St. Jean Baptiste holiday.

Trudeau campaigned under the slogan "One Canada, One Nation," and he had criss-crossed the country, addressing ever-larger crowds of captivated voters and swooning youngsters and leaving his main rival, Progressive Conservative leader Robert Stanfield, swimming in vain against a tide known as Trudeaumania. He had returned to Montreal on June 21, a Friday, to a rapturous reception. At noon, he addressed a vast crowd of thirty-five to forty thousand followers who packed the square in front of Place Ville Marie and the streets around it.

That evening, he spoke to 2,500 supporters outside the east-end Church of the Nativity. Separatist hecklers did their best to shout down Trudeau, but only managed to provoke him. "Look at these people," he said. "They put candidates in every riding [during the 1966 provincial election] and they couldn't even elect one. Now they want to tell

the people of Quebec how to run things. They say there will be disturbances at the St. Jean Baptiste parade. They're not content to discuss
issues, to hold meetings, to print publications. . . . They have the freedom to do that. We know what kind of republic we'd have with them—a
police republic."

The police were prepared for trouble on the evening of the parade.
Pierre Bourgault of the RIN, Reggie Chartrand of the Knights of Independence and other leading separatist agitators had spent the weekend
rallying their supporters and sympathizers. The parade began at 9 p.m.
and the lead floats did not reach the reviewing stand until 10:15, but the
trouble started well before that. By 7 p.m., an enormous crowd of young
people had gathered in La Fontaine Park, including several hundred agitators who were carrying placards, chanting slogans and handing out
leaflets urging people not to vote in the next day's federal election.

The first arrests occurred at 7:30 and there were more arrests shortly
after 8 p.m. Around 8:30, four men hoisted Bourgault to their shoulders
and began carrying him through the crowd. They were plainclothes
police and they whisked the startled separatist to a paddy wagon with
doors open. That's when the trouble started. Fierce fighting broke out
in the front lines between demonstrators and police. Demonstrators
elsewhere in the park began hurling stones and pop bottles. Dozens of
helmeted, baton-wielding officers charged the crowd and the battle was
on. It lasted until one o'clock in the morning.

Radio-Canada had four reporters on hand to cover the parade: Janine
Paquet and Gérald Lachance posted in a broadcast booth opposite the
reviewing stand, and Paul Racine and André Dubois amid the crowd.
The journalists unexpectedly ended up covering a riot. What follows is
a condensed version of their coverage:

Gérald Lachance: Hello, Paul Racine. Can you hear me, Paul
    Racine? Paul Racine, can you hear me?
Paul Racine: Hello Gérald Lachance, Paul Racine here, I can
    hear you well enough. There's a terrible racket all around

me. People screaming. Protesters chanting slogans. The
roar of police motorcycles. I will try to give you a summary
of the situation. . . . For half an hour, we have witnessed,
we and all the journalists present here, scenes of brutality
which . . . I have not personally seen before in Montreal.
Police and demonstrators are being injured. And in making
arrests, the least you can say is that the police have been
very rough. Several children have been slightly injured and
I have seen mothers who came with their children to watch
the parade leaving and returning to their homes.

GL: André Dubois, can you hear us?

André Dubois: Yes, hello Gérald, I am at the reviewing stand.
I see behind you, in Park La Fontaine, four fires have been
lit. . . . Three or four minutes ago a police officer was carried
to an ambulance on a stretcher and taken to hospital.

Janine Paquet begins to describe the parade, but Lachance abruptly
interrupts.

GL: Oh, one minute Janine! I see some demonstrators have
overturned a police car, two even . . . there are three police
cars, three patrol cars overturned on the extension of
Cherrier Street. . . . Paul Racine, you are on the spot. Can
you hear us?

PR: I hear you very well. I'm between two . . . two groups of
protesters who are attacking some automobiles. They're
throwing things. They've turned over two automobiles
right in front of me. The police are about to intervene.
Police on horses and motorcycles. They've turned over a
police car and another automobile. The demonstrators are
now attacking a third vehicle and trying to overturn it . . .
it's over. The police are on the spot now. It's very difficult to
see what's happening. Oh, projectiles are landing from all
sides. I'm going to have to take shelter behind an automobile. They're breaking the windows of a Montreal police

car. And here come the police. It's the police on horses who are charging the demonstrators, nightsticks raised and the crowd retreats . . . the crowd retreats leaving four vehicles overturned and completely demolished.

GL: And now the crowd, to avoid the police charge, to avoid being struck has completely invaded Sherbrooke Street and halted the parade. And another car has been overturned on Cherrier Street, Cherrier just behind Sherbrooke. . . . And there is another vehicle overturned and very, very badly damaged. There is broken glass all over the road. There are broken barricades and really an atmosphere of very, very great tension here this evening. Paul Racine, are you still there?

PR: Yes, I swear this is not funny. I'm actually, literally lying alongside an automobile near La Fontaine Park and they are bombarding us with projectiles that are landing non-stop around us. . . . I don't dare get up. We literally have to hide on the ground behind these vehicles.

GL: Thank you. And, well, it's the same here. There are police cars and motorcycles leaving their place in front of the reviewing stand and they're trying to push back the crowd in front of them. Nothing can move. Everything is absolutely immobilized. Janine, can you see anything?

Janine Paquet: I see three injured women who are being carried to a police ambulance. It's extremely dangerous for the crowd. The crowd cannot protect itself. We're on a platform facing the stage where the dignitaries are seated, the dignitaries and the prime minister of Canada, Mr. Trudeau. . . . Everyone on the stage is watching what is happening—the demonstrators in the crowd. The parade is temporarily immobilized. The crowd is booing and there are fumes in the air from Molotov cocktails and there is broken glass and bottles everywhere. The police are going from left to right. . . .

GL: Thank you Janine. . . . I don't know if it's caused by Molotov cocktails but there is a very, very acrid smell of smoke in the air. It is a veritable riot. . . . The young girls on the floats are leaving them, they're leaving the floats. The floats are abandoned in the middle of Sherbrooke Street.

JP: They've thrown something, I think, at Mr. Trudeau.

GL (voice halting): I don't think it hit him, eh Janine?

JP: No, not at all. . . . It looks like everyone wants to evacuate except . . .

GL: And there's another bottle which . . . which has come from the crowd and it landed at the foot of the reviewing stand. And the guests of honour are quickly seeking shelter, are leaving, are quitting the stage altogether. Mr. Trudeau is still there. He's seating himself and with a broad gesture of his hand seems to be saying to the other guests: "Choose for yourself, I'm staying." Paul Racine, are you listening?

PR (after a long pause): Hello, do you hear me Gérald Lachance? Janine Paquet?

GL: Yes, hello Paul!

PR: Ah well, I am actually at the edge of La Fontaine Park and the rumour circulated that the prime minister evacuated the stage. Then hundreds and hundreds of demonstrators rushed toward the police lines on Sherbrooke. I don't know whether the police will be able to contain them.

GL: Ah well, I can assure you that Mr. Trudeau is still there . . .

The attack on the reviewing stand occurred shortly before 11 p.m. It took police another two hours to put down the riot and restore order, and early the next morning Police Director J.P. Gilbert stood before some fifty journalists at a news conference. Many had been shocked at the sight of officers beating protesters with three-foot-long truncheons, and they posed questions about police brutality. Gilbert curtly dismissed them. "They always cry police brutality," he said, referring to the protesters. "There was no police retaliation until demonstrators started throwing projectiles, mainly pop bottles. It is a fact that the projectiles were being thrown everywhere, even into the crowd, and not just at the police. We had to protect the public."

Then Gilbert provided an account of the evening's events. Some of the demonstrators had hurled bottles filled with paint. A few had somehow obtained Jet Commando Tear Gas, a product only available in the United States, and had sprayed police with it. The department had a thousand officers on duty, including a cordon of uniformed and plainclothes officers in front of the reviewing stand. Police made 293 arrests—so many that the holding cells in nearby stations were quickly filled to capacity and prisoners had to be transported elsewhere. Forty-three officers and eighty-three spectators were injured. Seventeen horses also suffered injuries, though all later recovered. Twelve cruisers were damaged or destroyed, and an undetermined number of private automobiles were also damaged.

The demonstrators broke the police lines and got close to the reviewing stand only once, but TV cameramen and newspaper photographers captured images of several dozen dignitaries scrambling to safety inside the municipal library while Trudeau ignored all those who urged him to retreat. For a few moments, he sat alone at the front of the stand, smiling and leaning forward with his arms resting on the rail. The whole commotion lasted less than three minutes before police re-formed their line and pushed the demonstrators back and the other dignitaries returned to their seats, but in those three minutes a legend was born. Trudeau was forever cast as the fearless leader who would not be intimidated, even by an out-of-control separatist mob.

A second legend arose out of the St. Jean Baptiste Day riot, one created by the separatist side. Lawyers who were sympathetic to the cause collected eyewitness accounts of what happened that night. They took sworn statements from journalists, students, labour leaders, a doctor, a comedian, an ambulance driver, a soldier, a farmer and some who had been there simply to watch the parade.

Housewife and spectator Monic Cournoyer swore she saw two officers take hold of a teenager and pin his arms behind his back while a third and then a fourth struck him over the head. "I was sick at heart at the sight of such a disgusting spectacle," she told lawyer Bruno Colpron. Raymond Lanteigne, a merchant, attended the parade with his three children and the child of a friend. "An officer gave me a shove from behind," he said. "When I told him he had no right to push me, two others grabbed me, kicked me, struck me, took me by the hair and threw me in a paddy wagon." A Jesuit priest, Father Jacques Couture, who worked with the poor in Saint-Henri, was arrested and taken to a police detachment and thrown into a cell with sixteen others, including a young English-speaking Trudeau supporter who had a bloody gash on his cheek. The youth pleaded for medical attention, Father Couture said, but the officers ignored him and taunted the prisoners instead, saying, "Look at them. The dirty separatist dogs. They ought to go to the gas chambers."

Reggie Chartrand gave a long, detailed statement. He was in the park when the riot started, but claimed to be a mere spectator. He watched several officers beat three youths, one of whom lost consciousness and collapsed. "He took at least two more blows," Chartrand said. "It sickened me and I told the police to leave them alone. They weren't causing any trouble. That's when one of the officers noticed me and shouted, "It's Chartrand. Get him." Three or four officers surrounded him and kicked and beat him and hauled him off to a paddy wagon and then a police detachment, bleeding profusely from wounds to his face and scalp. He was allowed to wash up before being whisked to hospital, with his hands cuffed behind his back despite a badly swollen left wrist. From the hospital, officers escorted him back to the detachment and a crowded cell, where he spent the night and the following day—without being given anything to drink or being allowed to use the washroom. "In the afternoon," Chartrand told the lawyer Robert Lemieux, "around five o'clock, they treated me like a human being. They let me go to the washroom. It was about time. It had been twelve hours."[1]

The lawyers took sixty-one sworn statements and compiled them and

turned them over to Les Éditions Parti Pris, the small, left-wing, separatist publishing house, and the editors added an introduction, a condensed
version of the Radio-Canada broadcast, newspaper photos and editorial
comment and published it all in November that year under the title *Le
Lundi de la Matraque: 24 Juin 1968*. The publication was a small, square,
poorly bound paperback, printed on low-grade paper and illustrated with
grainy black-and-white images—mostly police manhandling protesters
or beating them or charging at them on horseback with sticks raised—
but it was the book's message, not its appearance, that mattered.

"The 24th of June 1968 will not be forgotten," the editors wrote in
their introduction. "That night will not be another of those dates that
our historians can only piece together with difficulty in thirty or fifty
years, like so many important dates in the tragic history of Quebec,
which are today forgotten, unknown and buried in the archives, but
which, assembled piece by piece, show that Quebeckers have always
demonstrated their discontent and their anger toward those who despise
them, exploit them or betray them.

"And the repression has been violent, bloody and sometimes mur-
derous.

"This small volume," they wrote, "is filled with the same violence
exercised by the established order or its representatives against those
who disagree with them, against those who want change or simply
want to express their ideas freely."

And so, in the annals of the separatist movement, Monday, June 24,
1968, became a day of infamy—the Monday of the Bludgeoning—when
police attacked peaceful, innocent protesters and clubbed them like
baby seals.

---

1. On January 20, 1969, Chartrand was convicted on three charges of assaulting police
   officers—he had sprayed tear gas in their eyes—and he was sentenced to three consecutive one-month jail terms.

Nine

"THIS WIND OF MADNESS"

DETECTIVE-SERGEANT ROBERT CÔTÉ ENDURED one restless night after another in the fall of 1968 and winter of 1969, and when he slept, he often slept poorly. He was troubled by images of poor Walter Leja. Leja reaching for a bomb in a mailbox a moment before it exploded. Leja lying on a Westmount street and a crowd of stunned onlookers uncertain whether he was dead or alive. Leja lying in a hospital bed, minus most of his left arm and rendered deaf and dumb by the force of the blast.

Côté saw himself laid out on a stretcher, his body battered and broken and his face blank and statuesque, or resting peacefully in a casket, in uniform of course, and dozens of fellow officers arriving at a funeral home and lining up to pay their respects. He saw such things and said to himself, *It could happen to me*—and he was not normally given to such disturbing thoughts. He was only thirty-two and was by nature a cheerful, outgoing, exuberant individual and he had good reason to be happier than usual that fall and winter. He had met his wife Pierrette Beaudry in January 1968, they had married in July, they had purchased their first home and they were expecting their first child. Their home— the first floor of a row house, with an external spiral staircase leading to the unit above—was located on one of the numbered, north–south avenues of Rosemont and was a fifteen- to twenty-minute drive from police headquarters. But Côté scarcely had time to enjoy his newfound status as husband, homeowner and expectant father.

Crude homemade bombs were exploding all over the city and, if they weren't exploding, it was because alert citizens had spotted them and called police and he or his partners on the bomb squad had dismantled them. Forty-six bombs were planted within Montreal or the surrounding municipalities between mid-August 1968 and the end of February 1969. Most were planted at night—the only concession the bombers made to public safety—and the targets were usually employers with labour troubles.

Côté had replaced Léo Plouffe as head of the squad in July 1966, and the position came with a car—a late model Chevrolet Biscayne station wagon. It was dark blue and unmarked and equipped with a siren and a portable magnetic flasher that could be attached to the roof when he responded to a call, and he kept a set of head-to-toe protective armour known as a Spooner suit in the rear of the vehicle. The department had acquired the eighty-five-pound suit from the Spooner Armor Co. of New York, a firm founded in the early 1920s by Bernard Spooner and his partner Leo Krause. Spooner and Krause had developed the first commercially successful bullet-proof vests. They created the armoured suit in response to a series of bombings that took place in New York between 1940 and 1957. The Montreal bombers used high-explosive dynamite, which created supersonic shock waves that were powerful enough to kill a person. Dynamite also produced a deadly shower of shrapnel. The Spooner suit provided no protection against such lethal forces and Côté seldom wore it, though when he did it made for good pictures in the next day's papers.

Côté and his men had another piece of protective equipment—a hinged screen made of half-inch-thick aluminum and tall enough for a person to stand behind. Two poles protruded from it that were eight feet in length and had hooks on the ends for manoeuvring a suspicious package. The screen was heavy and cumbersome and the poles difficult to manipulate, but the whole contraption was more useful than the Spooner suit, and it too made for good newspaper photos.

Most of the bombs had to be dismantled by hand, by an officer working alone and unprotected, and Côté almost always handled the job himself. He was the head of the squad and believed he had a moral obligation to put his own life on the line rather than endangering the lives of his men. The work was unnerving and it was unpredictable. He never knew when he would be called upon to investigate an explosion or dismantle a bomb. He wore a paging device on his belt when he was off-duty or out of the office, and it emitted a high-pitched beep that told him to call headquarters. He had a phone on the stand beside his bed, and when it rang in the middle of the night, he sat up, put the receiver to his ear and said, "*En route*" (I'm on my way).

There were usually other officers at the scene when he arrived, as well as fire trucks and ambulances, all with red lights flashing, and frequently there were reporters and curious onlookers as well. His fellow officers cleared a path when Côté pulled up in his big, blue Biscayne, and he would step out and announce, "The guest of honour has arrived."

The first bombs in this new wave of terror exploded in the early morning hours of Tuesday, August 20, 1968. One was placed behind the Victoria Precision Works at 2901 Rouen Street in the east end, and it detonated at 3:30 a.m. The second blew up half an hour later and about ten kilometres away at a north-end Régie des Alcools du Québec (RAQ) liquor store. The third destroyed a car parked outside the home of Alphonse Lagace, an RAQ advisor who lived in the Town of Mount Royal.

No one claimed responsibility, and Côté and his men found nothing in the debris that would disclose the identity of the bombers, but labour troubles appeared to be the only link among them. Victoria Precision Works, which manufactured Leader bicycles, tricycles and kids' wagons, had hired replacements after its employees had gone on strike several months earlier. And some three thousand RAQ employees had been on strike since June 26, resulting in liquor stores across the province being closed.

The bombers struck with renewed vigour in September and October. There were ten attacks, aimed at diverse targets—two liquor stores, the city's central post office, the armoury of the Black Watch Regiment, the statue of Sir John A. Macdonald in Place du Canada and two Sherbrooke Street political establishments—the Union Nationale's Renaissance Club and the Liberal Party's Reform Club.

Some of the bombs were poorly constructed and failed to explode. But others were assembled by more proficient hands and the police concluded that two gangs were behind the havoc. They also noted that one of them used the same timing device in almost all its bombs—a $3.95 Westclox Silver Bell alarm clock. And the bombers soon disclosed that they were operating under the banner of the FLQ. Côté observed those three letters scrawled in white chalk on the wall of a liquor store on St-Denis Street after an explosion on September 8. The same acronym was written on the exterior of the central post office after a package containing a stick of dynamite was deposited in a mail chute and on September 18 the bombers left a note signed "FLQ" after an explosion at the home of Albert Tanguay, governor of the Bordeaux Prison.

There was trouble at the prison that fall, and Pierre Vallières and Charles Gagnon were behind it. They went on a hunger strike and a large percentage of the institution's seven hundred prisoners joined them. Vallières was appealing his murder conviction and Gagnon was awaiting trial, and they both refused their food in order to protest the slow pace of the judicial proceedings. The other inmates wanted extended visiting hours, an increase in telephone privileges—two calls a week was the norm—and better food. By the time the strike had reached its tenth day, some of the inmates were almost too weak to appear in court. The *Gazette* reported that an accused car thief named Édouard Lefebvre was "baggy-eyed, colorless and wavered feebly" when he took his place in the witness box. After taking the oath, he whispered in a shaky voice, "I . . . I . . . I think I'm going to faint," and two court officers rushed to his side to prevent him from collapsing.

The bombers had no interest in the ordinary prisoner. They acted to demonstrate "concrete support for patriots Vallières and Gagnon," as they put it in a note left on the front lawn of the governor's large, two-storey home that stood on a quiet north-end street a few blocks west of the prison. The bombers placed a package of explosives under a porch at the rear of the residence and it exploded at 3:30 a.m. Côté and two other members of the bomb squad arrived a few minutes later. The porch was heavily damaged, the lawn littered with debris and twenty-seven windows had been blown out. The blast also broke an undetermined number of windows in nearby homes. The officers spent several hours searching for the remains of the bomb and that led them to the note, which provided a glimpse into the mindset of the perpetrators. It stated, "The FLQ has shown today the only way to abolish the regime of justice for the rich. This is directed at a representative of a rotten society."

The wave of terror intensified in November when there were fourteen bombing incidents. The bombers began by placing a small package of explosives under a bus owned by the Murray Hill Limousine Service— a show of support for the mostly francophone cab drivers who were protesting the company's taxi monopoly at Dorval Airport. The bomb exploded late in the evening on November 4 and caused minor damage.

The next attack occurred on Monday, November 11, and it was downright reckless. The terrorists placed a package of explosives in an underground passageway linking CN's Central Station with Place Bonaventure, a massive five-storey retail, commercial and convention centre. It exploded at 8:30 p.m. Côté found the floor littered with broken brick, bits of concrete and a coating of dust from the plaster on the walls, while reporters at the scene zeroed in on three people who had been in the passageway when the explosion occurred—a maintenance worker and a middle-aged couple who were visiting Montreal. The visitors refused to give their names, but told the reporters, "The floors were shaking and the walls were coming in at us."

The terrorists planted three more bombs that week, but Côté dismantled them all. The first—on November 12—was a small one, just two sticks of dynamite in a shoebox left at the entrance to the headquarters of Bell Telephone at 1080 Beaver Hall. The next two—on November 14 and 15—were larger. Each comprised eight sticks of dynamite that were eight inches long and one and a half inches in diameter. In both cases, the terrorists attacked companies in the midst of strikes—Domtar Ltd. and the Lord Steel Company—and they did so in the dead of the night. They placed one bomb under a tractor-trailer parked outside a Domtar Corrugated Products warehouse and the other against the wall of a warehouse owned by the Lord Steel Company.

All three bombs were of similar construction, and in one of his incident reports Côté noted, "Whoever assembled them appeared to be following the instructions and schematics found in the December 1967 issue of *La Victoire*, official organ of the FLQ." He and his fellow officers were lucky to find remnants of the bomb that exploded at 2 a.m. on Sunday, November 17, outside the premises of the Standard Structural Steel Company at 5330 Paré Street. Côte concluded that this bomb had been the biggest to date. It blew out thirty-five windows, gouged a crater two feet in diameter and thirteen inches deep, and left burn marks six feet high and ten feet wide on the wall of the building. Furthermore, an officer with the Town of Mount Royal police force arrived after hearing the explosion and feeling a slight tremor while sitting in his cruiser a kilometre away.

That was the start of another hectic week for the city's bomb squad. On Thursday, November 21, the terrorists hit a liquor store on St-Laurent Boulevard, the broad thoroughfare that spanned the island from south to north and traditionally divided French and English Montreal. It was the fourth such attack against an RAQ property, and this time the bomb was placed in a narrow laneway between the store and a four-storey apartment building.

It exploded about half an hour after midnight and the blast blew out the windows in the apartments across the alley. The temperature was several degrees below zero that night and Montreal had already received its first big dump of snow. Shocked and shaken residents wandered out of their apartments and into the street in nightclothes, winter boots and overcoats, and they huddled for warmth in the glare of the flashing lights of police cars and fire trucks. One resident stayed behind, and he leaned out his shattered window and told the reporters below, "It nearly threw me out of bed."

A little over twenty-four hours later—at 3:52 a.m. on Friday, November 22—another bomb exploded. The target this time was one of the symbols of English-Canadian commercial might—the grand, nine-storey T. Eaton Company department store at 677 Ste-Catherine Street West. The bombers had warned Eaton's, as well as other retailers, to stop selling Leader bicycles, tricycles and wagons built by workers hired to replace the striking employees at Victoria Precision Works. The other stores had heeded the warnings, but not Eaton's and the terrorists responded with a bomb placed in one of the small, square lockers in the basement of the department store, an amenity for customers who wanted to store their hats, coats and other things while they shopped. The blast caused some twenty-five thousand dollars' damage, and Côté later recalled that it looked like an earthquake had hit. There were thirty cleaners in the building, none of whom were hurt, and Eaton's opened for business at the usual hour that Friday, though it turned out to be anything but an ordinary day. An anonymous caller phoned the radio station CKAC at 3:20 p.m. and warned that a bomb was going to explode in the jewellery department in ten minutes. The station called police headquarters and the call went straight through to Côté. As it happened, he and some of his officers had spent most of the morning combing through debris looking for traces of the first bomb and he was writing his report on the incident. He dropped that and rounded up his men and a traffic cop on a motorcycle, complete with sidecar, and the latter led the small motorcade of police vehicles through narrow, congested, snow-covered streets. The store had been evacuated when they arrived, and police and firefighters had pushed hundreds of shoppers, as well as employees, to the opposite side of the street.

"I went in," Côté recalled in an interview, "and somebody yelled, 'It's on the floor.' It was between a water fountain and the wall, in a cardboard container about the size of a shoebox. I was all alone and I could hear the tick, tick, tick. I got on my knees and lifted the lid and there were four sticks of dynamite, but the clock was face down and there was so much tape around it I couldn't clip the wires.

"All I could do was push in the alarm button to stop the ticking and deactivate the clock. That neutralized the bomb and I picked it up and walked out with it under my arm and all I saw was this huge crowd of people and they all started to applaud. We took the bomb to a big park in Pointe-Saint-Charles and dismantled it. We looked at the clock and realized it had been set to blow five minutes after I neutralized it. That was my closest call."

Eaton's immediately offered a five-thousand-dollar reward for information leading to the arrest of the bombers, and a prominent civic official publicly denounced the bombings for the first time. "I pray to God," said Lucien Saulnier, chairman of city council's executive committee, "that these people will realize that all these attacks of violence and upheaval are costing much more than they hope to gain from these contemptible acts."

The following Monday—November 25—the MPD, the SQ and the RCMP announced the formation of yet another Combined Anti-Terror Squad. Their most senior investigators would be responsible for hunting down the terrorists, and the terrorists responded on November 27 by attempting to blow up a police cruiser. The vehicle was brand new and parked at a dealership called Trans Island Motors, which supplied the MPD with patrol cars. An employee spotted a package when he moved the cruiser and immediately suspected a bomb. One hundred members of the staff were hastily evacuated and the bomb squad arrived to handle the emergency.

There were three explosions in the first two weeks of December 1968, one at the residence of André Morceau, general manager of Lord Steel, a second at the Westmount home of Charles Herschorn, president of Murray Hill Limousine Service, and the third at the home of Herschorn's Westmount neighbour, Percy M. Fox, chairman of Great Lakes Paper Co. and a director of Domtar Ltd.

The attackers planted a fourth bomb outside the residence of Roger Brochu, owner of Canadian Structural Steel Co., in the early morning hours of December 12. Côté dismantled it and deemed it the largest he had handled to date. It comprised eight sticks of dynamite, two detonators and something new—a cylinder of C.I.L. Pento-Max II, which he described in his incident report as "an exceptionally violent explosive used mainly for blasting in quarries and mines."

The bombings set the entire city on edge. Jittery residents flooded the police communications centres with calls about bomb threats and suspicious-looking packages. Most proved to be false, but Côté and his squad had to respond to each one. Editorial writers were demanding that the authorities do something to maintain order and preserve the city's reputation. Questions were posed in the House of Commons and Quebec's Legislative Assembly, soon to be renamed the National Assembly.

The city offered a ten-thousand-dollar reward for information leading to the capture of the bombers, and the provincial government matched it, but two of the province's largest labour organizations, the Quebec Federation of Labour and the Confederation of National Trade Unions, refused to contribute. And, in his annual Christmas message, Mayor Jean Drapeau condemned the "dangerous, depressing and costly climate of violence" that pervaded the city, adding that "violence and disorder, rancor and conflict" were no way to change society.

The bombers took Christmas off, but they went into overdrive on New Year's Eve and brought a booming end to a holiday season that had been quiet for the city, for its police force and for Robert Côté and his wife Pierrette Beaudry. And the newlywed couple needed some peace and quiet. The wave of bombings in the autumn of 1968 had turned their lives upside down. It had put enormous stress on both of them, and it had taken a toll. On December 14, Pierrette had miscarried and lost the twin girls she was carrying. She spent a week in hospital and the rest of the holiday at home recovering, and she and Robert planned a quiet

New Year's. They began the evening by watching a movie on TV and at 11 p.m. tuned in to *Bye-Bye*, Radio-Canada's satirical send-off of the year just passed. A few minutes later, the phone rang. It was the communications centre at headquarters.

A bomb had just exploded on the east side of City Hall. Côté left immediately. He placed the magnetic flasher atop the Biscayne and headed downtown with his siren wailing. He drove south on d'Iberville Street, his customary route, and hadn't gone far when a message came across the police radio: "Forget about going to the east side. Go to the west side. There's an unexploded bomb waiting for you." Minutes later, he received a third message: "When you finish at City Hall, go to Dorchester and Bleury. The federal building just blew up."

Police and fire vehicles were on the scene when he reached City Hall, though a good way back from the brown paper bag that had been placed against the wall. Côté approached it, gently tore the paper to expose the bomb and observed nine sticks of dynamite and a cylinder of Pento-Mex II. He snipped the wires connecting the detonator, the battery and the Silver Bell alarm clock and looked at his watch. It was 11:45 and he later recalled that it was a lovely winter night—not too cold, a gentle snow falling—and the bells of Notre-Dame Basilica were already ringing in the new year.

Then he and another officer headed for Dorchester and Bleury, a few blocks northwest of City Hall, to begin the investigation at the federal building. The blast had occurred in an alley between the nine-storey office complex and the five-storey structure opposite, and the narrow thoroughfare was covered in broken glass, twisted metal, chunks of concrete and shards of wood. The shock wave had ricocheted from one building to the other, from the bottom to the top, and destroyed eight hundred to a thousand windows, and people thirteen kilometres away later reported hearing the explosion.

The motive for this attack was clear, the reasons for the City Hall bombings less so. Police and media speculated that the terrorists might have been driven by anger over the reward the city had offered for their capture. In any event, the bomb on the west side of the building had been placed directly under Mayor Drapeau's office and the mayor was indignant. On New Year's Day, he called Police Director Jean-Paul Gilbert and summoned Gilbert and Côté to a meeting to discuss the months-long bombing spree. They met on January 3, and it was apparent from the mayor's questions that Drapeau had been paying close attention and was deeply concerned about the safety of the citizenry and the image of the city. He said he and other civic officials had spent five years planning and preparing for Expo 67. Fifty million people had visited the world's fair in Montreal. It had brought the city world-wide acclaim. "Now," Drapeau said, "a bunch of hot-headed young crazies are ruining the reputation of Montreal." Then he added, "Monsieur Côté, this wind of madness has to stop." Côté agreed, but was in no position to halt the madness, as the mayor called it. His job was to dismantle the bombs or investigate the scene of an explosion. CATS detectives were responsible for tracking down the perpetrators, but their efforts were going nowhere.

The terrorists staged four attacks in January and five in February and they were becoming increasingly reckless. In the early morning hours of Wednesday, January 8, an anonymous caller contacted a French-language radio station and warned that a bomb was about to explode at the home of the police director, adding, "The FLQ has a long memory and hasn't forgotten the St. Jean Baptiste parade of June 24." Shortly afterward, an explosion occurred outside a semi-detached residence on Ernest-Lavigne Street in the east end. The attackers picked the right street but the wrong house. The victim was a contractor named Jacques Arbour.

In the weeks that followed, the terrorists planted a series of bombs in workplaces while people were at work. The first of these attacks occurred mid-afternoon on Tuesday, January 21, and was aimed at the Federation of Independent Canadian Unions, which had contributed one thousand dollars to the city's reward for the bombers' capture. The federation's offices were located on the top floor of a small, three-storey commercial building and faced the east–west Metropolitan Expressway.

Union vice-president Donat Martin spotted a plastic bag in the staircase outside the federation offices, peeked inside and saw a clock and four sticks of dynamite and called the police. Two constables barely had time to evacuate the building when the bomb exploded. One of them, Constable Lionel Boucher, was stepping out the door when the blast knocked him over and sent him skidding into the cruiser.

Three days later, the bombers attacked the Montreal office of Noranda Mines Ltd., which was located on the eighth floor of the eleven-storey Bank of Nova Scotia building in downtown Montreal. Charles Labarre, an employee with the brokerage firm Davidson Company, spotted a brown paper bag outside the door of the Noranda offices while returning from lunch. He heard a clock ticking inside and immediately notified the building's switchboard operator. She called the police first, then alerted Henri Passmore, a retired officer and the bank's head of security. Passmore took the elevator to the eighth floor, got off and calmly picked up the bomb. He walked to the end of the corridor and placed the explosives in the concrete stairwell, then closed the heavy metal door. Two officers arrived, inspected quickly and advised everyone in the Noranda and Davidson offices to lie on the floor. A few minutes later, the bomb exploded with enough force to shake the entire building.

The two brazen daytime attacks were front-page news in Montreal. The next one—the mid-afternoon bombing of the Montreal Stock Exchange on Thursday, February 13—made the front pages of major newspapers from Halifax to Vancouver. The exchange occupied the third and fourth floors of a forty-five-storey office tower and was equipped with a "revolutionary communications system," as one paper put it. The system included computerized records storage, closed-circuit TV and a big electronic display board on which the latest bids, asking prices and quotes were posted instantaneously. On a typical day, a million and a half shares traded hands. Over three hundred people worked there. Visitors were welcome to watch the market in operation from the gallery that overlooked the trading floor, with or without a publicity department tour guide to explain things. At some point that afternoon, the bombers slipped into the gallery and left their wares in a corner behind a concrete column. They alerted CKAC and the station forwarded the warning to the police and the exchange, but it arrived too late.

A few minutes before 3 p.m., a huge explosion occurred. Brokers with Cliché et Associés on the twenty-first floor later reported that the building shook. Jacques Dupuis, executive vice-president of the exchange, was seated in the boardroom and felt the floor lift. An employee named Danny Polson was working in an office near the epicentre of the blast and was hurled twenty feet and slammed into a wall. Exchange president Charles Neapole walked onto the trading floor expecting to see twenty-five people dead or grievously injured. Instead he saw dust-covered, spectral-looking traders milling about in a dazed state, and some of them bleeding from wounds inflicted by flying debris. Fifty women had been in the gallery enjoying a guided tour, when the bomb exploded and, against all odds, escaped injury.

Twenty-seven people were sent to hospital, most suffering from shock. Police estimated that the bomb contained fifteen pounds of dynamite. Exchange officials figured it caused one million dollars' damage. Remarkably, the exchange opened for business at 11 a.m. the following day, one hour later than usual. Stock quotes had to be written by hand on a chalkboard because the big electronic board had been badly damaged, but traders moved 860,094 shares before the bell sounded to signal the close of trading. "Opening up this morning was a great morale booster," Neapole said. "You have to admire the guts of our girls coming back here today. And the traders did a hell of a job."

Nevertheless, the bombings had taken an immeasurable toll on the city. An editorial in *La Presse* warned of a "slide into anarchy," while a second one described Montreal as "a city of fear." Ordinary Montrealers had become wary and fearful. "I'm always afraid the building where I work will be hit," an office worker named Rosa Feldman told a reporter on the afternoon of the stock exchange attack. William Klenk, who worked in the Sun Life building, said, "Everybody's frightened. Nobody trusts anybody who's carrying a package that looks suspicious. What city are we living in?" Civic and provincial leaders moved swiftly to reassure the public. The reward for information leading to the capture of the bombers was increased to sixty-one thousand dollars and Premier Jean-Jacques Bertrand addressed the crisis. "We will not allow these agitators to destroy Quebec," the premier said. ". . . .and the life of every citizen must be and will be protected."

The attack on the stock exchange was widely condemned, but not universally so. Parti Québécois leader René Lévesque described it as an "out and out barbarous act" and said the perpetrators were deluded if they thought such actions would change society. Then, he muddied the waters by adding, "Terrorism is a living symptom of illness, not its cause. It may well be—as the history of the last few years reminds us— that terrorism will threaten us until we have cured its underlying causes, which are first and foremost, gaping and neglected social wounds and the frustrations to which they give rise."

The radical left-wing labour leader Michel Chartrand blamed capitalism. "Terrorists didn't create violence," Chartrand said. "It created them. Some of them are just defending themselves against the violence they have suffered for generations, the violence of the capitalist system, which forces workers to live in poverty and pushes them into unemployment. What we need is a revolution. We must destroy the capitalist system and reorganize the economy to meet the needs of the people."

The next attack occurred at around 11 p.m. on Saturday, February 22. More property was damaged and more people were injured, including a seven-month-old infant named Dora Dorion. The target this time was the Reform Club, the three-storey stone structure at 82 Sherbrooke Street West that served as a social centre for the provincial Liberal Party. There were more than eighty people in the building, though only one, a Liberal senator, was politically connected. The others were there to celebrate the anniversary of Mr. and Mrs. Jean Lebroque, a celebration that ended abruptly when a bomb exploded in an exterior concrete stairwell leading to the basement.

The blast punched a hole in the wall, tore up the ceiling on the ground floor and blew out windows in eight other buildings on both sides of the street. Ten police cars and five ambulances raced to the scene. Bewildered and frightened guests spilled out of the building. Police attempted to control the crowds that gathered in the street while paramedics assisted the injured—two middle-aged women who had been working in the cloak room, a taxi driver who happened to be driving by the club when the bomb exploded and lifted his vehicle six inches off the ground, and little Dora Dorion, who was asleep in her crib in a third-storey apartment across the street when shards of glass hit her in the face.

Less than seventy-two hours later, the bombers hit the Queen's Printer Bookshop on Ste-Catherine Street West, which sold federal publications of all sorts. They placed a small bomb in a basement library that measured twenty by sixty feet. It exploded shortly before closing time. An employee and a customer were in the basement, but they were shielded from the full force of the blast, which, according to the *Gazette* report "sent hundreds of books flying in every direction, tore a gaping hole in the ceiling, ripped light fixtures from their moorings and demolished book racks."

By the time of the Queen's Printer bombing, police had received two hundred tips from the public. A bookstore employee provided a description of a young man who had come in that afternoon and asked what time the store closed. And informants had come forward, hoping they could lead investigators to the bombers and claim the sixty-one-thousand-dollar reward.

Ten

THE SILVER BELL BOMBERS

THE YOUNG MAN ON THE OTHER END of the line was insistent. He had information that would assist the investigation and could lead to arrests, and he was prepared to disclose what he knew, but he and the head of the bomb squad would have to meet. He had already called Robert Côté twice and both times Côté had asked, "Why me? Why don't you call the detectives in charge?" He offered to provide names and phone numbers. Both times the young man had balked. He had had bad experiences with the police. But he had seen Côté's picture in the newspapers and had thought, *This cop seems different.* Now he was back on the line and, this time, Côté relented. They would meet on Monday, March 3, in the evening, at the Club Car bar and restaurant in Place Ville Marie. Côté alerted the detectives leading the investigation and they provided a body pack equipped with microphones and a recording device and sent a small contingent of plainclothes officers as well.

The Club Car was a long, narrow place with a bar and stools against one wall and a row of tables against the wall opposite, and the men in civvies were seated discretely throughout when Côté arrived at around 8 p.m. His informant showed up a short time later, Côté waved him over, they introduced themselves, and then the informant began talking. He talked until eleven o'clock, and by then two things were apparent. The young man knew a lot and he was awfully eager to collect the reward.

As it happened, though, he was too late. He was still talking when Côté's pager began beeping. Côté excused himself, dashed to the nearest pay phone, called headquarters and was told that fellow officers had just arrested a suspect in a third-floor apartment at 3775 St-Dominique Street. They had burst in on him and caught him in the act of assembling a bomb and now they needed Côté to dismantle it. He arrived at 11:45 p.m. with two members of his squad, John Meloche and Marcel Joly. They all knew the neighbourhood. It had a large immigrant population, mainly Greek, and was dominated by old, rundown apartment buildings like the three-storey walkup at 3775 St-Dominique. Côté and his partners met Lieutenant-Detective Roger Cormier on the landing outside the suspect's unit and Cormier briefed them. The bomb was on the floor of the apartment and was a live one, Cormier said, but he had decided against evacuating the building. He wanted the premises searched quickly and quietly to avoid attracting attention. He was certain that the suspect had a roommate and accomplices who would turn up here sooner or later.

The suspect's two-bedroom apartment was grubby and disorderly. Once white walls had faded to murky grey. There were dirty dishes in the kitchen and ashtrays heaped high with cigarette butts. Empty pop bottles and old newspapers littered the floor of the living room. A four-shelf bookcase of bricks and boards was crammed with volumes on Marxism, communism and various recent revolutions, and there was a black-and-white poster of Che Guevara on the living room wall and one of Marx and Trotsky in the larger bedroom.[1]

Côté scarcely noticed any of it, though. He concentrated on the detonators, wires and other bomb-making paraphernalia scattered here and there. His men pried the padlock off a large, blue metal trunk and spotted two more bombs lying on top of a cache of dynamite. They opened a second trunk and found more explosives, and Côté told Cormier that the building, as well as the ones adjacent to it, had to be evacuated immediately. "*Tabernac*, Bob, you're not serious," Cormier replied. "If we evacuate, we'll need a whole parade of cruisers to shelter everyone.

His accomplices will never return if the street is full of police cars." Côté said they had no choice. There was enough dynamite in the two trunks to blow up the whole block. At that, Cormier and other officers began knocking on doors and rousing the residents. They escorted them outside on a chilly, late-winter night and moved them a safe distance away to await the arrivals of cruisers, which would ferry them to a detachment until the search was complete.

Meanwhile, Côté dismantled two of the bombs, but he had to pause at the third and examine it a moment before touching it. He could hear the clock ticking—the usual Westclox Silver Bell—and he could see a piece of cardboard wedged between two copper wires that had been attached to the terminals of a battery. This was new. He had dismantled fifteen bombs since the previous August without coming across anything like it, but he realized in an instant that it was a booby trap. Remove that piece of cardboard and the tips of the wires would touch. The circuit would be complete and the thing would blow.

Côté neutralized the bomb and then he, Meloche and Joly began emptying the trunks. One contained ninety-six sticks of dynamite. The second held sixty-five, as well as thirty-five cylinders of Pento-Mex and nearly one thousand feet of high-explosive detonating wire. They found 150 detonators in a clothes closet and they laid out everything on the floor of the living room. A police photographer took pictures, Côté and his assistants reloaded the trunks and hauled them out, and then Cormier and his men searched the premises for additional evidence.

Among other things, they found a handwritten list of the places that had been bombed, clothing belonging to two men, and copies of *La Victoire*, the underground journal of the FLQ. Its typewritten pages contained instructions on bomb-making, fighting in forested terrain, and purchasing weapons without a permit; and one issue provided the following view of Quebec society:

> We live under a regime of violence created by the English and the federalists. In order to preserve their interests and to

continue to exploit us, they have installed on our Quebec soil their federal police dogs [the RCMP] as well as their federal armed forces. These two elements constitute for all Quebeckers a revolver pointed at our heads. The English and the federalists are using a form of violence against us which is insulting, cruel and inhumane. Their violence is an odious blackmail existing ever since we were conquered by their arms.

We must combat violence by violence. This is why the FLQ uses the same violence against the English colonialists and their accomplices which they themselves have used against us since the conquest.

The officers continued the search until nearly 4 a.m. At headquarters, meanwhile, detectives Pierre Désrosiers and Berthier Bolduc questioned the suspect, who waived his right to counsel and his right to remain silent.

The suspect was a short, taut, tense-looking individual. He had tousled reddish-blond hair, a beard and a demeanour that projected anger. His name was Pierre-Paul Geoffroy. He was twenty-four and he had spent his childhood in Berthierville, a small town on the north shore, about sixty kilometres downriver from Montreal. The police had watched him for several days after receiving a tip from a shopkeeper near his apartment building and, as it happened, they also had a file on Geoffroy. He had been arrested, along with four others, during the violent protest at the 7 Up plant and the march through the Town of Mount Royal in February 1968. Since then, he had been a regular at demonstrations and disturbances and had clashed with police.

The detectives asked him why he had turned to bombs and Geoffroy told them, "I thought about this type of action for a long time to protest the social state of Quebec. I decided to make my first bomb in May 1968 and placed it against the wall of the 7 Up plant, the east wall, I think. I think there were three sticks of dynamite and a metal flashlight filled with black powder. I called Radio-Canada to warn them and the bomb was dismantled.

"Then at the RAQ on St-Denis Street in the north end, I deposited a bomb made of one stick and a jar of gasoline and black powder. . . . I put it in a garbage can in the alley behind the building but only the black powder detonated, I think. That's what the newspapers said because I read the accounts in the papers."

Then he acknowledged planting bombs at a second RAQ outlet on Sherbrooke Street West, at the premises of the Reform and Renaissance Clubs and at the Ministry of Labour building on McGill Street. He confessed, in short order, that he had planted bombs at the Westmount home of the president of the Murray Hill Limousine Service, at a Domtar warehouse, the Lord Steel Company plant, the Standard Structural Steel plant and the RAQ store on St-Laurent Boulevard. He was also responsible for the three bombs placed on the premises of Chambly Transport, a strikebound company with several South Shore locations, the two bombings at the T. Eaton Company department store on Ste-Catherine Street West and one at the Black Watch armoury on Bleury Street.

Geoffroy explained that he had attacked the home of Roger Brochu, proprietor of Canadian Structural Steel, to protest the dismissal of several workers who were attempting to organize their fellow employees. He had planted the bombs at City Hall to protest a dispute between the city and the police fraternity and to demonstrate his general displeasure with the administration of Mayor Drapeau. He explained in some detail the attack on the Canadian Federation of Independent Unions and his rationale. "I placed a bomb on the second floor, in the staircase near the door," he told the two detectives. "It was to protest against the Federation, which is, in fact, a front run by the bosses."

Geoffroy's rationale for attacking the offices of Noranda Mines in the Bank of Nova Scotia building was equally feeble. He was protesting the dismissal of a security guard at a Noranda mine in Mattagami, some 650 kilometres north of Montreal, an internal personnel matter that normally would have attracted no outside attention. But the employee in question happened to be an outspoken member of the Mouvement pour l'intégration scolaire, which was demanding unilingual French schools across the province, and nationalists assumed he had been fired for his political activities.

"In the month of February," Geoffroy continued, "I made a bomb composed of six sticks of dynamite, each of two pounds, and a cylinder of Pento-Mex and I put it in a black fibreglass briefcase and I went to the Stock Exchange building. I took the elevator to the fourth floor. There were two or three people there when I got off so I went to the washroom before going to the visitors' gallery.

"I primed the bomb . . . and went to plant it, but passed by a group of visitors. So, I went to the other end of the gallery because there was a column there that would absorb the shock and put the public in less danger. It would have been about twenty-five to three. I passed by the group of visitors on my way out of the gallery.

"I took the elevator down and went to the Metro station and phoned CKAC and I told them that there would be an explosion at the Stock Exchange. Then I called the exchange but no one answered. Then I went back to my apartment and I heard on the radio that they hadn't had time to evacuate the place."

Geoffroy finished his deposition by providing accounts of the last two bombings. "About ten days later," he said, "I made a bomb of eight small sticks of half a pound each and I planted it in the exterior staircase leading to the basement [of the Reform Club]. It was to protest the declarations of Jean Lesage against the terrorists and to hit a symbol of the Quebec bourgeoisie.

"At the Queen's Printer, it was a Tuesday, I think. It was really a fire bomb made from a beer bottle containing gasoline and two sticks of dynamite. I planted it in the basement, on the floor of the room, among the bookshelves. It was around 4:30."

Désrosiers and Bolduc then asked a series of questions. What follows is drawn from their record of the interrogation:

Detectives: When you made the bombs or when you planted them, were you acting alone or with others?

Geoffroy: I don't want to respond to that question.

Detectives: To the best of your knowledge, would there have been any other bombs planted by you, or by other persons besides those you mentioned in your deposition?

Geoffroy: I believe I have acknowledged all of them and I learned through the papers there had been other bombings, but I wasn't aware of who was behind them.

Detectives: Where did you get the dynamite for your bombs?

Geoffroy: It was dynamite that I stole from a quarry in Laval where it was stored in a little shed. I also took some from a quarry in Acton Vale.

Detectives: What brand of alarm clock did you use to make your bombs?

Geoffroy: Westclox. They were valued at $3.50 to $4.00. I bought them in different places so as not to be recognized.

Detectives: When you planted a bomb, how did you discover whether it exploded or was dismantled?

Geoffroy: Through the media, either radio or the newspapers.

Detectives: Were you part of any particular organization?

Geoffroy: I was part of the FLQ for several months.

Detectives: What mode of transportation did you use when you were planting the bombs?

Geoffroy: Most of the time I took the Metro or the bus.

Detectives: When you went to plant a bomb did you always call to warn that an explosion was going to happen?

Geoffroy: Yes. Usually it was radio station CKAC that I called.

Detectives: Can you give us an idea on the general structure of the FLQ?

Geoffroy: It works by cells. There are only a few members in each cell and the cells are independent from one another and don't know each other.

Detectives: How do you meet other members of your group?

Geoffroy: I received a phone call from someone who identified themselves by a nickname only and someone would come to my place.

Detectives: Can you give us the name of these persons?

Geoffroy: I only knew them by their nicknames.

The detectives concluded the interrogation with three routine questions: "Have you made this declaration freely and voluntarily?" "Do you know how to read and write French?" and "Will you sign this declaration freely after reading it?" Geoffroy said yes to each. Désrosiers and Bolduc noted the time—5:15 a.m.—and that ended the session.

The police could have laid charges immediately, but they held back. They badly wanted to nab Geoffroy's accomplices, and so conducted round-the-clock raids in Montreal and the surrounding suburbs over a three-day period. They came up empty-handed and the suspect refused to assist. The police detained Geoffroy under the Fire Prevention Act, a new piece of legislation which the National Assembly had passed the previous week. It allowed police to hold someone accused of arson or terrorism indefinitely without charging him or bringing him before a magistrate. However, the authorities were required to hold an inquiry under the office of the fire commissioner, and the accused had to appear once every twenty-four hours.[2]

Premier Jean-Jacques Bertrand, who also served as attorney general, ordered an inquiry under the new act—the rationale being that an explosion is a fire that occurs instantaneously—and he named Cyril Delâge, a Quebec City notary, fire commissioner for Montreal. The inquiry began late in the afternoon of Tuesday, March 4, less than twenty-four hours after the arrest. Robert Côté was the first to testify, but Geoffroy was the principal witness. He acknowledged that there were two FLQ cells operating within the city and that he had served as a liaison between them. Each cell had three or four members—all young men who had met through the youth wing of the RIN. They usually met at his apartment to plan their attacks, though he did not consider himself the leader. The stock of dynamite and other explosives belonged to the group and, when he went out, he always left a key under the mat at the front door, just in case a fellow member needed access to the material. But, he adamantly refused to disclose the identity of his accomplices and co-conspirators.

Fire commissioner Delâge adjourned the hearing after hearing two and a half days of evidence, and the police charged Geoffroy with 124 offences in connection with thirty-one bombings. In each case, they charged him with (a) making a bomb with the intent of causing an explosion that was likely to lead to injury, death or damage to property; (b) conspiring with unknown persons to make a bomb; (c) planting a bomb with the intent of causing injury, death or property damage; and (d) conspiring with unknown persons to plant a bomb. These offences were all punishable by up to life imprisonment. He was also charged with four counts of illegal possession of explosives and one of break and enter.

Geoffroy was arraigned before Chief Judge André Fabien of the Sessions Court on the morning of Friday, March 7. He wore a greenish tweed sports jacket, green turtleneck, black dress pants and expensive-looking glasses. He was represented by André Daviault, a Berthierville lawyer retained a day earlier by his family. The clerk of the court spent ninety minutes reading the charges, after which the judge asked Geoffroy how he pleaded—guilty or not guilty. To the astonishment of everyone present, he replied: "Guilty."

"These are very serious charges," Judge Fabien said. "Have you given enough thought before deciding to plead guilty?"

"Yes," Geoffroy said and, at that, the judge adjourned the hearing for two weeks.

In the interim, reporters interviewed Geoffroy's neighbours and his shaken and distraught parents, and a fuller portrait of the youthful terror-ist emerged. He was the second of three children. He had a sister, Louise, who was twenty-seven, married and teaching in Montreal, and a younger brother, Jacques, who was twenty-two and employed by the Company of Young Canadians, a federally sponsored community works program.

His father, Maurice Geoffroy, was secretary treasurer of the Berthierville school commission, and *La Patrie* reported that he and his wife lived in "a comfortable and spacious, architect-designed home with a view of the river." The Geoffroys had enrolled Pierre-Paul at age twelve in Collège Roussin, a private school run by a Catholic lay order in Pointe-aux-Trembles, on the eastern tip of the Island of Montreal. He stayed there until he was eighteen, at which point his parents sent him to a high school in Ottawa where he became so proficient in English that some Montreal acquaintances mistook him for an anglophone. Geoffroy's next stop was the Institut des arts graphiques. There, he completed a three-year program and became qualified to work as a printer, but in the fall of 1967 he enrolled at the Collège Sainte-Marie to study political science. He dropped out before the school year was complete, but in June 1968 he applied to the Quebec government for a bursary to resume his studies. He was turned down and, not long after, began making bombs and planting them all over Montreal.

When lawyer André Daviault met Geoffroy shortly before he was arraigned, Geoffroy's first question was, "What can my parents think of me?" The answer appeared in the Sunday, March 9 edition of *La Patrie*. Mrs. Geoffroy told the reporter Claude-Lyse Gagnon that she had read the first newspaper stories about the arrest of a suspect. Those reports did not name the individual, but she concluded that it was her son after seeing a photo of the police carrying a blue trunk out of 3775 St-Dominique. She knew that Pierre-Paul had lived at that address. And the trunk looked like the same one she and her husband had given him. "I haven't done anything since then," she said. "I'm not even capable of crying."

She and her husband opened their doors to a second Montreal reporter—Bill Bantey of the *Gazette*. Maurice Geoffroy described his son as a young man of average intelligence, who was in good health, liked sports and read a lot about national and international politics. "He had come to the conviction that independence was the only solution for Quebec," Geoffroy told Bantey. "He had been a militant member of the Rassemblement de l'indépendance nationale. But I never thought he would turn to violence. . . . It's impossible to explain. How can a child brought up to respect the established order become a terrorist?" Although his son's actions had caused him great sorrow, the elder Geoffroy told Daviault that he and his wife were anxious to see Pierre-Paul, and the lawyer relayed the message. To which the son replied, "It had better wait. I'm not ready and they're not ready yet either."

Only one member of the family—younger brother Jacques, an ardent separatist—attended Geoffroy's sentencing hearing, which was held on April 1. Chief Judge André Fabien had already heard the Crown and the defence submissions. Daviault had made a lengthy appeal for clemency, arguing that unlawful and sometimes violent protests were typical of the times and that Geoffroy was a young man who had taken such dissent to the extreme. The defence lawyer pointed out that unions had defied the law, teachers had engaged in civil disobedience and encouraged their students to rebel, priests and bishops had challenged the higher authorities of their faith and even the Montreal police had threatened an uprising amid a contract dispute with Mayor Drapeau and the city council. "I'm not saying that all these actions can be justified, but I am saying that all these made an impression on our youth," Daviault said.

But Judge Fabien did not buy the argument. "The community has a right to peace and public order," he said. "Geoffroy, by his violent acts, has violated this sacred right of the entire population. Coldly and deliberately, he has put in peril the lives of his fellow citizens by planting his devices in public places." He had acted in the name of a destructive and anarchistic ideology and had attempted to "destroy the established order by undermining the foundations and fundamental principles of our democratic society." The sentence, Judge Fabien added, had to be harsh enough to deter others and it had to take account of Geoffroy's character and temperament. "Can Pierre-Paul Geoffroy be rehabilitated?" the judge asked at the conclusion of his address. "Does Pierre-Paul Geoffroy want to be rehabilitated? The Court is strongly inclined to doubt it. Geoffroy has a political ideal which can only be accomplished through acts of terrorism." Judge Fabien imposed terms of five years for each of the five lesser charges of illegal possession of explosives and break and enter. Then he sentenced Geoffroy to life in prison on each of the 124 charges related to the bombings.

Geoffroy flashed a victory sign to his brother as he was led out of the courtroom to begin serving what was then the harshest prison sentence ever handed out in the British Commonwealth, and he took his secrets with him. The newspaper La Patrie suggested that Geoffroy was playing the martyr, and he eventually achieved something akin to that exalted status. A group of FLQ supporters and sympathizers, known as the Mouvement pour la défense des prisonniers politiques du Québec, organized a week of solidarity on his behalf in March 1970 on the anniversary of his arrest. Geoffroy wrote a letter from prison that was read at one of the week's events, in which he explained what had driven him and others to become terrorists. "The reason we are in jail," Geoffroy explained, "is because we acted when the time came. We committed ourselves totally to the revolution. We moved from the defensive to the offensive. We practised what we believed, we were willing to set an example for the revolutionary vanguard so that it could set an example for the whole population on how to win its freedom. We are the fuse to light a bigger fuse, which in turn will touch off the dynamite."

Geoffroy never disclosed the identity of his accomplices, but the police eventually zeroed in on four suspects—Pierre Charette, a Radio-Canada music librarian; Alain Allard, an electronics technician who worked at Canadian Marconi; and two students at Collège Sainte-Marie, Normand Roy and Michel Lambert. All four went underground immediately after Geoffroy's arrest. They fled Montreal for New York two at a time, Charette with Allard, Roy with Lambert, and hid out briefly with a chapter of the Black Panthers, the African-American liberation movement. On May 5, 1969, Charette and Allard left New York aboard a National Airlines flight destined for Miami, one armed with a revolver, the other with a knife, and shortly before the plane was due to land they burst into the cockpit and ordered the pilot to take them to Havana.

Both remained in exile for ten years. Journalists and family members greeted Charette when he walked into the terminal at Dorval airport on January 14, 1979, but several police officers were also waiting and they promptly arrested him. He was charged in connection with three bombings, for which he received a six-month sentence and served four. Allard returned home later that year with a Cuban wife and a five-year-old daughter, and he too earned a six-month sentence.

Roy and Lambert pursued a different course as exiles. Roy left New York for Cuba, then travelled to Algeria. Lambert returned to Montreal and stuck around long enough to take part in the Murray Hill taxi riot, a violent disturbance in October 1969 that shall be described in detail further on in this narrative. Lambert flew to Paris that December and then to Algeria, where he reconnected with Roy. Their next move caused a media sensation back home in Quebec. On August 15, 1970, the magazine *Perspectives*, a weekend supplement carried by *La Presse*, ran a cover story under the headline "Two Montreal terrorists in training with Palestinian commandos." Earlier that summer, the journalist Pierre Nadeau had visited the camp of the Palestinian Democratic Resistance Front in the mountains of northern Jordan. There were sixty commandos in the camp—a mix of Lebanese, Iraqis, Sudanese, Egyptians, Turks and the two Montrealers.

They were operating under the *noms de guerre* Sélim and Salem, and they concealed their identities from Nadeau. They had been there for about six weeks, and had spent their mornings attempting to absorb the front's hard-core Marxist-Leninist indoctrination, which was delivered in Arabic, and afternoons receiving instruction on guerilla tactics and how to handle AK-47s.

Roy returned home in 1972, enrolled in a history program at the Université de Montréal and took a job at a hospital. He was arrested on June 18, 1974, and charged with three bombing offences and sentenced to thirty months. Lambert ended his exile in September 1979 and evaded police until May 22, 1981, when he was arrested in Hull. He got off with a one-year suspended sentence.

As for Geoffroy, he served almost twelve years of his 124 life sentences. He was released on parole on February 15, 1981, and has never spoken publicly about his youthful reign of terror.

1. This description of the apartment is drawn from a report by *Gazette* columnist Bill Bantey, who was allowed in after the police had completed their search.
2. They had used a similar legal procedure in June 1963 after arresting the Westmount mailbox bombers and others involved in the first wave of FLQ terrorism, and it had caused an uproar in the press and among the city's defence lawyers. This time, no one complained.

Eleven

THE BRIEFCASE BOMBERS

AS SPRING GAVE WAY TO SUMMER in 1969, Claude Ryan surveyed the social and political landscape of his native province and drew some dark conclusions. As the editor of *Le Devoir*, the small but influential Montreal newspaper, Ryan was renowned for his trenchant commentary on Quebec affairs. He believed that a dangerous new radicalism had taken root, and he attributed it to a small core of professional protesters and agitators who routinely resorted to violence. Whether it was a labour dispute, a political convention, the St. Jean Baptiste Day parade or the Vietnam War, these professionals were always present. Though they did not always instigate violence, they joined in and they exacerbated it. "They have declared war on the established order," Ryan concluded in an editorial published on Saturday, June 28. "They have resolved to cause as much trouble as possible by all means at their disposal. . . . One can reject their views and positions. One can consider them dangerous and subversive. That cannot erase a brutal reality. The disturbances which they cause, the troubles which they incite, the windows which they break, are for them necessary stages in the realization of their vision of the world."

A day earlier, Ryan had gone even further. Speaking at the annual convention of the Canadian Consumer Loans Association, he said, "Social and political radicalism are here to stay. Authority has never been so weak in Quebec and the minds of the people have never been so much in search of values. Quebec, at this moment, has a climate of intellectual, spiritual, moral and social anarchy." Ryan could have cited as evidence the St. Jean Baptiste Day riot of June 24, 1968. Or the disruptive protests that had shaken Montreal's two English-language universities in early 1969. The first of these began on January 29, when two-hundred-odd protesters—most, but not all of them students—occupied the seventh-floor faculty lounge and ninth-floor computer centre of an academic and administration building at Sir George Williams University—the culmination of a dispute that had simmered for months after six black students accused a biology professor of racism. The two-week occupation ended when the university asked the police to remove the protesters, who responded by trashing the faculty lounge and setting fire to and destroying the computer centre—a rampage that caused one million dollars' damage.

Then there was Opération McGill français—the prolonged assault on McGill University by an odd alliance of militant separatists, radical students and the political science lecturer Stanley Gray, a twenty-four-year-old Ontarian and self-described Marxist revolutionary with a shaky command of French. The group viewed the century-and-a-half-old institution as a bastion of Anglo privilege and elitism. Their immediate objective was to rally French-Canadian opposition, though their larger goal was to transform McGill into a French-language university.

Opération McGill activists had burst into meetings of the Senate and board of governors—shouting, *"Révolution! Vive le Québec socialiste! Vive le Québec libre!"*—and they had spent weeks organizing a demonstration that occurred on the evening of Friday, March 28, 1969. Some nine thousand chanting, whistle-blowing college students and union members as well as the separatist organizers marched fifteen blocks west on Sherbrooke from St-Denis Street to the gates of the university.

The authorities expected the worst and had taken every precaution to prevent a demonstration from turning into a riot. The MPD had posted 1,000 of its 3,700 officers at various points on the campus, the SQ had 400 officers on site and another 200 in reserve at its downtown training centre, and the RCMP had a contingent of 200 ready to move if necessary. McGill deployed 150 faculty members to watch key buildings and report any trouble, and over 100 doctors and dozens of nurses were on standby to treat the injured at two nearby hospitals. Ominously, a police helicopter with two huge searchlights attached to the undercarriage hovered over the crowd at a height of six hundred feet.

Demonstrators taunted police in riot gear, as well as the estimated four thousand McGill students and supporters gathered behind the officers, but the massive security operation worked. The next day's papers deemed Opération McGill a peaceful protest, by Montreal standards, the toll being several dozen broken windows in shops along Sherbrooke, isolated looting, several damaged police vehicles, thirty arrests, thirty-six injured, half of whom were police officers, and fistfights between demonstrators and spectators when a few of the latter repeatedly sang "O Canada" in English.

The spring of 1969 brought more turmoil and turbulence and inspired Ryan's warnings that radicalism and anarchy were threatening the political and economic stability of Quebec. Eleven thousand construction workers went on strike in early June, paralyzing the industry at the height of the building season and using violence and intimidation to shut down job sites. In mid-June, some four thousand demonstrators converged on the Union Nationale leadership convention in Quebec City, but they met a cordon of police officers one thousand strong. They hurled rocks and insults while seventy-member squads of specially trained riot police, equipped with helmets, facial protection and shields, advanced and retreated in sequence and lobbed canisters of tear gas into the crowd. Violence erupted again at Montreal's St. Jean Baptiste Day parade, and this time the demonstrators achieved a symbolic victory. They overturned the float carrying a large papier-mâché statue of the saint, yanked off the head and marched away holding it aloft in triumph.

And amid all this, another wave of bombings had begun.

— — —

The first attack occurred on Thursday, May 2. Robert Côté investigated, and in his report he described the blast as more spectacle than disaster. The bomb was a small one. It had been placed at the rear of a three-storey brick office building that housed a number of tenants, including the Montreal Construction Association. It exploded at 10:20 p.m. and startled the night watchman, who was inside and shielded from the blast that left the parking lot littered with broken glass and other debris. The police assumed that the construction association was the target, given the labour troubles brewing in the industry, but the perpetrators later released a communiqué that revealed mixed motives. Among other things, they said, "We will avenge the imprisonment of the patriot Pierre-Paul Geoffroy and carry on his work to decolonize the people of Quebec. Anything that contributes to the cause of independence and socialism in Quebec will have the FLQ's support."

The bombers struck again on successive nights in mid-June. At 2 a.m. on June 15, a Sunday, a powerful bomb exploded behind the offices of the St. Jean Baptiste Society (SJBS) in the mid-sized city of Sherbrooke. It destroyed the rear wall of the two-storey building and damaged homes and cars on both sides of the street. Afterward, the perpetrators issued another communiqué, this one promising that the FLQ would continue "the struggle for the decolonization and liberation of the people of Quebec, the struggle for true independence, which can only come about as a result of a total revolution." The SJBS's Sherbrooke branch had apparently interfered with those objectives by inviting Prime Minister Trudeau to attend its St. Jean Baptiste Day parade, an invitation it quickly rescinded. That infuriated Trudeau, who told reporters, "This is not democracy, it is armed confrontation. These people are creating a police state and they will be the first to complain about it."

A little over twenty-four hours after the Sherbrooke bombing, a bomb exploded at the front entrance of the two-storey headquarters of Fitzpatrick Construction Ltd. in the west island suburb of Notre-Dame-de-Grâce. A passerby, George Sarapoulous, was thrown from the sidewalk to the street and suffered minor injuries, and the blast sprayed bits of wood and grey brick for one hundred feet. Côté and his officers conducted a meticulous search and discerned that the bomb had been concealed in a cheap brown briefcase of fake leather. But more important, they recovered fragments of the battery, the detonator and the timing device. The components were similar to those recovered after two earlier bombings—the attack on September 18, 1968, at the residence of Albert Tanguay, governor of the Bordeaux Prison, and the attempt on January 18, 1969, to bomb the home of police director Jean-Paul Gilbert.

This confirmed what investigators already believed—that a second group had been operating at the same time as Geoffroy and his accomplices, but independently of them. Geoffroy's arrest, and the harsh sentences he received, had checked the others temporarily. But they were back and they became increasingly brazen. In the early morning hours of July 7, the group attacked five construction companies. They placed the bombs at the front entrance of each firm's business premises and the devices exploded at 5:15 a.m., 5:30, 5:45, 6:30 and 7:30. Fourteen people were at work on the first floor of one of the buildings, though no one was injured, and Côté and his men found the remnants of inexpensive, fake-leather briefcases at three of the sites.

These bombings were a mere warm-up for the spate of attacks that occurred within a single week in mid-August. The first bomb exploded shortly before midnight on Saturday, August 10, outside the premises of a finance company in the Town of Mount Royal. The next target, the Department of National Revenue building on Bleury Street in downtown Montreal, had been bombed on New Year's Eve by Geoffroy and friends. They had placed their explosives in a laneway between the federal structure and an adjacent one. This time the terrorists concealed them in a small cardboard box and left it outside the front doors. The night watchman spotted the package around 2:30 a.m. and called the police, and two officers arrived just as the bomb exploded—with sufficient force to lift their cruiser off the road.

The terrorists completed the week by planting a dozen incendiary bombs in the Eaton's store on Ste-Catherine Street, which were discovered before causing any damage. They bombed a union office on St-Denis Street and a provincial Ministry of Labour building in Quebec City, at which point Premier Jean-Jacques Bertrand and his minister of justice, Rémi Paul, decided stern measures were needed. "We will use every means at our disposal to crush these extremists, these revolutionaries and these little bearded Castros," Bertrand said. "If we are obliged to, we will respond to their violence with force."

Meanwhile, Justice Minister Paul convened a meeting with his senior officials and high-ranking officers from the RCMP, the SQ and the MPD. They met for most of the week and drafted a ten-point plan. Among other things, they promised heightened surveillance on individuals suspected of terrorism, increased co-operation among police forces and improved security measures around government buildings. They called on private companies to do more to protect their property and asked news organizations to play down coverage of the attacks, which, they believed, only encouraged the perpetrators. They also advised the public to be watchful and to report any suspicious activity. The minister reminded the populace that there was a fifty-thousand-dollar reward for information leading to arrests, and then denounced the revolutionary extremists. "The anonymous terrorist is not even a human being," Paul said. "He lacks that which makes a person whole in the full sense of the word: an identity. I refuse to believe that the political goals which these criminals pretend to be pursuing are in the interests of a healthy, hardworking and democratic populace like the people of Quebec."

The minister's rant and the ten-point plan led to a lull in the bombings—followed by the most audacious attack since the bombing of the Montreal Stock Exchange.

Shortly after 5:00 a.m. on September 29, a powerful bomb exploded at 5700 Des Plaines Street—the Rosemont residence of Mayor Jean Drapeau.

The mayor wasn't home, but his wife Marie-France and their twenty-year-old son Michel were asleep upstairs in the modest one-and-a-half-storey cottage-style dwelling. They escaped unharmed but badly shaken, leaving their shattered home in nightclothes and standing bare-foot in a cold drizzle while neighbours gathered round them and police cars, fire trucks and ambulances converged on the normally tranquil tree-lined street.

The bomb had been placed at the bottom of an exterior concrete stairwell leading to the basement. Robert Côté led the investigation, and everything he saw spoke to the power of the explosion. There was a crater three feet in diameter and sixteen inches deep at the foot of the stairwell. There were cracks throughout the ten-inch-thick concrete foundation and a chunk of the foundation measuring five feet by four feet had been ripped loose and hurled into the basement. The furnace had been knocked off its base. Doors were torn from their hinges. The ground floor hardwood had buckled and the furniture had been upended and tossed about, and nineteen neighbouring homes had sustained minor damage. Côté and fellow investigators recovered fragments of an ivory-coloured alarm clock, an Eveready battery and twisted metal hinges that appeared to be from a briefcase.

Mayor Drapeau said nothing publicly, but the city's newspapers roundly denounced the bombing. The *Gazette* described it as "a symbol of hate, ugliness and ruin," and went on to say, "The question will be asked everywhere: what sort of area is this that can have 100 bomb-ings in only 24 months, with even the Mayor's house now added to the long list?"

The police, meanwhile, stepped up their efforts to protect public fig-ures and to catch the bombers. Plainclothes officers were posted out-side the homes of leading municipal, provincial and federal politicians, including the Outremont residence of Prime Minister Trudeau. Secu-rity guards searched everyone entering courthouses. CATS carried out nineteen raids and interrogated fifty people suspected of either support-ing the bombers or participating in terrorist activities. However, they made no arrests and the hunt for the bombers was swept aside by one of the most infamous events in the city's history—a sixteen-hour work stoppage by police that led to a rash of armed robberies, a rampage of vandalism and looting on Ste-Catherine Street and a riot that left two men dead, including a provincial police officer.

On the morning of Tuesday, October 7, police officers deserted the department's seventeen detachments and joined their off-duty colleagues at Paul Sauvé Arena for what their union euphemistically called a "day of study." Members of the force were studying a recent arbitrator's report on contract negotiations with the city, and firefighters, who were in the midst of equally contentious bargaining, walked off the job as well. Some four hundred provincial police officers were pulled from their regular duties and posted to various parts of Montreal, though that number rose to eight hundred as the day wore on and the chaos mounted.

By early afternoon, masked and armed bandits began to hit banks, commercial establishments and private homes. Most of the bankers were wise enough to keep minimal amounts of cash on hand and were robbed of less than a thousand dollars. A branch of the Banque d'Épargne failed to take that precaution and three men in balaclavas smashed plate glass windows with iron bars, walked in and made off with $28,845.

Meanwhile, Premier Jean-Jacques Bertrand adjourned the regular business of the National Assembly and summoned his ministers to an emergency meeting. They drafted, and the Assembly promptly passed, a back-to-work law that provided for prohibitive penalties against officers or union officials who defied it. For good measure, the government requested the assistance of the Canadian Army, and the army agreed to send 106 members of the 22nd Regiment, the Van Doos, from its Valcartier base just outside Quebec City, but the troops arrived too late to stop the looting and rioting that occurred in the evening.

The trouble began at around 6 p.m., when some seventy-six taxi drivers in company cars assembled on a residential street north of La Fontaine Park to begin an ostensibly peaceful protest against the Murray Hill Limousine Service. The drivers were members of the militant Mouvement de libération du taxi (MLT). They vehemently opposed the Murray Hill monopoly on service from Montreal-Dorval Airport, which meant that regular cabbies, most of them French Canadian, could drive passengers to Dorval but had to make return trips with empty cars. The MLT had organized a number of anti–Murray Hill demonstrations and had attracted the support of FLQ militants, who had on one occasion planted a bomb under a company bus and, on another, had bombed the Westmount home of the president.

This time, they formed a convoy of cabs and drove to City Hall and several large downtown hotels to demonstrate their displeasure, and then on to the Murray Hill garage at the corner of Barré and Versailles Streets in Griffintown, southwest of the city centre. They set out with an escort provided by the Popeyes motorcycle gang. A number of journalists accompanied them, as well as several dozen youthful separatists from the radical fringes of the independence movement.

The protest was peaceful until the convoy encountered a Murray Hill limousine with four passengers aboard. The lead drivers halted the limo. Those behind them stopped. Everyone got out and the limo driver and his passengers found themselves surrounded by an angry, shouting mob. MLT leaders allowed the passengers to leave with their luggage, and then their followers pummelled the vehicle with sticks until it was badly dented and the windshield, windows and headlights had been smashed.

Their next stop was the Murray Hill garage. The place appeared deserted. The big doors at the front were closed. The exterior was illuminated by high-powered lights along the roof line, and there were four buses parked side by side below. The cabbies parked in the yard. Most got out and stood back while their youthful passengers immediately showered the buses with stones, bricks and whatever else they could lay their hands on.

The ensuing riot lasted over two hours. The rioters smashed windows in the garage and hurled Molotov cocktails at it. The ruckus attracted hundreds of onlookers, as well as dozens of young people who joined the frenzied attack. The rioters approached the building, but gunfire suddenly erupted from the roof and they retreated. A *La Presse* reporter, whose byline did not appear above his story the next day, wrote that the mob advanced and retreated like an army laying siege to a fort. The volleys of gunfire from 12-gauge shotguns continued and several rioters were hit and wounded. A small contingent of firefighters arrived and doused some of the fires, but not those closest to the building. Then a team of eight provincial police officers showed up and were immediately surrounded by a hostile crowd, and all but two retreated. These two attempted to stop the riot, the journalist from *La Presse* reported, but "were shouted down, roughed up, had their caps thrown in the air and their badges ripped off" before firefighters pulled them from danger.

As the officers looked on, the mob set fire to the building and pushed an already burning bus through a garage door while one enterprising young rioter got behind the wheel of a Murray Hill car and rammed it into five limousines and three buses. Then a cry rose abruptly—"The police are here!"—and forty anti-riot officers equipped with helmets and batons marched with military precision toward the rioters, who initially jeered and then scattered and fled. Many proceeded to Ste-Catherine Street and disappeared into another mob that was engaged in an orgy of window-smashing and looting. Montreal's "day of anarchy," as some commentators called it, ended shortly after midnight when the police returned to duty and members of the Van Doos took up positions around a number of public buildings.

The toll was immense. The damage was estimated at two million dollars. Over a hundred people were arrested. Looters stole half a million dollars' worth of merchandise. A dozen people were wounded by gunfire in the Murray Hill riot. Two provincial police officers were badly beaten by a mob on Ste-Catherine Street. And there were two fatalities. One of the dead was Robert Dumas, a thirty-two-year-old provincial police corporal and father of four who had a wife and a modest home across the river in suburban Longueuil. Dumas happened to be among the rioters, in plain clothes rather than uniform, when the rooftop snipers began firing indiscriminately into the crowd.

There was another riot in Montreal in the fall of 1969, in the northeastern suburb of Saint-Léonard—this one over the emerging and explosive issue of language rights. It was the culmination of a dispute that had simmered and festered for two years. Saint-Léonard had grown exponentially in the post-war era. The population had risen from eight hundred in 1955 to thirty-five thousand in 1968, and by then some 40 percent of its residents were recent arrivals from Italy. They wanted their children educated in English, and the Saint-Léonard Catholic School Commission accommodated them. Like many of Montreal's Catholic school commissions, it offered classes in both French and English—at least from grades one through eight.

However, the commissioners of Saint-Léonard feared that bilingual schools were contributing to the decline of the French language and culture, and in late 1967 they announced that they would phase out English-language instruction, starting with students entering grade one the following September. Italian immigrant parents and their anglophone counterparts were outraged. They formed the Saint-Léonard English Catholic Association of Parents to fight the measure. A group of francophones—led by a thirty-three-year-old architect named Raymond Lemieux—formed the Mouvement pour l'intégration scolaire to fight for unilingual French instruction in Saint-Léonard and throughout the province.

The two sides first squared off when a seat on the commission came open and a vote was scheduled for June 10, 1968. The association fielded a pro-bilingual candidate while Lemieux's group put up a French-only candidate. Meanwhile, separatists and nationalists in Montreal and elsewhere saw the conflict as part of a broader fight. "The problem raised by the referendum in Saint-Léonard is not a quarrel of the local school commission," a reader named Simone Landry wrote in a letter to the editor of *Le Devoir*. "It is the life of the Québécois nation that is in play here." In the same edition another reader, Jacques Poisson, wrote, "A battle has begun in Saint-Léonard that no Québécois can afford to lose." But the nationalist side lost the election on June 10, and for two years it continued to lose the battle of Saint-Léonard. In the fall of 1968, over two hundred families refused to send their first graders to the local schools. Instead, they set up their own, English-language classrooms in the basements of seven private homes with help from the Provincial Association of Catholic Teachers.

The anglophone rebellion took a more ominous turn in September 1969. Students from grades three through seven boycotted the start of classes and the parents of four hundred grades one and two students went looking for space for a temporary English-language school. The Protestant School Board of Greater Montreal offered them classrooms in two east-end schools and that provoked the riot that occurred on the evening of September 10 in the heart of Saint-Léonard's Italian district.

Lemieux's now renamed Ligue pour l'intégration scolaire (LIS) scheduled a protest march along a commercial strip lined with Italian businesses, followed by a public meeting at a local elementary school. A crowd of 1,500 nationalists, including a contingent of Reggie Chartrand's Chevaliers de l'indépendance and dozens of other radical separatists, assembled in the parking lot of a shopping centre then began marching along Jean Talon Boulevard toward the school. Saint-Léonard's entire forty-two-member police force formed two lines across the street and attempted to stop the demonstrators but stood no chance.

Police chief Sylvio Langlois had appealed to the SQ for reinforcements in advance, and the provincial force sent five hundred officers equipped with riot gear. However, the march was already in progress when they arrived in a convoy of school buses, and the demonstrators spilled past and around them as the officers attempted to form units. The police threw tear gas canisters into the mob, but the protesters lobbed them back, along with Molotov cocktails. Many in the unruly throng carried placards tacked to four-foot poles and used them to smash windows. They encountered gangs of young Italians on street corners and fistfights and brawls broke out. As they neared the school, they met another crowd of Italians who had strung a chain across the road. The Italians charged, hurling stones and rocks, but the demonstrators counter-charged, wielding their poles like baseball bats.

The provincial police formed a cordon four deep around the school where the LIS intended to hold its meeting. Shortly after 9 p.m., Saint-Léonard mayor Léo Ouellet read the Riot Act—the first time that had occurred in the Montreal area since 1949—and Lemieux told his supporters they had made their point and advised them to go home. Most took his advice, but some three hundred others retreated along Jean Talon, smashing more windows as they went. It was 11 p.m. before the police managed to subdue the remnants of the mob. By then, windows had been broken in 118 businesses along a three-kilometre strip. Eighteen people had been injured and thirty-seven arrested. And in the aftermath of the riot, Premier Jean-Jacques Bertrand's Union Nationale government concluded that the province needed a language law to clarify both majority and minority rights.

The government introduced Bill 63, a "Law to Promote the Teaching of the French Language in Quebec," on Thursday, October 23. It gave parents the right to choose between French and English as a language of instruction for their children, but also stipulated that the children of Anglo-Quebeckers must acquire a working knowledge of French. And immigrants would be required to do the same.

Four members of the government immediately announced that they would vote against the bill, and that weekend, representatives of one hundred organizations from across the province gathered in Montreal and formed the Front du Québec français to oppose the legislation. "A new Battle of the Plains of Abraham has begun," declared

François-Albert Angers, president of the St. Jean Baptiste Society's Montreal chapter. "Already, the doomed forces in defense of the Anglophones are in place. General Wolfe is called Jean-Jacques Bertrand." The labour leader and social activist Michel Chartrand pushed things further. "If Bill 63 is passed, English universities and colleges in Quebec are likely to be dynamited," Chartrand said, and the provincial attorney-general Rémi Paul had him charged with sedition.

There were two massive, generally peaceful protest marches the following week, one in Montreal that attracted a crowd estimated at twenty-five thousand and another outside the National Assembly in Quebec City that drew some twenty thousand people. There were three weeks of debate in the National Assembly that ended with an impassioned speech by the premier, who described Quebec as "a land of liberty" where minority rights were respected. The assembled deputies approved the legislation by a margin of sixty-seven to five on November 20, and that night Montreal's briefcase bombers struck again. Their target was a prominent English-language educational institution.

At around 8:45 p.m., police received a warning that a bomb was about to explode at the four-storey F.X. Bryan building at Loyola College, an all-male, Jesuit-run high school and post-secondary institute. The five hundred students attending night classes were hastily evacuated. Sergeant Aurelle Gaudet was the first officer on the scene, pulling up in front of the building moments before the blast occurred. It nearly destroyed the cruiser and Gaudet later told a reporter, "If I had stepped out of my car two minutes later, I would have been a dead duck."

Robert Côté arrived to conduct the investigation, and in his incident report he wrote, "On entering the building by the main doors, which had been ripped apart, we could see that the interior of the building had been heavily damaged. Bricks and pieces of concrete and wood were scattered everywhere. The broad concrete steps leading to the basement had been ripped apart and there were fissures throughout the brick walls of the staircase. The characteristic odour of dynamite permeated the basement and the damage there was more spectacular."

Two brick walls had been completely destroyed. The landing between the upper and lower level of the staircase—a slab of concrete six inches thick, eleven feet long and five wide—had been torn loose and overturned. Broken water pipes flooded the basement and the power had been knocked out. Côté detected a crater on the floor under the landing, which was where the bombers had placed their wares, and he managed to find the remnants of an alarm clock and fragments of material that likely came from a fake leather schoolbag. That was enough to lead him to conclude that these were the same bombers who were responsible for the wave of attacks that had begun in early May.

There were two more bombings before the year's end. On November 30, terrorists planted a small bomb in a greenhouse at McGill, which destroyed the structure but otherwise caused minimal damage. Three days before Christmas, they resorted to an old tactic. They deposited a bomb in a mailbox on Pie-IX Boulevard, a major north–south artery in the east end. Around 6 p.m. that day, a twenty-six-year-old postal employee was making his rounds in a small van and collecting the mail. He stopped at the box that had been targeted, stuffed the contents into a canvas bag and tossed the bag into the rear of the van. At that moment, a powerful explosion tore the vehicle to pieces, but the driver suffered only minor cuts and bruises.

No one was arrested for the postal bombing or the attack on McGill. Nor were the briefcase bombers apprehended. Their crimes remained unsolved for nearly three years, until one evening in early May 1972, when a young firefighter walked into the Côte-des-Neiges police detachment next door to his firehall and said he had something to confess. He said it was about bombs. He said he had planted a lot of bombs in Montreal. This was no case for a suburban detachment, so the officer in charge called the Section de récherche sur la criminalité, a branch of the force that included the anti-subversive unit, the organized crime section and the bomb squad.

Gilles Forgues, a lieutenant-detective at the time, took the call from Côte-des-Neiges. "We went to the station," Forgues recalled in an interview, "and we started talking to this firefighter and we decided we better bring him downtown. We took him to a quiet room on the second floor and the detectives who were with me started talking to him. It was about 9:30 by then.

"He kept talking and talking and said I was the one who planted this bomb and I was the one who planted that bomb, but all of a sudden he stopped. The detectives came to me in the other room and said, 'He doesn't want to talk anymore. He wants to see a priest.' He looked bizarre, but he spoke fluently.

"So I said 'No problem,' and I went downstairs and I got a white scarf that resembled the stole that priests wear and I put it around my neck and I went back upstairs and I sat with him. And he said he wanted to pray so we got down on our knees and we prayed—in Latin. Then he wanted to make a confession so I said: 'Okay my son, go ahead.' So he started talking, but he was talking so fast that I raised my hand and I said: 'Whoa, my son. God won't be able to understand you. We'll have to write it down so it's exactly like you're talking to me, but you're talking to God.'"

And the young man agreed. His name was Georges Dubreuil. He was twenty-nine and lived at that time Saint-Eustache, northwest of Montreal, though he had resided in the city during the bombing spree. His confession took twelve hours and proceeded in fits and starts. He would provide Forgues and his fellow detectives with an account of a bombing, then he would stop and insist on more prayer. He and Forgues would kneel and pray while the other detectives retrieved Côté's reports to confirm that the two accounts matched.

By the time he was done, Dubreuil had taken responsibility for fifteen bombings. He acknowledged that he had been the leader of a gang and he disclosed the identities of his accomplices. He had worked most closely with his friend Jocelyn Bonneville and to a lesser extent Bonneville's brothers, Paul, then a Hydro-Québec employee, and Alain, a student and former president of the RIN's youth wing. Dubreuil implicated his wife Murielle, as well as his brother Jean-Claude and another friend, Jean Marsot. He stated that he always drove when they were out planting bombs and several times said that he had owned a beige 1966 Ford Galaxie 500.

The Dubreuil gang launched their wave of bombings with an attack in August 1968 on a strike-bound liquor store. They hit the home of a 7 Up company executive, the home of the general manager of Lord Steel and the home of an adviser to contract negotiators for the Régie des Alcools. They bombed the home of Albert Tanguay, governor of the Bordeaux Prison, in September 1968 to support Pierre Vallières and Charles Gagnon, and Dubreuil provided the following account of that incident:

"We (Jocelyn and I) put the bomb in a fake leather briefcase and during the night, around 3:00 in the morning, we went there in my car. I parked on a side street south of Mr. Tanguay's residence and we went to his place on foot. We wanted to plant the bomb at the front, but it wouldn't have done enough damage so we went to the back and put it under the verandah then we went back to my car.

"Then we went to the Dunkin' Donuts on Salaberry Street and when we left there, about an hour later, we heard the boom. We were happy with our work. We went back to my place and Jocelyn took his scooter and left. Me, I went in and listened to the news on the radio. In the morning, my wife went to work and I went by the governor's residence and saw that the damage was not so bad."

Dubreuil acknowledged bombing the offices of construction companies in the spring and summer of 1969 and that he had assembled the bombs, usually comprising ten sticks of dynamite, in the apartment where he and his wife lived, along with some of their friends. He told the detectives that his wife had accompanied him on two bombing runs—the attacks on the St. Jean Baptiste Society building in Sherbrooke and the home of the 7 Up executive. (Murielle Dubreuil made a brief confession of her own and acknowledged the attempt in January 1969 to bomb the home of police director Jean-Paul Gilbert, whom her husband and Jocelyn Bonneville regarded as a fascist.)

Through a long night of prayer and confession, prayer and confession, detectives periodically asked Dubreuil questions.

Q: Where did you learn to make bombs?

A: I read an article in *Allo Police!*[1]

Q: Where did you purchase the alarm clocks used to make the bombs?

A: My wife and I bought them in different places—pharmacies, hardware stores.

Q: Who is this individual R——L———, whom you've mentioned several times?

A: He's a guy who worked for the CSN[2] and he provided the dynamite and suggested places to plant the bombs. He got the dynamite from construction workers and he hid it for us in two places where we picked it up, an empty field alongside Henri Bourassa Boulevard East and near a tree he had marked on Île Bizard.

Q: Where did you keep the dynamite?

A: For several years I lived on Salaberry Street. I was the caretaker and I lived there with my wife. I stored the dynamite in a locker, but I found that dangerous so I took it and hid it on the roof of the apartment block, under the sun deck. I lifted the plywood and hid the dynamite underneath. One time I went up and got the dynamite and I made a bomb in my apartment, on the kitchen table.

Q: Were you responsible for bombing the mayor's house?

A: Non.

They posed the question several times and several ways, but the answer remained: "Non."

"He answered all our questions, but at Drapeau's residence, no," Forgues recalled, all those years later. "We never found out who planted the bomb at Drapeau's place."

Dubreuil was arraigned along with five accomplices on May 5, 1972. A photo that appeared in the next day's *Gazette* shows the six men standing in the prisoner's dock and facing the bench. Dubreuil is on the far left. He is clean shaven, his hair is short and neatly trimmed and he has a look of profound anguish on his face. The others—Paul Bonneville, Jocelyn Bonneville, Jean-Claude Dubreuil, Alain Bonneville and Jean Marsot—look more like typical young men of the day with an assortment of long or longish hair, thick, bushy sideburns, moustaches and wire-rimmed glasses. They were all facing charges that could have landed them in prison for a long time.

That didn't happen, however. By the end of May, the case against them had collapsed. A psychiatrist, Dr. René Charbonneau, testified for the defence at the start of a preliminary inquiry and told Sessions Court Judge Maurice Rousseau that Dubreuil was schizophrenic. On top of that, he suffered from "a marked state of anxiety," believed he had "a divine mission to change the world," and had been using hashish and LSD for two years. Charbonneau asked Judge Rousseau to excuse Dubreuil from testifying and the judge agreed, saying that the firefighter looked as if he were "carrying the weight of the sins of the world on his shoulders."

Alain Bonneville said he had given a statement corroborating some of Dubreuil's confession only because the police had intimidated him and threatened him with multiple charges. Murielle Dubreuil, who was twenty-eight and pregnant, then told Judge Rousseau that the statement she had given police was false, that she had acknowledged a role in the bombings to help her husband. "I would say anything, sign anything [if it helped him]," she said. "I answered to satisfy the police. I didn't know what was going on."

Without the testimony of Dubreuil or his wife, the Crown had no evidence to present against Jean-Claude Dubreuil, Jean Marsot or the Bonneville brothers, and the charges were withdrawn. Although he had made a detailed confession, Georges Dubreuil was never prosecuted. The Crown stayed the charges because he had been co-operative, because of his mental state, because he had had a spiritual awakening and because he had declared his intention to join the Trappist fathers at Oka, Quebec, and devote himself to the monastic life.

---

1. *Allo Police!* was a lurid weekly tabloid published in Montreal between February 1953 and July 2004. It was devoted almost exclusively to crime and, according to one former editor, covered every murder committed in the province during the paper's half century of publication. *Allo Police!* routinely featured gruesome photos of the bodies of bullet-riddled gangsters, strangled rape victims and others who had died violently.

2. The Confédération des syndicats nationaux, or Confederation of National Trade Unions, is a province-wide federation of labour unions, organized by business sector and by region.

Twelve

——————

PRELUDE TO A KIDNAPPING

GEORGES DUBREUIL AND HIS GANG began their attacks in 1968, and their campaign of terror escalated the following year—one of the most tumultuous in the city's history. However, 1969 ended peacefully in Montreal. No bombs exploded at City Hall or elsewhere on New Year's Eve. Nor were there any of those shattering, middle-of-the-night explosions in January 1970—and February, March and April were quiet as well. The city's newspapers—French and English, daily and weekly—were filled with news typical of more normal, terrorism-free times.

The weather was awful to start the year, thirty-eight straight days of sub-zero temperatures, the longest cold snap since 1901. That put a dent in the city's crime rate, with armed robberies in January 1970 down 50 percent from the single-month record of 325, set in December 1969, but Montreal's reputation as the holdup capital of Canada remained secure. And the Canadiens, winners of two straight Stanley Cups, were having a miserable season, one plagued by injuries, suspensions and dissension, and they would, in fact, miss the playoffs for the first time in twenty-one years.

There were also labour troubles galore. The city's outside workers, the mostly male employees who cleaned the streets, tended parks and maintained civic buildings, were threatening to strike in late February. Interns and resident physicians at hospitals in Montreal and across the province were embroiled in a contract dispute with the government, and they responded by withholding their services at night and on weekends. Some 450 mail truck drivers, employees of the G. Lapalme Company, were furious at the prospect of losing their jobs, effective April 1, after the federal government awarded delivery contracts to five other private companies. The drivers staged rotating strikes, mountains of mail went undelivered and, when that failed to win them any concessions, they vandalized hundreds of street-corner letter boxes and other postal property.

On a more uplifting note, Mayor Jean Drapeau launched Montreal's bid for the 1976 Summer Olympics and the Quebec Liberals chose a new leader. Three candidates had entered the race to replace Jean Lesage, the father of Quebec's Quiet Revolution. They were Pierre Laporte, former journalist, former cabinet minister and then house leader and caucus chair; Claude Wagner, another former cabinet minister best known as a crusading prosecutor and crime-busting judge; and the quiet, bespectacled but brilliant economist Robert Bourassa, who was thirty-six, represented the Montreal riding of Mercier in the National Assembly, and had earned a master's degree in economics and political science at Harvard, a second master's in finance at Oxford and a law degree at the Université de Montréal. Bourassa won a resounding first-ballot victory. Wagner finished a distant second and Laporte an even more distant third. Wagner quit in a huff, but Laporte stayed on to help patch the rifts caused by a bruising campaign and to prepare the party for the next election.

The Union Nationale premier, Jean-Jacques Bertrand, was feuding with Pierre Trudeau and dropping hints of an early election. Trudeau had flatly rejected Bertrand's demands for an increased share of the federal social development tax, and the premier had returned to Quebec and told a gathering of party faithful, "No more nos from Ottawa. Quebec is finished compromising with Ottawa." Bertrand believed his scrap with the feds was just the issue to take to the people. Besides, the Liberals had a new, untested leader; René Lévesque's Parti Québécois (PQ) had nominated candidates in only 36 of 108 ridings; and the Créditistes, who were running provincially for the first time, were totally disorganized. The time was right to seek a fresh mandate, the premier concluded, and in mid-March he called an election for April 29.

Bertrand launched the Union Nationale campaign in the local arena in Cowansville, a small town ninety kilometres southeast of Montreal. There was two feet of snow in the woods surrounding the rink, and the building itself was unheated. The premier delivered a hot, impassioned speech on the province's constitutional demands before some three thousand party faithful. "If we don't get the results we want," he roared, "we'll report back to the people and, through a referendum, the electorate will decide the future of Quebec." But the premier's passion failed to stir the crowd, most of whom huddled and shivered in a frosty rink where the temperature hovered just above freezing, and it was a sign of what lay ahead. His party quickly tanked and the election became a two-horse race between Bourassa's Liberals, who had a five-point plan to create a hundred thousand jobs, and Lévesque's PQ, which stood for one thing: Quebec independence.

The PQ was unprepared for the election, but it didn't matter. The party had a charismatic leader and energetic, emotionally charged, mostly youthful supporters behind it. The campaign kickoff was held in Maurice Richard Arena in east-end Montreal. Thirteen thousand people packed the place an hour before the official start, according to newspaper reports, and another four thousand were trying to get in when party officials closed the doors. Lévesque appeared on stage and a thunderous chant arose: "*Le Québec aux Québécois!, Le Québec aux Québécois!, Le Québec aux* . . . ." He began to speak and the crowd rose and applauded wildly. The ovation lasted thirteen minutes. Lévesque stood motionless, tears welling in his eyes, and, four minutes in, the house lights dimmed—"leaving him," as a *Gazette* writer put it, "a small, silent figure in a pool of light."

Lévesque embarked on a four-day, 6,400-kilometre tour of the province that took him through the Eastern Townships, through the Beauce region south of Quebec City, around the Gaspé Peninsula, into Quebec

City and along the north shore, and he spoke to eight hundred supporters in Drummondville, a thousand in Thetford Mines, six hundred in
Arthabaska County and six hundred in the textile town of Grand-Mère,
north of Shawinigan in the Mauricie region. He wrapped up the tour
by addressing three thousand people in the parking lot of a shopping
centre in Cap-de-la-Madeleine, near Trois-Rivières. Lévesque told voters
what a PQ victory would mean, and he sketched two scenarios. "If the
party wins with less than fifty percent of the popular vote, we'd have
to call a referendum to make things clear," he said. "If we gain fifty percent or more, this [election] would in effect be a referendum."

The party's position was enough to scare some voters and terrify
others, especially anglophones. Nevertheless, by mid-campaign a *La
Presse* poll put the PQ half a point behind the front-running Liberals
and way ahead of the fading Union Nationale. Bourassa attacked the
PQ's sovereignty-association scheme, but without the fist-swinging
harangues favoured by some fellow Liberals, both provincial and federal. Instead, he relied on astute propositions and piercing questions,
such as, "We need a billion dollars in foreign investment next year. Is
independence the best way to get it?" Or: "Lévesque says he can make
Quebec independent, but he can't create 100,000 jobs. Where is the
logic in this?"

Others used a big, blunt stick to clobber the PQ. They maintained
that all the terrorism of the past seven years had been committed for
the cause of independence. Bertrand's justice minister, Rémi Paul, told
audiences, "Not all *péquistes* are terrorists, but all terrorists support the
PQ." Réal Caouette, leader of the federal Créditistes, said, "The PQ has
recruited all the revolutionaries. If the PQ came to power, there would
be a bloody revolution within a year." Pierre Laporte told voters that
the dollar would plummet to sixty-five cents if the PQ formed the government, and some wealthy Quebeckers took the charge seriously,
which was evident when, a few days before the vote, Royal Trust loaded
eight armoured trucks with cash, securities and other valuables and
shipped them to Toronto for safekeeping.

Lévesque shrugged it all off and campaigned at a blistering pace. In the final hours of the forty-five-day race, he spoke to five thousand supporters in Laval, seven thousand at an arena in Montreal North and eight thousand at Paul Sauvé Arena in the city's Rosemont neighbourhood. Another crowd of exuberant PQ faithful filed into Paul Sauvé twenty-four hours later, hoping for a historical breakthrough, but they left heartbroken and, in many cases, angry and disillusioned. Their party captured 23 percent of the vote, but only 7 of 108 seats. Lévesque was defeated. So was Jacques Parizeau, the party's top economic adviser. The Liberals took 45 percent of the vote and seventy-two seats—ten times as many seats with only two times the votes.

As he and his party were going down to defeat, Jean-Jacques Bertrand had warned Quebeckers, "There are youths of nineteen and twenty who are ready to stage a revolution here. The germs of revolution already exist in our society." Desperate politicians say such things in the heat of a campaign, but in this case Bertrand was right. While thousands of young, independence-minded Quebeckers put their heart and soul into the PQ campaign, others had no faith in the party or in electoral politics.

Charles Gagnon was one. Pierre Vallières was another. Both were by then in their early thirties. They had been in jail since their arrests in New York in September 1966, but they remained the revered ideological leaders of the revolutionary fringe of the independence movement. Gagnon was still facing three conspiracy charges arising out of the bombings that led to the deaths of Thérèse Morin and Jean Corbo. Vallières had been convicted of manslaughter in the death of Morin, appealed successfully, been found guilty of manslaughter a second time and sentenced to thirty months, and was appealing again.

Gagnon was released on bail in late February, and Vallières near the end of May. The Conseil central des syndicats nationaux de Montréal, a major labour organization, put up bail money for both men while the

Syndicat des journalistes de Montréal contributed to a bail fund for Vallières. As well, supporters of Vallières and Gagnon had formed the Mouvement pour la défense des prisonniers politique du Québec, and had organized street demonstrations and other events to press for their release.

In his first public appearance—at a separatist meeting in Saint-Henri—Gagnon denounced the PQ as a "dangerous illusion" and warned his audience that "we must not allow the Parti Québécois to dominate the protest and revolutionary movement." Vallières announced that he was committed to "revolutionary violence as part of a precise strategy for a broad national liberation front." But violence was only part of the equation. Vallières went on to say, "The FLQ wages its struggle on many other fronts, both secretly and openly. Revolutionary action . . . includes radicalizing trade unions, citizens' committees, student associations, etc." There were, in fact, all sorts of committees, fronts and movements attempting to radicalize workers, students and others, and these groups spanned the spectrum from moderately socialist to doctrinaire Marxist. Supporters and sympathizers could belong to one or more of these simultaneously or migrate with ease from one to another. Or they could quietly join those who were forming secret cells and plotting attacks on the established order.

The numbers involved in clandestine activity and their levels of commitment were always matters of conjecture, given the fluidity of the movement. But one credible estimate, compiled later by Gérard Pelletier, a Trudeau cabinet minister and former editor of La Presse, put the number of extremists—those ready at any given time to commit violent acts—at no more than forty to fifty. A smaller, more durable group published and distributed propaganda advocating violent revolution. The extremists and propagandists could count on two hundred to three hundred active sympathizers who would provide financial aid or harbour fugitives, and perhaps two thousand to three thousand passive supporters who approved of the terrorist acts.

The early propagandists, the anonymous publishers of La Cognée, had viewed French Quebeckers as an exploited and oppressed minority who could be liberated through independence alone. They saw no need for an economic or social revolution, and some even contended that independence could be achieved with the support of the Québécois bourgeoisie, or business class. By the end of the 1960s, though, the leading voices of the movement were preaching an entirely different gospel, one heavily influenced by Vallières and Gagnon. That was clear from an anonymous and clandestinely circulated document entitled *Stratégie révolutionnaire et rôle de l'avant-garde.* "The strategic objective is clear to all [revolutionaries]," the authors wrote. "It is the destruction of the capitalist society and the construction of an egalitarian, just and free society based on the collective practice of self-government at all levels. . . . Here in Quebec the struggle for the overthrow of capitalism is inseparably linked to the struggle for independence. Independence is understood as something other than the paper sovereignty promised by René Lévesque, supported by the parasitic petty bourgeoisie of Quebec, who aspire only to replace the English as administrators of American capitalism in Quebec."

> True independence is inseparable from total revolution and its attainment will always and everywhere demand a war to the finish against imperialism. . . . This war involves three major stages. . . . Since 1963, ever since the explosion of the first FLQ bombs, we have been in the first stage of revolutionary struggle and it will continue until agitation becomes widespread and culminates in a general economic, political and social crisis.
>
> The strictly military phase will come later when the masses are ready to revolt. . . . And to attain this, we must wage . . . a host of partial battles that gradually sensitize the masses to the common enemy and provide them with the reasons and the means to rise up *en bloc* against capitalism, colonialism and imperialism.

Such was the thinking among Québécois revolutionaries in early 1970, when a new network of *felquistes* was preparing for action. The authorities got a glimpse of where they were headed on February 26, during Quebec–Palestine Solidarity Week, when two constables on a routine patrol spotted a van with a faulty tail light on St-Denis, north of Sherbrooke. Pulling it over, they inadvertently uncovered a kidnapping plot. The occupants, Jacques Lanctôt, a twenty-five-year-old labourer, and Pierre Marcil, a twenty-four-year-old taxi driver, had rented the vehicle. The officers searched it and found a sawed-off rifle and an unusually large wicker basket, one capable of holding a man. They patted down both men and recovered from one of them a document entitled "Operation telephone." It contained the names and phone numbers of prominent radio and TV journalists and a news release announcing the kidnapping of Moise Golan, the Israeli consul and trade attaché based in Montreal. The document included Golan's address and the following statement: "Details will be found in an envelope under the shelf in a telephone booth located at . . ."

The constables charged the pair with illegal possession of a firearm and turned over the curious document about the kidnapping of Golan to their superiors in the anti-terror squad, and one month later, detectives laid charges of conspiracy to kidnap. But Lanctôt had no intention of sticking around for his trial. He had been released on bail, and so went underground and rejoined his comrades in plotting the next round of terrorism, which began almost immediately after the April 29 provincial election.

In early May, three bombs were planted outside Montreal postal depots, two of which exploded, in a show of support for the Lapalme drivers, who had by then lost their jobs. The perpetrators soon turned to other targets, their bombs bigger and their attacks more audacious. The first occurred on Sunday, May 24—during the long-despised Victoria Day holiday weekend. The target was a symbol of commercial might—the former Board of Trade building, a seven-storey, U-shaped stone structure on St-Sacrement Street in the financial district. Terrorists placed a bomb at the foot of the steps leading to the front door. It exploded shortly after 4 a.m., shattered hundreds of windows in the targeted building as well as those nearby, and left a crater that was five and a half feet in diameter and eighteen inches deep. Those responsible issued a communiqué, which appeared in *Le Journal de Montreal* and which made clear their motives: "By the attack of May 24, 1970, at the Board of Trade Building, the Front de libération québécois has expressed its determination to fight by all means the exploitive capitalist system and to demonstrate solidarity with the workers of Quebec."

Four days later, on Thursday, May 28, members of the FLQ launched a daring and sophisticated mid-morning attack. At 10:20 a.m., a small bomb exploded behind a Canadian General Electric building on Jean Talon Boulevard West, scorching a brick wall and heavily damaging several cars parked against it. Five minutes later, and less than three kilometres away, another bomb exploded outside an aging two-storey building that served as an intern's residence at Queen Mary Veterans' Hospital in Côte-des-Neiges. Police, fire and ambulance squads raced to both sites and, while they were thus occupied, bandits staged an armed robbery at the Université de Montréal, a few blocks from the hospital. Three masked men brandishing sub-machine guns burst into the caisse populaire in the university social centre and made off with $58,775.

The bombers completed a week of havoc by returning to a favoured target—the wealthy, Anglo-dominated community of Westmount. *Felquistes*, as members of the FLQ were by then known, had visited twice before: first in May 1963, when the mailbox bombers planted ten one-and-a-half-pound charges; and again in December 1968, when Pierre-Paul Geoffroy and his gang planted much larger bombs outside the homes of two corporate executives. This time, the attackers prowled the serpentine streets of Westmount shortly after midnight on Sunday, May 31, and left behind seven powerful bombs, five of which exploded, the first at 2:10 a.m. at the rear of a Sherbrooke Street office building occupied by a company called Financial Collection Agency.

The Westmount Police Department summoned Robert Côté and his bomb squad. The bomb experts were by then at the beck and call of every police department on the island of Montreal whenever there was trouble involving explosives, and they were examining the debris behind the Financial Collection building when four more explosions occurred outside private homes between 4 a.m. and 5 a.m.

The *felquistes* had hit an unoccupied mansion in Upper Westmount. They placed another against the foundation of a two-storey cottage-style dwelling at 5 Lansdowne Ridge, the residence of prominent business-man Peter Bronfman, his wife and their three children. The explosion wrecked a playroom in the basement and made a shambles of the family's elegant living room. The bombers then attacked the home of Hugh McCuaig, a partner in the brokerage firm Doherty, Roadhouse and McCuaig, and the blast nearly buckled a side wall.

Two bombs failed to explode. The first was discovered under a parked car at around 10 a.m. that Sunday. Côté dismantled it and found that it contained thirteen sticks of dynamite, weighing about fifteen pounds, and was set to go off at 4:10 a.m., but the detonator had failed. Some five hours later, a ten-year-old boy named Maurice Samuels stum-bled upon the other one behind the home that his parents were in the process of buying. Decades later, Stella Samuels, the boy's mother, viv-idly recalled the incident. "I decided to come with the children to have a look at the home," she said. "We pulled up to the front and Maurice and his two younger siblings ran around back and suddenly they came running back and Maurice put his arms up and said: 'Mom, you can't go back there. There's a funny-looking package on the porch.'

"We had heard about the bombings on the news that morning so I went next door and called the Westmount Police Department. I said: There's a suspicious looking package on the back porch.

"The guy who took the call said: What did it look like?

"I said: I didn't see it. My son did.

"He said: How old is your son?

"I said: Ten.

"He said: Lady, we're really very occupied with bombs today. Could you please go back and have a look at it?

"So I said to myself: So be it, and hung up. I stepped out of the house and the whole street was an armada of emergency vehicles, every one imaginable, and the police were evacuating all the residents."

The package contained a bomb all right—the biggest dismantled in the Montreal region over the previous several years. According to Côté's incident report, it comprised thirty-one sticks of dynamite, each one eight inches long and one inch in diameter.

The Bourassa government responded swiftly to the latest wave of bombings. On June 2, Quebec justice minister Jérôme Choquette announced a fifty-thousand-dollar reward for information leading to the arrest of the terrorists. Three days later, Choquette unveiled a tough new explosives control law—something that was long overdue, given that the administrations of Jean Lesage, Daniel Johnson and Jean-Jacques Bertrand had done nothing to update Quebec's decades-old and unusually lax laws regulating the distribution and handling of explosives.

Under the new law, everyone who purchased or possessed dynamite or similar products would require a permit issued by the SQ, and unused explosives would have to be returned to the vendor. Choquette added that forthcoming regulations would stipulate how dynamite was to be stored in order to prevent thefts. As well, he promised stiff penalties for violations of the law and for careless handling or storage.

The announcements did nothing to halt the terrorism that had, once again, shaken the city of Montreal. In fact, the perpetrators appeared bent on demonstrating their defiance of authority. Seven cases of dynamite, 350 pounds of the stuff, were stolen from a quarry in Laval on the day that the government announced the fifty-thousand-dollar reward. And shortly before 5 a.m. on June 6, a powerful bomb exploded in an alcove between a medical centre and a rooming house on Sherbrooke Street East, though the presumed target was nearby Club Canadien, a social club popular with francophone businessmen.

South Shore residents later reported hearing the blast. A Montreal transit driver, who happened to be passing by at the moment the bomb exploded, said his bus had been pushed sideways by the shock waves. A middle-aged Greek couple living in the rooming house had the most harrowing experience. "The bed shook and glass from the light fixture above us littered the bed," the woman, who was not named in newspaper accounts, told reporters. "I didn't know what had happened and found myself screaming hysterically."

On June 8, terrorists placed a small bomb in a night deposit box at a branch of the Canadian Imperial Bank of Commerce, which blew a hole in the side of the building. Then they took a break to plan their next operation, and it was a big one. Shortly after midnight on June 16, an anonymous caller alerted radio station CKAC that a bomb had been planted behind the IBM plant in Ville Saint-Laurent, a suburban municipality northwest of Montreal-Dorval Airport. The local police department called in Côté, who arrived at 1:30 a.m. with constables in tow.

They found two bombs, each in a blue canvas kit bag similar to those that kids used to carry their hockey equipment, and the bags had been placed in a horizontal position under a railway loading platform. Côté approached cautiously. He got down on hands and knees. He used a pocket knife to slit the side of one bag, and then the other. He peered inside and he saw a lot of dynamite—about forty pounds in each bag. He noticed something else—one small glitch that had prevented the bombs from exploding.

The bombers had used open-faced timing devices that were often found on kitchen counters before stoves came with built-in timers. These gadgets had a single, manually operated dial that could be set from zero to sixty minutes. The bombers had modified the timers by attaching one nail to the dial, inserting another into a bicycle brake pad, and then fastening the pad to the face of the timer. They had cranked the dials after planting the bombs, anticipating that a few minutes later the dials would move toward zero, the nails would touch, the electrical circuit would be complete and the bombs would blow.

But in both cases, folds in the canvas of the bags had become wedged between the nails. "If I had lifted one of the bags and jarred the fold loose," Côté reflected years later, "well, I wouldn't be here to talk about it. The first bomb would have exploded and that would have set off the other one too."

After dismantling the IBM bombs, Côté immediately raced back downtown. At 2 a.m., a powerful bomb had exploded between the engineering and the chemistry buildings at McGill University, and a blast in such a confined space maximized the damage. The explosion ripped a gaping hole in the brick wall of the engineering building, tore off two huge doors, ruptured a steam pipe that was part of the heating system and shattered dozens of windows. Steam billowed from the pipe while Côté and some of his men sifted through the debris, looking for fragments of the bomb. They were still down on their hands and knees conducting their search when another officer informed them that there was an urgent call from the communications centre at police headquarters. Security guards had discovered a suspicious-looking package behind a newly opened Domtar Tar and Chemicals research laboratory in Senneville, a suburb at the western tip of the island, some thirty-five kilometres from downtown Montreal, and the local police department had requested Côté's assistance.

Provincial police officers provided a high-speed escort along Autoroute 40 with emergency lights flashing. A contingent from the Senneville force, including the chief, was waiting for Côté. These men had no experience with bombs, and besides, large quantities of high-explosive liquids were stored on site. The bomb had been placed in a niche under an electrical transformer and it was another big one—six sticks of dynamite weighing a total of about thirty pounds. After dismantling it, Côté concluded that it had been set to explode at 1:15 a.m. but had malfunctioned due to faulty wiring.

The bombers hit the post office in Longueuil, across the river from Montreal, on June 18, and the following night they struck the Outremont residence of Jean-Louis Lévesque, one of the country's most successful

French-Canadian businessmen. By then, though, CATS was about to strike a decisive blow against the bombers—some of them at any rate.

Choquette's offer of a fifty-thousand-dollar reward had produced results. An informer had come forward and provided police with several names. The police began following some of those individuals and their associates, and one of the suspects led investigators to a secluded two-storey red-and-white summer cottage in the town of Prévost, up in the Laurentians, about fifty kilometres north of Montreal.

Police watched the place for two weeks and saw young men coming and going. They placed a listening device inside to eavesdrop on conversations, concluded that the chalet was a terrorist hideout, and raided it on the morning of Sunday, June 22. Thirty plainclothes officers emerged from the woods surrounding the cottage and apprehended the startled occupants—André Roy, twenty-three, an unemployed taxi driver, and his wife Nicole, twenty-six, who had their two-and-a-half-year-old daughter with them; Claude Morency, a twenty-one-year-old labourer; and François Lanctôt, who was also twenty-one and the younger brother of Jacques Lanctôt.

The officers searched the premises and found a carton containing $28,620, about half the loot from the Université de Montréal robbery, as well as a list of everyone who had received a cut of the money. They found twelve balaclavas, a sawed-off double-barrel shotgun, two pistols, two revolvers and ammunition for each of the weapons, as well as detonators, clocks, batteries and wires that could be used to assemble bombs, and some curious odds and ends—namely a large syringe, a small vial of liquid anaesthetic and a set of handcuffs.

Police subsequently discovered seven cases of dynamite, some 350 pounds in all, in the basement of Morency's father's home in Laval, and a search of the Montreal apartment he shared with Lanctôt turned up something entirely unexpected—250 copies of a crudely produced communiqué that revealed a plot to kidnap a diplomat. It began with the following statement: "The sickening representative of the U.S.A. in Quebec, Consul Harrison W. Burgess, is in the hands of the Front de Libération Québécois. Here are the conditions on which the life of Consul Burgess depends . . ."

The document went on to detail the would-be kidnappers' plan to demand the release of thirteen so-called political prisoners, including the murderers François Schirm and Edmond Guénette, the bandit Robert Lévesque and the serial bomber Pierre-Paul Geoffroy. They would also demand the reinstatement of the G. Lapalme Co. drivers, the payment of a "voluntary tax" of five hundred thousand dollars in gold bars, and passage to Cuba for themselves and the political prisoners, along with two journalists and two lawyers to ensure that they made it safely.

The police released Nicole Roy, but charged her husband and Lanctôt with a dozen offences and laid twenty charges against Morency. Premier Bourassa told reporters that his government would stamp out terrorism, and Justice Minister Choquette held a press conference in his office at the court house and among the items on his desk was a slim, maroon-coloured booklet entitled *Manuel de la guérilla urbaine*, later published in English as *Minimanual of the Urban Guerrilla*. It was among the items seized at Prévost, and copies of the booklet, which numbered no more than forty pages, had been circulating for several months among Montreal's aspiring revolutionaries.

The author, a Brazilian revolutionary named Carlos Marighella, had published his manual for mayhem in June 1969. It was intended for rebels and insurgents in Brazil and referred specifically to circumstances there, but the thinking behind it was clearly capable of inspiring readers in Quebec who saw themselves as members of an oppressed and colonized minority. "To be an assailant or a terrorist," Marighella wrote, "is a quality that ennobles any honourable man because it is an act worthy of a revolutionary engaged in armed struggle against the shameful military dictatorship and its monstrosities.

"The urban guerilla follows a political goal and only attacks the government, the big capitalists and the foreign imperialists, particularly the

North Americans. . . . The principal task of the urban guerilla is to distract, to wear out, to demoralize the militarists, the military dictatorship and its repressive forces and to attack and destroy the wealth and property of North Americans, the foreign managers and the Brazilian upper classes." The types and nature of actions Marighella recommended included armed robberies of banks, thefts of explosives and weapons, strikes and work disruptions, sabotage, executions, armed propaganda and kidnapping.

Brazilian police in São Paulo shot and killed Marighella in November 1969. But by then, his compatriots had kidnapped C. Burke Elbrick, the U.S. ambassador to Brazil, who was released in exchange for fifteen imprisoned insurgents. That was the start of a wave of politically motivated kidnappings. In the first six months of 1970, rebels in Brazil, Argentina, Guatemala and the Dominican Republic abducted nine individuals, all but one of them diplomats or embassy officials. One of the hostages was murdered and another escaped, but the rest were released in exchange for prisoners—ninety-three all told—including forty who were freed on June 1 to secure the release of the West German ambassador to Brazil.

For the radical young Montrealers who were attempting to launch a revolution, the Latin American kidnappings seemed a spectacular success. And if it worked there, why not in Quebec?

In late June, a writer for the Montreal weekly *Le Petit Journal* observed, "Terrorism seems to be a malady of which Quebec is not near being cured. Everything indicates that, as soon as one FLQ cell has been dismantled, another takes its place." There were, in fact, other *felquistes* lurking in the shadows, and they emerged immediately after the Prévost raid and made a mockery of Bourassa's promise to wipe out terrorism. They bombed the Banque Canadienne Nationale in Tracy, a south shore town forty kilometres downriver from Montreal, and the branch happened to be managed by the premier's cousin. On June 24—Quebec's

St. Jean Baptiste Day holiday—*felquistes* hit the headquarters of the Department of National Defence on Lisgar Street in downtown Ottawa and they took another life.

Wilfrid O'Neil, Alfred Pinisch, Leslie McWilliams, Thérèse Morin and Jean Corbo had died in previous waves of FLQ violence. The victim this time was Jeanne d'Arc Saint-Germain. She was fifty, had three children and two grandchildren, and lived quietly in an apartment in Vanier, a largely French-speaking quarter of the capital. Saint-Germain worked in the department's communications centre, located on the ground floor of the sprawling World War II–era complex. She was scheduled to finish her night shift at 7:15 a.m., but died instantly when a powerful bomb exploded at 6:28 a.m. and tore the centre to pieces.

The death of Saint-Germain did not stop the bombers. They waited a little over a week before planting a bomb that exploded outside the security fence at a Petrofina refinery in Pointe-aux-Trembles at the far east end of the island. After that, they took another week-long breather, but then struck three times in three nights.

Shortly after 3:00 a.m. on Friday, July 10, a garbageman named Henri Béliveau was part of a crew collecting the trash in the financial district. He walked into the alley behind the twenty-two-storey office tower at 360 St. James Street West—the former headquarters of the Royal Bank of Canada. Béliveau spotted a bulging, almost new olive-green knapsack resting on top of a trash can. He picked it up and began walking toward the garbage truck waiting on the street. That's when he heard the tick-tock, tick-tock of an alarm clock. He lifted the flap and reached inside and pulled out a bomb consisting of two long, fat sticks of dynamite, the clock and a battery all taped together. He immediately dropped it, glanced inside the knapsack, saw more dynamite and dropped the pack. Then he hailed a passing cab and asked to be taken to the nearest police station, where he reported the incident.

Côté was summoned and arrived at 3:40. He determined that the bomb had been set to explode at 4:00 a.m., but the wire running from the clock to the battery had been jarred loose when the device hit the sidewalk, which, in effect, neutralized it. He found another six sticks of dynamite in the knapsack, each one sixteen inches long and three inches in diameter and weighing five pounds apiece.

The next incident occurred at 8:00 a.m. on Saturday, July 11. The head office of Wawanesa Insurance in the Town of Mount Royal was the intended target. An employee had parked her car behind the building and was walking toward the entrance when she spotted a package with dynamite protruding from it. She walked right past it, entered the building and phoned the Mount Royal police. They ordered the employees to evacuate and called in Côté, who dismantled a bomb containing two five-pound sticks. It was set to explode six minutes later.

Côté answered one more call that day. The SQ requested his assistance after an explosion destroyed a Buick Wildcat on the Metropolitan Expressway and killed the driver. This was a mob hit. Police found the mangled remains of a career criminal named Danny Polansky inside the shattered vehicle. The investigation lasted hours. Côté arrived shortly after 6 p.m. and returned home completely exhausted at 11:30. He took a hot bath and fell into a deep sleep, but was awakened by his wife half an hour after midnight. There was a call from the communications centre at headquarters. A bomb had been discovered at 129 St. James Street—head office complex of the Bank of Montreal.

The bank complex comprised three nineteenth-century buildings and one constructed in the twentieth. They occupied an entire block, and an enclosed alleyway ran through the centre of them. A security guard had alerted police after finding a Volkswagen Beetle parked in the alley with the key in the ignition and dashboard lights on. The first officer on the scene slid into the driver's seat to examine the vehicle. He heard a clock ticking under the passenger seat and realized there was a bomb aboard and called for reinforcements.

Côté and fellow officer John Meloche arrived within minutes. The flashing red lights of police cruisers, fire trucks and ambulances lit the alley like a casino as the two men approached the Volkswagen. It was parked in an east–west direction, with the passenger door against the north wall. Côté had no alternative but to lean across the driver's seat to get at the bomb. He slowly and gingerly pulled a green garbage bag from the floor beneath the passenger seat. He attempted to ignore the ticking of the alarm clock as he slit the garbage bag, located the wires that formed the electrical circuit and snipped them with his nail clippers.

The white cotton gloves Côté wore to avoid leaving his own fingerprints behind were soaked with sweat when he emerged. He was about to shout "All clear" when Meloche said, "Bob, *sacrément*, come and see this." There was a box full of dynamite—fifty pounds all told—in the back seat. Meloche lifted the lid of the trunk and discovered an identical box and then they looked at each other and laughed like fools. The car contained 130 pounds of dynamite, a "super bomb," as the next day's papers put it. They all agreed that an explosion would have been catastrophic and hailed Côté as a hero for dismantling it. He was, by then, perhaps the best-known police officer in the city. His name and photograph had appeared in the papers after almost every bombing incident, but he had never been quoted and had never given an interview.

Côté agreed to speak to the *Gazette* in late July only because police director Marcel Saint-Aubin had nominated him for the Order of Canada, and he was admitted as an officer, the first member of a municipal police force accorded that distinction. During the interview, Côté explained his three simple rules for handling a bomb: don't pay any attention to the ticking of the clock; never take anything for granted; and always look for the unsuspected, the hidden mechanism, or the hidden booby trap. Côté also pointed out that he and his men had recovered almost seven hundred pounds of dynamite by dismantling bombs planted in the wave of terrorist attacks that had begun in early May.

The bomb squad's success apparently annoyed the bombers, who sent a letter to police headquarters dated July 21. It was addressed to "Sergeant Robert Côté of the anti-terrorist Gestapo" and said, "A mass will be celebrated soon to honour the memory of Sergeant Côté. With sincerest condolences from the AFQ [Anarchist Front of Quebec]." Police identification technicians lifted several fingerprints from the document, but were never able to determine who had sent it. Nor were investigators able to apprehend those responsible for the bombings. The Bank of Montreal super bomb was their final attempt to sow havoc and mayhem. A calm settled over Montreal, although it was an uneasy one, as *Le Journal de Montreal* reported.

Reporter Pierre Bouchard had tapped his police sources, and they had several theories on why the bombings had stopped. Perhaps the terrorists had run out of dynamite or had been unnerved by increased surveillance. Perhaps they were frustrated by their recent failures. But maybe they had decided it was time to change tactics. This was what most concerned the authorities. They knew the FLQ was still alive and well. They knew there were *felquistes* out there and they would be back. They feared that future attacks would be better planned, more dangerous and more spectacular. And they were right.

Thirteen

———

THE OCTOBER CRISIS LAID BARE

"BIRTHDAY PRESENT FOR MR. CROSS"

James Cross arrived in Montreal in February 1968 with his wife Barbara and their twenty-year-old daughter Susan to take up the important and prestigious position of senior trade commissioner in the British government's Montreal office. His mandate was to increase commerce with Canada, and he and his wife and daughter moved into a fine two-storey stone home located on Redpath Crescent—high on the south slope of Mount Royal.

Cross enjoyed a brisk walk to start the day, and if the weather was clement, he could amble along the pleasantly wooded pathways of Mount Royal Park, which abutted the back fences of the homes on Redpath Crescent and extended across the summit of the mountain. Or he could walk to the office, which was located in the Prudential Assurance building on Dorchester Boulevard, below Ste-Catherine Street, so it was downhill most of the way. Cross was in charge of a team of twenty-eight employees—some of them trade commission officials like himself, others Montrealers who performed clerical and administrative duties—and all took to their new boss. He was smart, diligent and reserved, but nevertheless charmed those around him with his wit— "a fine, Irish, racy sense of humour," as one colleague put it.

Cross was a British civil servant, but was Irish by birth and had been blessed with a top-notch education. He had begun his schooling in his hometown of Nemagh in County Tipperary and completed it at the King's Hospital, a three-hundred-year-old Anglican-run school in Dublin. Then he earned a degree in political science and economics, with first-class honours, from Trinity College Dublin. He graduated in 1944 and spent three years in the British Army, then joined the Board of Trade. He began his career in England before being sent abroad, first to Winnipeg and Halifax, then Kuala Lumpur in Malaysia and then Montreal.

A newspaper report described the affable Irishman, who went by the nickname Jasper, as "an urbane, highly educated man who mixes easily with people and has a light touch in his dealings with the British government's Montreal office." He enjoyed monthly lunches with fellow members of the city's consular corps, spoke to Rotaries and other service clubs, attended trade shows and conventions, and kept up a steady round of meetings with businessmen and corporate executives. He was in Montreal to promote trade and commerce, but the city's business community was preoccupied with all the uncertainty swirling around the province's political future. The subject came up repeatedly and consumed a disproportionate amount of Cross's time. He listened carefully and filed detailed reports to the British High Commission in Ottawa. And early in his tenure, he had had his own encounter with the politically inspired violence that had rattled Quebec throughout the sixties.

Cross attended the St. Jean Baptiste Day parade on June 24, 1968, with the American consul, Harrison W. Burgess. Both had brought their wives and they joined Prime Minister Trudeau, Mayor Jean Drapeau and a host of other dignitaries on the reviewing stand. But their attention quickly shifted to the riot that erupted across the street at La Fontaine Park, and the two couples exited along with everyone except Trudeau when the mob briefly broke through police lines and began hurling rocks and pop bottles at the reviewing stand.

The next two years were filled with turmoil and upheaval—labour strife, the rise of the separatist Parti Québécois and its charismatic leader René Lévesque, the relentless terrorist bombings that mostly targeted private businesses, the Sir George Williams riot, the Opération McGill français movement, the police work stoppage of October 7, 1969, that led to looting and rioting, the Murray Hill taxi riot, and the fight over language rights that erupted in the suburb of Saint-Léonard but soon engulfed the entire province.

Cross took a leave in the summer of 1970 and spent it in England, and upon returning he learned that the police had broken up a terrorist plot to kidnap Harrison W. Burgess. Police provided protection for the American consul but made no effort to safeguard other members of the city's diplomatic corps. Life went on as usual. Before the summer was out, the trade commissioner and his wife celebrated the marriage of their daughter to a Montrealer, and on September 29 they observed Cross's forty-ninth birthday.

Cross skipped his morning walk on Monday, October 5. It was the start of an unusually busy week and he was reviewing his itinerary with his wife. The president of the Confederation of British Industries was scheduled to visit Montreal and Cross had organized a round of appointments and special events. "We were discussing the week ahead as I walked between the bedroom and the bathroom dressing," Cross said in a 1998 interview with researchers at Cambridge University's Diplomatic Oral History Programme. "I then heard a ring of the doorbell and was surprised that anybody would arrive that early in the morning. My wife suggested that it was probably Quebec Hydro come to read the meter so I took no further notice." The maid, a Portuguese woman named Anilia Santos, answered the door. She cradled her baby in one arm. A young man, dressed as a deliveryman, stood on the step holding a long, gaily wrapped package. "Birthday present for Mr. Cross," he said, then added: "You'll have to sign for it."

Santos said she didn't have a pen.

"Here's one," the man said, and pulled a revolver from under his coat and forced himself into the house. Two accomplices who had hidden below by the corner of the house dashed up the long set of concrete steps. One grabbed the package, ripped off the paper and pulled out a sub-machine gun. The gunmen mounted the staircase leading to the second floor while the third man guarded the front door.

"I was walking towards the bathroom dressed only in shirt and underpants," Cross told the Cambridge researchers. "A man came through the opposite side holding a gun and said: 'Get down on the floor or you'll be fucking dead.' I backed into the bedroom, lay on the floor and he then made me turn over onto my face and put handcuffs on me.

"He then called out another man who came up the stairs into the bedroom carrying a sub-machine gun and shepherding the maid and her daughter in front of them. The first man took me into the dressing room beyond the bathroom, put my trousers on and shoes and slipped a jacket over my shoulders. He then led me back through the bedroom. My wife said 'You must let me say goodbye to my husband' and came over and kissed me."

The kidnappers tore the bedroom phone from its socket and ordered Barbara Cross not to call the police for an hour. Then they made their way downstairs and out the front door and descended the steps to a taxi idling in the street.

"The only other person I could see was a gardener collecting leaves on the far side of the road," Cross recalled in his 1998 interview. "I was pushed into the taxi and shoved down between the front and back seats and a rug thrown over my head.

"Then we drove for about five to ten minutes and stopped in what was clearly some sort of garage or workshop. I was taken out, made to stand against the walls with my eyes closed and a gas mask with the eye pieces painted black was placed over my head.

"I was then taken back and pushed into another car in the same position between the seats and we drove possibly fifteen to twenty minutes. We finally drew up in what was clearly the garage of a house. I was taken out, led upstairs, the handcuffs were transferred from behind my back to the front and I was put lying down on a mattress in a room where I was to spend the next fifty-nine days."

A WILD GAMBLE

So began Canada's October Crisis. What started on a pleasant fall morning ended on a cold, snowbound night in late December. Cross's kidnappers seized the attention of the nation and briefly set the agenda, but they unleashed a chain of events that they could never have foreseen and that, once unleashed, they had no hope of controlling.

In the first days of the crisis, the kidnappers issued communiqués laden with ultimatums and outrageous demands and threats to kill James Cross. They anticipated that the Bourassa administration in Quebec City and the Trudeau government in Ottawa would yield to save a life, but both refused to bend to the whims of a violent minority—though they made one concession. They allowed the gang's manifesto—released with one of the communiqués—to be broadcast over the Radio-Canada television network. The Cross kidnappers watched with delight, but from that point on they were mere spectators in a deepening crisis that took one unpredictable turn after another.

First there was the second kidnapping, the brazen Thanksgiving weekend abduction of the Quebec cabinet minister Pierre Laporte, who was snatched from the street in front of his suburban, South Shore home while tossing a football with his teenage nephew. The gang holding Cross knew the men responsible, in fact had worked closely with them on kidnapping plots throughout 1970, though this one had never been part of their plans. It took the authorities by surprise as well. No one in Montreal or Quebec City or Ottawa had any idea what to expect next or whether there might be a fresh wave of bombings, and another 575 sticks of dynamite had been stolen from a warehouse and a quarry on successive nights in late September. The authorities concluded that diplomats and parliamentarians, as well as public buildings, had to be protected and they called upon the Canadian Army.

Soldiers appeared on the streets overnight, first in Ottawa, then in Montreal, a sight so far from the norm in our generally placid country that some wondered—was this necessary? Had the governments overreacted? And one skeptical journalist—the CBC's Tim Ralfe—cornered Pierre Trudeau on the way into the House of Commons and provoked an extraordinary outburst of political candour. Ralfe began by asserting, "My choice is to live in a society that is free and democratic and that means you don't have people with guns running around in it. . . . And one of the things I have to give up for that choice is the fact that people like you might be kidnapped."

Trudeau replied, "Yes, well there's a lot of people with bleeding hearts around that just don't like to see people with helmets and guns. All I can say is, go on and bleed. But it's more important to keep law and order in society than to be worried about weak-kneed people who don't like the looks of a soldier's helmet."

"At any cost?" Ralfe asked. "How far would you go with that?"

"Just watch me," Trudeau said.

The prime minister's defiance stunned the kidnappers, but the intervention of sixteen distinguished Quebeckers—a mix of journalists, lawyers, academics, labour leaders and opposition politicians—gave them cause for hope. The sixteen believed no price was too high when two lives were at stake. They urged the governments to negotiate, and to press their point they drafted a petition that they released at a press conference, signed publicly and then published in *Le Devoir*.

Agitators and provocateurs posed a new threat. The self-proclaimed *felquistes* Pierre Vallières and Charles Gagnon believed a rare opportunity had arrived. This could be the moment envisioned in the document *Stratégie révolutionnaire et rôle de l'avant-garde*, the moment when "agitation becomes widespread and culminates in a general economic, political and social crisis."

Vallières and Gagnon and a number of fellow travellers, including the hard-left labour leader Michel Chartrand and the flamboyant lawyer Robert Lemieux, who had made his reputation defending accused terrorists, set out to drum up support for the kidnappers and the revolutionary upheaval they had long dreamed of, and they found receptive audiences in Montreal's French-language universities and CEGEPs.

Meetings were held, rallies organized, strikes planned, classes boycotted and some institutions closed briefly.

Quebec authorities envisioned thousands of students, labour leaders and others spilling into the streets and causing havoc. They feared clashes between demonstrators and riot squads, and worried that unrest would spin out of control. The Montreal police, the Drapeau administration and the Bourassa government turned to Ottawa, requesting emergency powers—powers that included arbitrary arrest and detention—and Ottawa complied. At 4 a.m. on Thursday, October 16, the Cabinet declared that a state of apprehended insurrection existed in Quebec and proclaimed the War Measures Act, a decision that would be discussed and debated, derided and denounced from that day to the present.

Within an hour of the proclamation, police began arresting actual and suspected FLQ members, supporters and sympathizers. Before the day was done, dozens had been detained; and before the week was over, Pierre Laporte was dead—strangled with the gold chain he wore around his neck, his body dumped in the trunk of a car and the car abandoned in a parking lot within sight of the Canadian Armed Forces airport in the South Shore suburb of Saint-Hubert. "The FLQ has sown the seeds of its own destruction," Trudeau said in a nationally televised address after the murder, and he was right.

The police quickly identified four suspects in the Laporte kidnapping and two in the Cross kidnapping, and they distributed thousands of "WANTED" posters bearing photos and concise descriptions of the men. For the kidnapping and murder of Pierre Laporte, they wanted "ROSE, Paul, age 27; ROSE, Jacques, age 23; SIMARD, Francis, age 23; LORTIE, Bernard, age 19." And for the kidnapping of James Cross, "LANCTÔT, Jacques, age 25; CARBONNEAU, Marc, age 37." The police captured Bernard Lortie in early November. By the end of the month, they had located the apartment where Lanctôt and Carbonneau and their accomplices were holding James Cross, and this gang accepted exile to Cuba in exchange for releasing their hostage. Simard and the

Rose brothers remained at large until arrested on December 28 in a farmhouse southeast of Montreal.

That ended the October Crisis. Nothing like it had occurred in this country prior to the autumn of 1970 and nothing like it has occurred since. Jacques Lanctôt and Paul Rose led this misguided enterprise, and Rose explained their motives many years later in an interview with the Montreal writer Ann Charney. "Our goal was never to overthrow the government," he said. "How can a handful of people take power? What we hoped for was to speed up the process of change by bringing people to the point where they desired it. . . . The violent strategy of previous FLQ groups—bombs, dynamite—did not interest us. We felt that such acts, particularly when they created innocent victims, tended to alienate the very people we hoped to reach."

In the WANTED posters, Rose appeared to be a scruffy figure with a thin, dark moustache, a hint of a goatee, dishevelled hair and a sunken and withered left eye—the result of a childhood accident that had left him partly blind. Rose spent his early years in the impoverished Montreal neighbourhood of Saint-Henri, not far from the Redpath Sugar plant where his father worked, but the family moved across the river to the South Shore community of Longueuil when he was on the cusp of adolescence. Rose, the eldest of five children, early on displayed leadership and organizational skills and was the first member of his extended family to advance beyond high school. He earned a baccalaureate in political science from Collège Sainte-Marie in Montreal, went on to the Université du Québec à Montréal (UQAM) and paid for his studies by working as a longshoreman and hotel bellboy and elevator operator. Afterward, he spent two years teaching special needs children with the Chambly Regional School Commission.

Lanctôt grew up in the Montreal neighbourhood of Rosemont, the third of ten children, and the talk around the dinner table often focused on politics. His father, Gérard Lanctôt, had once been a a close associate and ardent supporter of the anti-Semitic journalist, Hitler admirer and fascist agitator Adrien Arcand. Lanctôt despised his father. In a memoir written years later, he described him as a racist who believed that whites were superior to blacks, that Jews were to blame for most of the world's problems and that the Catholic faith would keep the world safe for believers. Every evening at 7 p.m., the whole family knelt together and recited the Rosary.

The elder Lanctôt and his wife could not afford college educations for their sprawling brood, but their son Jacques was admitted to the Jesuit-run Collège Saint-Ignace. "If you said you wanted to become a priest, you were accepted," he told the journalist Monique Roy in a 1990 interview. "Me, I wanted to become a Jesuit missionary in Africa." He soon changed his mind. He found Camus and Sartre more appealing than Catholic theology, and was more inspired by Third World liberation movements than missionary work. He joined the RIN, but contributed little. He hung out at cafés and restaurants frequented by artists and intellectuals and, as he told Roy, "I was ready for anything. I dreamed of being the first at the barricades."

"Anything," in the summer of 1963, when Lanctôt was seventeen, meant forming an FLQ cell with two other youthful firebrands and hurling incendiary bombs at two Montreal armouries, a Legion Hall and a CN building. All three perpetrators were arrested and later received suspended sentences, and the Jesuits of Collège Saint-Ignace showed Lanctôt the door. Nevertheless, he pursued his studies elsewhere and taught French for two and a half years at the Séminaire de Saint-Hyacinthe, located in the small South Shore town of the same name. Then he returned to Montreal and worked part time as a taxi driver and immersed himself in left-wing causes and activities.

Lanctôt and Rose met purely by chance during the St. Jean Baptiste Day riot of June 24, 1968. That was the occasion of Rose's political awakening. The police brutality sickened him, he later told Ann Charney. He was arrested with dozens of others and thrown into a crowded paddy wagon. Landing next to a young demonstrator who had been badly beaten and was unconscious and bleeding, he used his own shirt to clean him up. Rose inadvertently came to the aid of Lanctôt, and that was the start of a partnership that would lead, albeit circuitously, to the events of October 1970.

Both were regulars at picket line protests and street demonstrations. Both were usually in the front lines. Both became known to police. A police photo from the Saint-Léonard school riot of September 1969 captured Rose bearing a large sign, staring straight into the camera and standing between Reggie Chartrand of the Chevaliers de l'indépendance and Raymond Lemieux, founder of the Ligue pour l'intégration scolaire. Lanctôt, meanwhile, threw himself into the campaign against the Murray Hill Limousine Service and the company's Montreal-Dorval Airport monopoly. He was a leader of the militant Mouvement de libération du taxi. He was injured in the riot at the Murray Hill bus barn in October 1969 and wound up on crutches and with one foot in a cast.

By that fall, the Montreal police were applying intense pressure on left-wing activists and organizations. They raided offices, seized documents and questioned individuals, all in response to the riots, protests and bombings that had rocked the city. On top of that, the Drapeau administration passed a bylaw in November 1969 prohibiting street demonstrations and protests—a measure later overturned by the courts. "It finally reached the point where I became convinced it was no longer feasible to work openly," Rose told Charney. "The margin for action had become too restricted. We felt ourselves hemmed in on all sides and the only recourse left was to move our operation underground."

They formed a new FLQ network that grew to some thirty-five members and two branches—one led by Lanctôt, the other by Rose. Lanctôt's group included his brother François; his sister Louise; her husband Jacques Cossette-Trudel, a supply teacher and the son of a senior official in the federal Department of Energy; and Marc Carbonneau, a taxi driver, a founder of the Mouvement de libération du taxi and the father of four children aged seven to fourteen. Rose's branch, alternately known as the Longueuil Group or the South Shore Gang, included his brother Jacques, a CN mechanic; Francis Simard, a RIN activist and electrician who worked briefly for CN; and Simard's childhood friend Yves Langlois, a Superior Court stenographer.

PLOTS AND PREPARATIONS

Initially the Rose and Lanctôt groups operated independently, but both were determined to carry out a spectacular action of some sort. They would need to be much better organized and equipped than the stealthy FLQ bombers who planted their explosives and then went back to their jobs or their studies. This new network would need weapons, vehicles, hideouts and money and the Rose group served as the fundraising arm of the network.

"Fundraising" was a euphemism for various frauds, credit card scams and bank robberies, and Francis Simard provided an illuminating account of the *felquistes'* activities in his 1982 memoir *Talking It Out: The October Crisis from Inside.* "We had to find a way to finance ourselves," Simard wrote. "I have to admit we didn't spend a long time looking. We were fighting against a certain form of social organization, so it seemed logical and natural to take back the money that belonged to that society's institutions. We had no problem with our consciences. We considered them thieves and exploiters living off the poverty of the people. Ripping them off was a sort of duty. We weren't going to shed any tears for Household Finance, Esso, Imperial or the Bank of Commerce."

They began by obtaining loans under their own names from finance companies like Household. They applied for credit cards, went on shopping sprees, sold the goods to friends and neighbours at a discount and kept the proceeds. In six months, Simard wrote, they had run up multiple balances of a hundred thousand dollars, but went through the money in a hurry. They used some of it to support themselves since most had quit working to devote themselves full time to their national liberation project, and they spent some of the funds on such things as printing leaflets and pamphlets promoting the cause. They then needed more money and the old scams wouldn't work anymore. Too many people were after them. So they began robbing banks.

"Borrowing from a finance company is one thing," Simard wrote. "Walking into a bank with a gun in your hand and robbing it is another. It took us weeks to decide and it wasn't easy. We'd never had weapons before. . . . There were plenty of questions. How do you rob a bank? How do you react once you've got a gun in your hand? . . . None of us had even seen a revolver. We didn't know how to get our hands on one." But they overcame their scruples and acquired a revolver, two M1s and two 12-gauge shotguns. "We learned about bank robberies by robbing banks," as Simard put it. "Security was strict. We didn't want anyone wounded, let alone killed. Everything was planned to keep unpleasant surprises to a minimum. The first guys in never carried loaded guns. You could never tell how they would react. Every hold-up is a different story. Something always happens. That's normal. Every time we learned something new. Our confidence grew. We never made the same mistakes twice. It was serious business. No one ever got involved for kicks."

The group committed twelve armed robberies. Paul Rose later told an interviewer that the loot totalled about two hundred thousand dollars, which they used to buy properties and rent apartments that would serve as bases of operation. In January 1970, the Rose group bought a house on the outskirts of Longueuil. They also purchased a farm in Saint-Anne-de-la-Rochelle in the Eastern Townships, about eighty kilometres east of Montreal, which they planned to use as a base for training militants and as a "people's prison," where one or more hostages could be held. "The farm was huge with all its buildings and completely isolated at the end of a country road," Simard wrote. "It seemed perfect. The whole group moved in. We worked there for part of the winter, until the spring of 1970. A couple lived there and raised sheep, which provided our cover."

In February, Lanctôt rented a second-floor apartment at 3955 St-André Street, two blocks west of La Fontaine Park. The following month, Rose and a young woman named Lise Balcer, posing as a married couple, rented a single-family dwelling at 5630 Armstrong Street, an isolated, semi-rural road near the Canadian Armed Forces air base in Saint-Hubert. Soon enough, kidnapping plots began to take shape, and these enterprising *felquistes* had weapons, vehicles, hideouts and enough money to sustain them for a while. Jacques Lanctôt's group was behind the plots, but the first two ended in failure. As we saw in the previous chapter, Montreal police nabbed Lanctôt and an accomplice on a weapons charge in late February 1970. The following month, they charged both with conspiring to kidnap the Israeli consul, Moise Golan, and Lanctôt had been on the run since then. In late June, the police arrested his younger brother François and his co-conspirators at their Prévost hideout and inadvertently discovered the plot to kidnap the American consul Harrison W. Burgess.

The failure of the Burgess plot was a devastating setback that set in motion a chain of events that led straight to the crisis in October 1970. The arrests and the seizures of money, weapons and dynamite were bad enough. Worse still, though, one of the suspects had a crudely drawn map of the Saint-Anne-de-la-Rochelle farm and the next day—a Sunday—police raided the place. There was a crowd in the kitchen, as Simard recalled in his memoir. The Rose brothers were there and Carbonneau and the fugitive Lanctôt, as well as his pregnant wife Suzanne and their infant son Boris. Lanctôt and the Rose brothers slipped out of the house and into a granary. Others hid on the second floor of the sprawling, ramshackle dwelling. Simard and Carbonneau greeted the police and gave false names. The officers searched the place but found nothing suspicious and left.

"The previous months' work collapsed in a single day," Simard wrote. "It was a rough blow. The farm was unsafe now. We had a truck and two cars there. They were useless too. Finances were in rough shape. What little money we had was running out." The house at 5630 Armstrong in Saint-Hubert became their base. Everyone went to work on a new kidnapping plot. Lanctôt's sister Louise and her husband Jacques Cossette-Trudel handled surveillance. They visited the Queen's Printer

Bookshop in downtown Montreal and checked the *Who's Who* directory, which listed all the diplomatic figures residing in the city, along with their home and business addresses. They initially watched several diplomats, but then focused on the American consul and the British trade commissioner, both of whom lived on Redpath Crescent—and they spent hours observing their daily routines. Others resumed fundraising activities, but their efforts were much less successful than before.

By late August discord had arisen between Lanctôt and Rose. Lanctôt was desperate to press ahead. He was wanted by police. His wife was expecting. His brother was in jail. He had even considered turning himself in after the farmhouse raid, but the others had dissuaded him. He was running out of time and options. Rose wanted to wait. He feared the police knew too much about them after the Prévost and Saint-Anne-de-la-Rochelle raids. He maintained they didn't have the money or the resources necessary to carry out a kidnapping. And he was opposed to abducting Cross, who was, in his mind, a symbol of cultural colonialism. He preferred the American consul or someone like him who represented foreign domination of Quebec's economy.

The dispute came to a head during a meeting in early September at 5630 Armstrong, in which nine key members of the network participated. They debated for hours and then voted. Five favoured the kidnapping, four were opposed and, with that, the sides parted. Rose and his group intended to continue organizing and fundraising. Lanctôt and his supporters returned to Montreal and planned to act by the end of September or start of October.

Somewhere along the way—and accounts vary—the hostage-taking project had been dubbed Operation Liberation, and the Lanctôt group now became the Liberation Cell. It had six members—Lanctôt; Jacques and Louise Cossette-Trudel; Marc Carbonneau; Yves Langlois, who went by the alias Pierre Séguin; and a young woman of nineteen who was a minor figure, was never charged and was only referred to as "*la jeune femme*" in future government inquiries and reports. The cell's

Members of the FLQ, including Francis Simard and Paul Rose (centre), in Percé, Quebec.

The FLQ attacked a Montreal armoury on the 1963 Victoria Day holiday with its largest bomb to date—seventy-five pounds of dynamite planted under a car.

Pierre-Paul Geoffroy's mother gave him this trunk when he was a student. Det.-Sgt. Robert Côté found the bombs and dynamite inside on the night of Pierre-Paul Geoffroy's arrest, March 3, 1969.

Police display the dynamite found in the trunk and elsewhere in the third-storey apartment that served as a base for Geoffroy and his accomplices, who were responsible for thirty-one bombings.

Shortly after 5:00 a.m. on September 29, 1969, a powerful bomb exploded at the Rosemont residence of Mayor Jean Drapeau (left). Inspecting the damage with him is Det.-Sgt. Robert Côté.

At 4 a.m., Thursday, October 16, 1970, the federal government invoked the War Measures Act in response to an unprecedented peace-time crisis. Nearly five hundred people were detained, though most were never charged.

RECHERCHÉS

ROSE, Jacques

23 ans, masc., t: 5-9
p: 180 lbs., t: clair
ch: bruns y: bruns
Canadien Français

LORTIE, Bernard

19 ans, masc., t: 5-9
p: 155 lbs., t: clair
ch: bruns y: bruns
Canadien Français

SIMARD, Francis

23 ans, masc., t: 5-7
p: 140 lbs., t: clair
ch: châtains y: bleus
Canadien Français

ROSE, Paul

27 ans, masc., t: 6-0
p: 210 lbs., t: pâle
ch: noirs y: bruns
Canadien Français cic.:
cataracte oeil ga.

CARBONNEAU, Marc

27 ans, masc., t: 5-5
p: 145 lbs., t: médium
ch: bruns y: bruns
Canadien Français

LANCTOT, Jacques

25 ans, masc., t: 5-10
p: 160 lbs., t: médium
ch: bruns y: bruns
Canadien Français

Recherché pour conspiration
d'enlèvement. Mandat: 1718-70
Cour des Sessions.

TOUS RECHERCHES POUR ENLEVEMENTS (CROSS & LAPORTE)

TRES GRANDE VIGILANCE A ETRE PORTEE - CHAQUE POLICIER DOIT AVOIR EN SA POSSESSION LA PRESENTE
CIRCULAIRE.

POUR INFORMATION: ADRESSEZ-VOUS A LA SECTION ANTI-TERRORISTES: 872-5720

Wanted poster, issued by the Montreal police department.

Prime Minister Pierre Trudeau attending the funeral of Pierre Laporte, October 20, 1970.

A police poster issued by the Quebec police seeking information on the whereabouts of Pierre Laporte. His body was later discovered in the trunk of Paul Rose's car.

PERSONNE ENLEVEE

Transmettre toutes informations à la
SURETE DU QUEBEC
1701 rue Parthenais, Montréal 133, P.Q.
Tél.: 395-4120

Dossier: 047-101070-011

KIDNAPPED PERSON

Transmit all informations to
QUEBEC POLICE FORCE
1701 Parthenais street, Montreal 133, P.Q.
Tel.: 395-4120

Montréal, le 11 octobre 1970
Montreal, October 11th, 1970

Ministre Pierre LAPORTE

SIGNALEMENT

Age	: 49 ans
Sexe	: masculin
Date de naissance	: 27-02-21
Taille	: 5'9''
Poids	: 180
Yeux	: bruns
Teint	: rougeaud
Nez	: prononcé
Corpulence	: trappu
Dents	: naturelles
Cheveux	: châtain grisonnant avec une cavité centre arrière - cheveux clairsemés - peignés sur le côté et front dégagé
Mains	: grosses
Doigts	: gros et courts
Vêtements	: chemise sport de couleur vert et blanc rayée à la verticale - pantalon vert foncé - souliers bruns - ne portait ni cravate, ni veston

DESCRIPTION

Age	: 49 years
Sex	: male
Date of birth	: 27-02-21
Height	: 5'9''
Weight	: 180
Eyes	: brown
Complexion	: ruddy
Nose	: pronounced
Build	: stocky
Teeth	: natural
Hair	: light brown thinning (greying) bald rear center of head. Combed sideways and high forehead.
Hands	: large
Fingers	: big and short
Clothes	: coloured sport shirt, green and white vertical stripes - dark green pants - brown shoes - he was not wearing a jacket nor a tie.

Le véhicule qui a servi à l'enlèvement serait un "Chevrolet" sedan 1968 de couleur vert ou bleu immatriculé 9 J 2420 Qué. 70.

The get-away car used in the kidnapping was reported as being a "Chevrolet" sedan 1968 green or blue in colour and bearing licence plates 9 J 2420 Qué. 70.

Circ: 74/70

P.A. Benoit, Insp-chef
Chief Insp.

Jacques Lanctôt's Liberation Cell included this photo of James Cross in its eleventh communique, released on November 7, 1970. A copy of Pierre Vallières's *Nègres blanc d'Amérique* rests on the table.

Thousands of Montrealers watched on the afternoon of December 3 as a police motorcade led James Cross and his kidnappers to the former Expo 67 site.

Paul Rose remained defiant while under police escort and in the
courtroom. He was cited for contempt twenty-nine times during
his January 1971 murder trial.

primary objective was to liberate imprisoned *felquistes*—not the people of Quebec—and they had to work fast.

The Cossette-Trudels made most of the arrangements. On September 5, they vacated the apartment at 3955 St-André Street, Jacques Lanctôt's residence until he'd gone into hiding in March. On the twelfth, Jacques Cossette-Trudel rented another, under an assumed name, at 10945 Des Récollets Street in Montreal North, some twenty-five kilometres from the heart of downtown. On September 15, he and his wife moved into the place—a first-floor unit in a two-storey walk-up—and they began preparing it for the arrival of a hostage. At about the same time, they put all their furniture and possessions into storage at the home of a friend, one Denise Quesnel, and Cossette-Trudel abandoned his car, a sporty red Renault 10. The couple rented a second apartment on St-Hubert Street, near the Metropolitan Expressway, to serve as a hideout for Lanctôt and Carbonneau and as a base for preparing communiqués.

In the latter half of the month, the group began rehearsing the kidnapping. They practised seizing the hostage, getting him into a car, getting him out and transferring him to another vehicle, and shuttling him into the apartment at 10945 Des Récollets—and they realized they would need a seventh participant. Cossette-Trudel suggested someone he had met the previous year, a young man who wanted to join a terrorist network. He arranged a meeting and told his acquaintance that there was a group planning a *"coup d'éclat,"* or something really big. The acquaintance agreed to participate—no questions asked.

The new recruit added a strange twist to the entire October Crisis. As events unfolded, word gradually circulated among FLQ sympathizers and supporters that one of the kidnappers was an anglophone from McGill, and the same information reached the police. But eight years elapsed before his name was revealed publicly, and a full decade before he was charged. The anglophone was Nigel Hamer, who had grown up in an affluent west island suburb. He earned an electrical engineering degree from McGill and by some accounts was a brilliant student, but his thinking took a radical turn under the influence of Stanley Gray of the Opération McGill français movement.

Cossette-Trudel put Hamer to work immediately. The Liberation Cell wanted a supply of dynamite and Cossette-Trudel directed him to another group of FLQ militants, led by Robert Comeau, a young professor of history at UQAM. On successive nights in late September, Hamer and the members of this cell stole a total of 1,100 pounds of dynamite from a quarry in Saint-Hyacinthe and a CIL paint warehouse in the South Shore village of McMasterville. Cossette-Trudel arranged a second meeting with Hamer on Saturday, October 3, this time at a downtown park, and he disclosed the exact nature of the planned *"coup d'éclat."* The next day, Cossette-Trudel picked up Hamer at an agreed-upon location, blindfolded him and drove him to 10945 Des Récollets, where he met the rest of the Liberation Cell.

The conspirators spent the evening reviewing their plans for the following morning, but a dispute arose. They were split on who to kidnap—the American consul or the British trade commissioner. An account of the rift later appeared in the union-sponsored weekly, *Québec-Presse*, based on a taped summary made by two members of the Liberation Cell. In it, one of the kidnappers disclosed the following rationale for choosing the British trade commissioner: "We believed that the impact of kidnapping a British citizen would be much greater, first with the government and secondly . . . with the people. Equally, we hoped that kidnapping a British diplomat would crystallize the positions of the two communities that exist in Montreal, that is to say, the French Canadians and the English. We hoped that once and for all the English would show their hand, that the big racist dailies, like the *Star* and the *Gazette*, would play the French card and that the French Canadians themselves would finally see and understand the real face of English power."

There was another reason why they opted to target Cross. His daily routine was more predictable than that of the American consul. In any event, once the matter was settled, the conspirators parted for the evening. Lanctôt, Carbonneau, Langlois and Hamer spent the night at the

St-Hubert Street apartment, the Cossette-Trudels and the young woman remained at Des Récollets, and everyone was ready for their rendezvous at 1297 Redpath Crescent—the home of James and Barbara Cross.

MONDAY, OCTOBER 5

Jacques and Louise Cossette-Trudel left 10945 Des Récollets in a wine-red 1962 Chrysler that Marc Carbonneau and Yves Langlois had purchased in September and they took up their assigned positions. Carbonneau left the St-Hubert Street apartment and went to a Diamond Taxi stand at the corner of St-Denis Street and St-Joseph Boulevard, where he had previously worked. He headed straight to the table where the keys for the fleet were kept, grabbed a set and left unnoticed. Then he drove back to the apartment. He picked up Langlois, Jacques Lanctôt and Nigel Hamer, who was disguised as a deliveryman, and he removed the portable Diamond roof light and replaced it with one from LaSalle Taxi, a ruse intended to sow confusion among the authorities.

When they reached Redpath Crescent, Louise Cossette-Trudel was waiting for them, seated in the front passenger seat of a car driven by another woman. She gave a signal indicating that James Cross was home, then the driver sped away. The job was complete in under five minutes. Cross's kidnappers put him into the back seat with Hamer, made him lie down, and threw an old piece of carpet over him. Then Carbonneau made for Édouard-Montpetit Boulevard—a few minutes away on the north side of Mount Royal—and a garage that Jacques Cossette-Trudel had rented the previous month.

Cossette-Trudel was there when they arrived. The kidnappers removed Cross from the cab and slipped a gas mask over his face—one with the eyes blacked out—and then they placed him face down in the back seat of the Chrysler and stowed their weapons in the trunk. Langlois, Cossette-Trudel and Hamer (blindfolded again) left for 10945 Des Récollets. Lanctôt and Carbonneau returned the cab to the Diamond

Taxi stand, and Lanctôt retreated to the St-Hubert Street apartment while Carbonneau completed the morning's work by dropping off the group's first communiqué.

By then the hunt for the kidnappers had got off to a shaky start. Barbara Cross had called police on a second phone in their home, but was so distraught that the French-speaking officer who took the call at a district detachment misunderstood her. He sent officers to the nearby Greek consulate. Domenico LaSource, a gardener who had been working across the street from the Cross residence, told detectives that the kidnappers had arrived in a LaSalle cab. There were three hundred LaSalle taxis operating in the city core, but police found nothing to indicate that any of them had been used in the abduction.

The police quickly established checkpoints on all the bridges leading off the island and checked hundreds of vehicles, but again found nothing. By mid-afternoon they had posted or distributed three thousand copies of a black-bordered leaflet with a small head-and-shoulders shot of Cross and the following description: "height 6'0"; weight 190 pounds; blue eyes; greying black hair; wearing a green checkered sports jacket and black pants." And by then, the police had found the group's first communiqué and an eight-page manifesto, both sealed in a plain, brown ten-by-fourteen-inch envelope retrieved from a mailbox at a UQAM pavilion at La Fontaine Park.

The communiqué was a stylish document that had been printed on high-quality paper shaded in red, green and white—the colours of the Patriote flag during the 1837–38 rebellion against British rule. And each page bore a silhouette-like image of *The Old Man of '37*, the artist Henri Julien's iconic depiction of a French-Canadian farmer bravely strutting into battle—wearing a toque, smoking a pipe and armed with an aged, muzzle-loaded musket.

Lanctôt had written the communiqué, and he began by stating, "Here are the conditions that the ruling authorities must fulfill in order to preserve the life of the representative of the ancient, racist and colonialist British system. . . ." The Liberation Cell's demands were, for all intents and purposes, the same as those contained in the communiqué seized during the Prévost raid. The authorities were instructed to halt their investigations of the FLQ; publish and broadcast the manifesto; release twenty-three *felquistes*, who were either serving sentences or awaiting trial, and provide an aircraft and their safe passage to either Cuba or Algeria; pay a "voluntary tax" of five hundred thousand dollars in gold ingots; rehire the Lapalme mail truck drivers; and disclose the identity of the informer who had led police to the Prévost hideout.

The conditions were non-negotiable and had to be met within forty-eight hours—otherwise James Cross was a dead man. Federal, provincial and municipal authorities responded cautiously. None had ever imagined that such a kidnapping could happen in Canada. Furthermore, all three levels of government had crowded agendas. A municipal election campaign was underway in Montreal. The Bourassa government was dealing with a doctors' strike over the adoption of Medicare and the premier was scheduled to spend three days in New York, meeting with investors and talking up his grand plans for James Bay hydro projects. The Trudeau government, meanwhile, was preparing a Throne Speech to begin a new session of Parliament.

Apart from all that, the Montreal police anticipated that the kidnapping crisis could be resolved quickly. On the afternoon of October 5, they had brought Barbara Cross to headquarters and shown her mug shots of a number of accused and convicted *felquistes*, and she immediately recognized Jacques Lanctôt as one of the kidnappers. Furthermore, the police had lifted two sets of fingerprints from the back side of the eighth and final page of the FLQ manifesto. They sent the prints to the RCMP identification division in Ottawa, and technicians there identified the prints as those of Jacques Lanctôt and Marc Carbonneau.

———

STALEMATE

The kidnappers had hustled James Cross into the back bedroom of 10945 Des Récollets. They removed the gas mask and replaced it with a hood. They undid the handcuffs and allowed him to move his arms from back to front and slapped on the cuffs again and then ordered him to lie on a mattress that rested on the floor. Cross asked his captors about their intentions, and they responded by reading their manifesto and the first communiqué. Cross was far from fluent in French, but he understood the threat in the final lines of the communiqué. The authorities had to accept all seven conditions and meet them within forty-eight hours. The conditions were non-negotiable and his life depended upon "the good will of the ruling authorities." Upon hearing this, Cross told his captors, "In that case, I must compose myself for death."

But there was a lot to distract him from this ghastly task. He was never alone. Someone stood guard, weapon in hand, around the clock. By the second or third day, the kidnappers allowed him to sit—handcuffed—in an armchair for a few hours at a time and they adjusted the hood so he could watch television. The TV and radio were on constantly elsewhere in the apartment, and someone was always dashing out to buy the morning and afternoon editions of the newspapers, which the kidnappers read closely.

They had no other way of knowing how the authorities were responding or whether the group had any support outside the movement itself. The best they could hope for was a willingness on the part of the authorities to negotiate, and on this, the two leading French-language dailies in the province were split. Claude Ryan of *Le Devoir* argued that the recent rash of politically motivated kidnappings in Latin America showed that intransigence led to tragic consequences. He urged those in government to make some concessions, even minor ones, to save Cross's life. Jean-Paul Desbiens, lead editorial writer for *La Presse*, was unequivocally opposed, insisting that concessions would lead only to escalating demands, maybe even more abductions. "One can imagine some other victim," he wrote. "A young girl would do very nicely. That would really shock the most sensitive among us. That is why neither the municipal government, the provincial government, nor the federal government should give in to this blackmail."

There was a third voice capable of swaying public opinion, and it belonged to René Lévesque. The PQ leader had failed to win a seat in the April election and was writing a daily column in *Le Journal de Montréal*. He risked alienating his own supporters if he lined up with the Trudeau and Bourassa governments, and risked offending the broader public if he supported the kidnappers. So, he equivocated. In his first column on the crisis, he denounced the kidnapping while refusing to call for the unconditional release of Cross. He said that disaffected young Quebeckers were resorting to terrorism due to the "blind brutality of the bureaucracy" and the "hypocrisy of the ruling circles." As he put it, "Their smug inaction in the face of social and economic injustice, and their haste to cover this inaction with the cloak of law and order at the first sign of danger, resorting to slander and lies whenever it suits them, that more than anything else is what has given rise to the FLQ."

The official response became clear late in the day on Tuesday, October 6, when Mitchell Sharp, the federal minister of external affairs, made a televised address in both English and French. The two senior levels of government had agreed to work together to resolve the crisis, but since Cross was a foreign diplomat, federal officials played a lead role. Regarding the seven conditions, Sharp said, "Clearly, these are wholly unreasonable demands and their authors could not have expected them to be accepted. I need hardly say that this set of demands will not be met. I continue, however, to hope that some basis can be found for Mr. Cross's safe return. Indeed, I hope that the abductors will find a way to establish communications to achieve this end." Sharp delivered another statement on French-language radio and TV the following evening. He informed the kidnappers that no discussions would take place until the government had received assurances that Cross would be released.

The kidnappers ignored the minister and continued to issue communiqués. By mid-afternoon on Thursday, October 8, they had issued five of them. They sent each dispatch to one of two French-language radio stations—either CKLM or CKAC. Carbonneau delivered at least one of them in person, while the rest were hidden in phone booths or garbage bins throughout the city, after which one station or the other was alerted by an anonymous telephone call.

This response put the municipal, provincial and federal authorities in an awkward position, as George Radwanski and Kendal Windeyer noted in *No Mandate but Terror*, their account of the October Crisis. Radwanski and Windeyer were *Gazette* reporters who had witnessed the bedlam unleashed by the arrival of each new communiqué. "The moment one of these missives was discovered, it would be rushed into the radio newsroom and read instantly on air," they wrote. "The public was informed of developments even before the authorities. Before the newscaster had finished, the station would be thronged with reporters and cameramen from other media. Then the newscaster would hold the crowd at bay while a secretary bolted herself into another office to make photocopies. It got to the point where one newspaper finally appointed a staffer to sit full time at CKLM just waiting for communiqués."

The authorities might have been embarrassed, but they were not moved. Instead, the kidnappers steadily yielded ground as the week progressed. The forty-eight-hour deadline expired on Wednesday at noon and they were forced to extend it another day. By noon on Thursday, when they issued Communiqué No. 5 (so titled), they had dropped several of their original conditions. But they stuck to their demands that imprisoned *felquistes* be released and that their manifesto be published or broadcast, and the federal government conceded on the latter.

Sharp allowed Radio-Canada to broadcast the manifesto on the evening of October 8—even though Trudeau staunchly opposed any concessions, especially one that might win the terrorists some measure of public approval. He needn't have worried about that. Radio-Canada's Gaétan Montreuil read the manifesto in a flat, uninflected voice and later said, "It was a very bad commercial." The document was almost identical to the manifesto seized after the Prévost raid of June 21, which had led to the discovery of the plot to kidnap Harrison W. Burgess. Jacques Lanctôt had a hand in writing both versions, although Francis Simard maintained in his memoir that he and the Rose brothers spent two days in mid-summer revising and polishing the text. In any event, everyone involved was immensely proud of the finished product. The authors described themselves as "a group of Quebec workers" dedicated to the "total independence of the people of Quebec in a free society."

They were advocating a revolution that would rid the province of capitalism and capitalists—in their words, "the clique of ravenous sharks, the big bosses of business and politics and their lackeys who have turned Quebec into their preserve of cheap labour and unscrupulous exploitation." These "lackeys" included Bourassa, whom they called a hypocrite, as well as "Drapeau the dog and Trudeau the fairy." The authors hoped to arouse and awaken the blue-collar workers of the steel plants, the textile mills and the shipyards, as well as the downtrodden of Montreal's poorer districts—and they addressed them directly. They urged them to "make your revolution yourselves in your own neighbourhoods, your places of work. Only you are able to build a free society." Yet, they demeaned these very people, describing them at one point as "terrorized slaves, terrorized by the big bosses" and at another as "faithful servants and bootlickers of the bigshots from Westmount, Town of Mount Royal, Hampstead and Outremont."

The kidnappers were triumphant after the broadcast of the manifesto. "We can speak of victory at this point since one of our principal demands has been accepted," a member of the Liberation Cell stated in the taped conversation provided to *Québec-Presse*. "For the first time, the patriots of the Front succeeded in expressing themselves practically by stepping into each household by means of Radio-Canada. They [Quebeckers] were in touch with us for the first time, a contact that was quite direct and blunt." The morning after the broadcast, the kidnappers issued Communiqué Nos. 6 and 7 to CKLM. One contained a clipping from that day's *Journal de Montréal* and a note from James Cross to his wife to prove that he was still alive. They announced the temporary suspension of the threat to execute him, but persisted in demanding the release of the imprisoned *felquistes*. They gave the governments until 6 p.m. Saturday to respond and they ordered the police to suspend their investigation.

The police had no intention of doing that. CATS had been working on the case round the clock since Monday morning. The squad was based on the third floor of Station 18, a combined police detachment and fire hall located at the corner of St-Dominique Street and Shamrock Avenue. "I arrived at the office at eight o'clock Monday morning," retired Lieutenant-Detective Julien Giguère recalled in an interview many years later. "I didn't go home till Saturday morning. We slept on bunks provided by the army."

Giguère occupied one of the key positions in the entire operation. He was in charge of intelligence for the MPD's own anti-terror squad, though he had only taken over the position the previous week. He had six city detectives working under him, as well as three from the SQ and another three from the RCMP. The team began shadowing suspects and contacting informers, several of whom fingered Jacques Lanctôt, Nigel Hamer and the Rose brothers, among others.

At dawn on Wednesday, October 7, the police arrested and questioned twenty-seven suspects. They also paraded them before Barbara Cross and her maid, but the women were unable to identify any of them and most were released by the end of the day.

Montrealers provided hundreds of tips, and the police checked those that seemed most promising. They announced on Friday, October 9, that Lanctôt was wanted in connection with the kidnapping, but they were no closer to capturing him. Nor did they know who else was involved, other than Marc Carbonneau, and they had no idea where Cross was being held. After five fruitless days, police, political leaders and kidnappers were stuck. The police investigation was stalled. The political leaders were not prepared to give in and the kidnappers were not prepared to give up. And there was another deadline looming, this one on Saturday at 6 p.m., amid the Thanksgiving holiday weekend.

Sharp decided to let the deadline pass. On Saturday morning, he phoned Quebec justice minister Jérôme Choquette and conveyed his decision to him. Choquette agreed. A short while later, Choquette called back. He had changed his mind. He intended to hold a press conference at 5 p.m. and to issue a statement clarifying his government's position. Sharp asked Choquette to send the text to his office by teletype. Then he huddled with his officials in the Operations Centre, which the government had set up in the East Block at the outset of the crisis. "When we read Choquette's statement we were dismayed," Sharp recounted in his 1994 memoir *Which Reminds Me. . . .* "He proposed saying that the government of Quebec was prepared to release certain 'political prisoners' who had been found guilty of violent crimes."

Sharp and his team revised the text and sent it back. Choquette said he would go with the original, and Sharp told him he would dissociate the federal government from it. Then he sat surrounded by tense officials, "contemplating the chaos if the Quebec and federal governments were to make conflicting statements," as he put it in his memoir. Sharp made a last call to Choquette and asked: if he stuck to his position, could he say with certainty that Cross would be released? Choquette could not.

Minutes before the Liberation Cell's 6 p.m. deadline, the justice minister walked into the downtown studios of a French-language television network. The place was packed with reporters. Choquette looked tense and exhausted. He spoke in French first and he was clear. The two governments would stand together. Their position had not changed. They would not—and could not—negotiate, and Choquette explained why: "No society can expect that the decisions of its governments or its courts of law can be questioned or can be erased by blackmail . . . because this signifies the end of all social order." They would guarantee the kidnappers safe conduct to a foreign country. That was all. "If you refuse," he continued, "I can assure you that you will benefit before our courts of all possible clemency in view of any humanitarian gesture you make to spare the life of Mr. Cross. . . . I therefore ask you, as a gesture of absolute good faith: release Mr. Cross immediately."

Members of the Liberation Cell listened intently. They had listened to each public utterance from the authorities and each had been another setback. They had anticipated that one government or the other—or both—would bend within four or five days and agree to negotiate. They had no Plan B and, as Cross later disclosed, quarrels and disagreements had broken out among them. And now this: another NO.

Choquette finished speaking about 6:15 p.m., and a few minutes later, radio and TV stations all over the city—indeed across the country—interrupted their regular programming to announce that armed men had just kidnapped Pierre Laporte, the Quebec minister of labour and immigration. The news came as a complete surprise to the kidnappers at Des Récollets, but they were thrilled, as Cross later recounted, and they knew who was behind the abduction of Laporte. It was Paul Rose, his brother Jacques and some of their associates, and this surprised them too. Rose had hesitated in August, but now he and his South Shore Gang had intervened. The Cross kidnappers assumed this would force the authorities to negotiate.

But events in the coming days would prove them wrong again. The Rose gang had acted rashly and carelessly, and that would lead to the undoing of all.

RETURN OF THE ROSE BROTHERS

The kidnapping of James Cross had been a shock to the Rose brothers and their associates. They had spent the first part of September planning their next fraudulent scheme to raise money. It would begin with the purchase of several series of traveller's cheques. Then they would take a trip to the U.S. and visit different cities, and at each stop they would go to a bank or a branch of the issuing company and claim that their cheques had been lost or stolen. They would cash the replacement cheques, and then repeat the same charade at the next stop.

The brothers left on September 24, along with their sister Claire, who was eleven, their mother Rose and Francis Simard, but they apparently concealed the real purpose of the trip. Rose Rose later testified that her sons were both deeply in debt, were unable to repay their creditors or buy a car and had decided to leave Quebec and settle in Texas. They drove Mrs. Rose's yellow 1969 Plymouth Valiant and travelled fast, but stopped at gun shops here and there hoping to purchase revolvers, explaining to her that carrying a firearm was commonplace in Texas. Investigators later retrieved postcards they had sent to relatives back home, and the cards revealed that they had visited Philadelphia and Baltimore on September 25, Nashville on September 29 and Dallas on October 1 and 2. They visited several gun shops in Dallas, but as non-residents, were unable to make a purchase. They got around the problem by paying a local resident thirty dollars to acquire firearms for them.

They were in Dallas when they learned from a local radio newscast that terrorists in Montreal had kidnapped a British diplomat. They immediately headed for home, and by the evening of October 7 were near Albany, New York. They managed to pick up Montreal radio station CKAC just as the journalist Louis Fournier was about to read the FLQ manifesto—twenty-four hours ahead of the province-wide broadcast on Radio-Canada. They pulled over and listened. "That moment was something special," Simard recalled in his memoir. "We knew the manifesto by heart. We'd helped write it. We'd fought over every word, for hours at a time, every comma, every sentence. Nobody talked. Nobody could have."

Early the following afternoon—Thursday, October 8—they were back in Longueuil. They feared the police would be watching the Rose family home, so they dropped Mrs. Rose and her daughter at a local shopping centre. Then Simard and the brothers took a motel room on a commercial strip called Taschereau Boulevard and spent the rest of the day assessing the week's events. They concluded that the Liberation

Cell was losing the battle with the authorities. Lanctôt and his gang had twice pushed back their deadlines and both times had dropped some of their demands. Something had to be done to stop the backpedalling, and there was only one option. They had to kidnap someone—either another diplomat or an influential politician—and they would hold their hostage at 5630 Armstrong, the bungalow in Saint-Hubert which Paul Rose had rented under a false name in the spring of 1970.

They considered the American trade consul or one of the diplomats who lived on Nun's Island, a small plot of land in the St. Lawrence, several kilometres west of the city centre. But the police would immediately establish checkpoints on all the bridges and cut off their escape. A diplomat was out of the question, so they settled on Pierre Laporte—a leading member of the freshly elected government of Robert Bourassa.

Laporte was forty-nine, married with two children and a native Montrealer. He had earned a law degree from the Université de Montréal in 1945, but never practised and spent the next fifteen years as a journalist and political reporter for *Le Devoir*. The newspaper sent him to Quebec City to cover the Legislative Assembly, as it was then known, and he quickly earned a reputation as a dogged investigative reporter and a relentless critic of Maurice Duplessis. The premier came to loathe Laporte and in 1958, after Laporte had uncovered a stock scandal involving several ministers, Duplessis barred him from the Press Gallery. Six months after Duplessis's death in September 1959, Laporte published *The True Face of Duplessis*, a devastating critique of the former premier and his government that contributed to the defeat of the Union Nationale in the election of June 1960.

Laporte's political career began when he won a seat in a by-election in December 1961. Jean Lesage made him minister of municipal affairs in 1962—a position he held until 1966, when the Union Nationale defeated the Liberals. Laporte spent the next four years as an opposition member, and then ran for the leadership of the party but lost to Robert Bourassa. He remained loyal to the younger, less experienced Bourassa and was rewarded when the Liberals won the April 1970 election. Bourassa made him Parliamentary Leader as well as a minister with two portfolios—labour and immigration.

Laporte's prominence would make him a high-value hostage. And he represented Chambly—a South Shore constituency. This was critically important, as Simard recalled. "Chambly riding was next to the St. Hubert military base. He had to live close by. We looked in the telephone book. A Pierre Laporte lived in Saint-Lambert. We had to find out if it was the same one. We called; his wife answered. . . . Yes, Pierre was at home but he couldn't come to the phone just now. . . . We were amazed. Incredible. . . . One of the most influential politicians in Quebec was at home. It seemed impossible to us . . . for a minister to be at home—nice and secure—we couldn't get over it."

The Rose brothers spent the night of October 8 at the motel on Taschereau Boulevard while Simard stood in a farmer's field behind 5630 Armstrong until well into the early hours of Friday, October 9—watching the place to ensure that the police did not have it under surveillance. Paul and Jacques Rose arrived the following morning and the three of them began planning the kidnapping. They figured out the best routes between 5630 Armstrong and the Laporte family home at 725 Robitaille Street in Saint-Lambert. It was a mere ten- to fifteen-minute drive and they could take side streets and back roads most of the way. The bungalow on Armstrong Street had an attached garage and they cut a large hole in the wall so they could park in the garage and get their hostage into the dwelling without being seen by any neighbours.

They realized they would need a fourth participant and enlisted Bernard Lortie, a nineteen-year-old youth from the Gaspé Peninsula. Lortie had met the Rose brothers and several other members of the network in the summer of 1970 in the village of Percé, where they were running a youth hostel called Maison des Pêcheurs, or Fisherman's House. He had briefly attended a trade school called l'École des arts et métiers, but had dropped out and was staying with his sister Rita, who lived with her boyfriend in Longueuil. Lortie joined them at the Armstrong Street house and, later that Friday, they all went into

Montreal to buy wigs, false moustaches and balaclavas with which to disguise themselves. They also acquired two M1 semi-automatic rifles at one of the pawn shops on Notre-Dame Street, and the owner of one of those stores later told a journalist that buying a gun there was as easy as purchasing a pair of shoes.

On Saturday afternoon, Simard and Jacques Rose drove to and from 725 Robitaille to check the Laporte home and the routes they had planned. Otherwise, they spent a long, tense day waiting for Jérôme Choquette's press conference and his response to the demands of the Liberation Cell. "We didn't need to discuss the kidnapping much," Simard wrote. "But the whole time, every second there was a kind of reticence . . . a fear . . . a refusal to go through with it. You feel you're preparing for a kind of suicide action. . . . We never sat down, all four of us staring into each other's eyes, and said: If the government refuses, what do we do then. . . . You tell yourself everything's going to work out. . . . That's what you want, what you hope for, you've got to believe it. . . .

"But the other possibility won't go away. . . . You know it might not work out. We would glance at each other, we felt a kind of embarrassment. We knew, but didn't say it out loud. We weren't up to talking about it."

They didn't wait for Choquette to finish speaking. They donned disguises and left their hideout in the car that Paul Rose had purchased under a false name in the spring—a pale blue 1968 Chevrolet Biscayne with a vinyl roof. Jacques Rose drove. Lortie—armed with a sawed-off shotgun—sat in the passenger seat. Simard was in the back seat, on the left. Paul Rose was on the right. Both carried M1 semi-automatic rifles. They had the address of the Laporte residence and the phone number written on a piece of scrap paper. They stopped once. "Jacques called the Laportes from a phone booth at a restaurant situated opposite the Tropicana in Longueuil," Paul Rose told police in the statement he provided on the night of his arrest. "A woman answered and said Pierre Laporte was about to leave. We took Tiffin Road until Logan then took a side street to Robitaille and went by the Laporte residence. Then finally someone saw Mr. Laporte playing football in a field across the street from his home. . . . When we pulled up in front of Mr. Laporte, Jacques hit the brakes so hard that the tires squealed."

THE LAPORTES

Pierre and Françoise Laporte had spent a pleasant day around their spacious and comfortable suburban home—a one-storey, executive-style bungalow with a single-car attached garage at one end and a front yard that sloped gently to the sidewalk. There was a park across the street and, beyond that, the Eulalie-Durocher convent. Their children were both away—Claire, then twenty, was attending university, and her brother Jean, who was only ten, was off with friends. Pierre Laporte had watched a hockey game early in the afternoon. Then he and his wife had dropped in for coffee and a visit with her sister Louise Laporte, who lived on a side street nearby. Afterward, the Laportes drove home and Louise Laporte and her eighteen-year-old son Claude accompanied them.

Laporte and his wife had planned to go out for dinner, and toward the end of the afternoon Françoise excused herself and went to get dressed. Her husband picked up a football and invited his nephew outside to play catch, and Louise Laporte went with them. She was the first to see the pale blue Chevrolet pull up. "I was waiting for my sister to get ready and join us," she said in the witness statement she provided to police. "I was seated in Pierre's car and the door was open and I had my feet outside the auto to watch Pierre tossing the football with Claude. All of a sudden a car came down Berkley and turned on to Robitaille and stopped abruptly. I said to myself it must be someone who wants to speak to Pierre." At that moment, Françoise Laporte stepped out the front door to announce that they could leave. Instead, she witnessed the abduction. "I was on the porch and I saw two men behind the vehicle pointing sub-machine guns at my husband's stomach," she told police. "One of them said: 'This isn't a joke. We're not fooling. Get in. Right now.' Pierre bent over and got in. I didn't wait for the car to leave. I immediately went in and called police."

Claude Laporte had the closest view, and he had the presence of mind to note the licence number but nearly everything else was a blur. "The vehicle took off quickly and immediately disappeared," he told police. "My uncle was wearing a white striped shirt with long sleeves, open at the collar, casual pants and brown shoes. I don't have a description of the kidnappers, only that they wore black masks. As the vehicle went past, I caught a glimpse of the people inside. They were young, twenty to twenty-five. . . . I'm not sure I could identify them."

The police department in Saint-Lambert instantly broadcast news of the abduction over its communications network. Some officers on patrol headed for the Laporte residence. Others set up checkpoints throughout the community, but not quickly enough to catch the kidnappers.

Meanwhile, a chaotic scene unfolded outside the Laporte family home. Journalists, photographers and cameramen arrived almost on the heels of the police. The *Gazette*'s George Radwanski was among them and later described the evening in his book *No Mandate but Terror*. "The lurid red of police cruiser flashers and the nerve-jangling yellow news mobile blinkers . . . turned the thronged street into a diabolical discotheque," he wrote. "People milled aimlessly. Many had tears streaming down their cheeks. 'Pas Pierre, c'est pas vrai,' a neighbour sobbed. Three photographers dashed over to capture her anguish [and] the flash of their cameras bounced off the well-groomed hedge and attracted a covey of darting reporters." Officers continued to arrive and had to ease their cruisers through the crowds. A slender young man in a buckskin jacket—Claude Laporte—came out of the house and was immediately surrounded by jostling reporters. Later, Pierre Laporte's mother left as well, "bent double with age and grief and supported by two younger women," and the cameras began flashing again. "Late into the night," Radwanski wrote, "the street scene remained frozen. Cars. Crowds. Flashes. Murmurs. And silences. The long silences of horror and grief."

ONE WILD WEEK
Sunday, October 11

In the first moments after the abduction, Pierre Laporte was shocked and terrified. "He had no idea where he was," Francis Simard wrote. "He hadn't seen anything. During the ride, he had been lying down, face to the floor. He didn't know where he was being taken. The guys drove the car into the garage on Armstrong Street. Nobody went outside. He was blindfolded and taken into a bedroom through the hole in the wall. Inside he was put on a bed and handcuffed." Simard, Jacques Rose and Bernard Lortie took turns guarding Laporte. Paul Rose left at 7:30 a.m. on Sunday to deliver the first of the group's communiqués. The four of them had proclaimed themselves the Chénier Financing Cell in honour of Dr. Jean-Olivier Chénier, a Patriote leader who died in the battle at Saint-Eustache during the Lower Canada Rebellion of 1837–1838. Rose took a taxi from Saint-Hubert to Montreal, arriving via the Jacques Cartier Bridge, the most easterly of the four bridges crossing the St. Lawrence. He got out at the Papineau Street Metro station and then rode six stops west to Peel Street—conveniently located close to the downtown studios of radio station CKAC.

Rose dropped the communiqué in a garbage can near the station, placed an anonymous phone call to alert the staff, and then took the Metro back to Longueuil and a taxi to the cell's hideout. He was en route when CKAC broadcast the communiqué, which read, "Faced with the stubborn refusal of the ruling authorities to comply with the demands of the FLQ, and according to plan three set beforehand to respond to such a refusal, the Chénier Financing Cell has kidnapped the minister of unemployment and assimilation of Quebec—Pierre Laporte. The minister will be executed at 10 p.m. Sunday if the ruling authorities do not respond favourably to the seven demands issued following the kidnapping of James Cross. Partial acceptance will be considered a refusal."

Rose wrote and delivered two more communiqués that day—both repeating the threat to execute Laporte. CKAC journalists retrieved the first at 1 p.m. and the second shortly before 4 p.m. The first included a letter from Laporte to his wife, assuring her that he was in good health and thinking of her and the children constantly, while the second came with a letter from Laporte to Robert Bourassa. "My dear Robert," he began, "I am writing the most important letter of my life. . . . You have the power to decide my fate. . . . We are faced with a well-organized escalation that will not end until the political prisoners are liberated. After me, it will be a third, then a fourth and a fifth [hostage]. Therefore act immediately and thus avoid a useless bloodbath and panic. Decide— my life or my death. I am counting on you and thank you for it. Regards, Pierre Laporte."

The abduction of Laporte created a dreadful crisis for the youthful premier and his largely inexperienced Cabinet. They had played a subordinate role to the federal government in the Cross kidnapping. Bourassa had even travelled to New York to meet with investors and had allowed Jérôme Choquette to speak for his government. Bourassa was in Sorel, spending the Thanksgiving weekend with his wife's family, when the news broke about Laporte. He rushed back to Montreal and took over the twentieth and top floor of the Queen Elizabeth Hotel. He installed himself in suite 2045 and some of his ministers took adjoining suites, and that floor became the new seat of government in Quebec, as one newspaper put it. Three plainclothes police officers stood guard outside the door of Bourassa's quarters. Fellow officers, also in plainclothes, patrolled the lobby and kept close watch on the reporters who tried—without success—to penetrate the security barrier that sealed the twentieth floor.

Bourassa and his Cabinet met all afternoon and into Sunday evening at the Hydro-Québec headquarters, where the premier kept his Montreal office, but their deliberations yielded divisions rather than consensus, according to William Tetley, the minister of municipal affairs. Tetley kept a diary and later published extracts in his book *The October Crisis: An Insider's View.* "I am for negotiating and so are most of the others, so is Bourassa," Tetley wrote in his diary. "I pronounce a long speech in

English (the first time ever to the Cabinet) to say 'We have a life at stake.' Choquette says he will quit the Cabinet if we give in. He is in a minority. We are all angry with the federal government and Trudeau for taking a high-minded position. They do not know the personal feelings toward Laporte. Nor do they have the decision to make.

"Both Bourassa and Choquette cool us with ice water. We pay for our own chicken charlie at night, $2.00 each. . . . We are still meeting at Hydro."

Bourassa intended to make a province-wide televised address ahead of the 10 p.m. deadline, and he and a few trusted advisers worked on the text. They went over it word by word and Bourassa reviewed it with Trudeau. Bourassa spoke a few minutes before ten—not on television, but into a radio microphone in a studio hastily arranged in his suite. His voice was calm but firm. He finished in four minutes and then waited for a response from those holding Cross and Laporte.

Monday, October 12

The kidnappers had listened closely in their respective hideouts, and what they heard gave them hope. Bourassa had said, "We wish to save the lives of Mr. Laporte and Mr. Cross." And ". . . we desire, before discussing the demands that have been made, to establish mechanisms to ensure . . . that the liberation of the political prisoners would result in the safety of the two hostages." And to eliminate any uncertainty, he added, "We ask the kidnappers to enter into communication with us."

The two cells responded separately. Lanctôt's Liberation Cell issued their communiqué first and CKLM went to air with it at 2 a.m. on Monday. The communiqué from Rose's Chénier Cell reached CKAC around 10 a.m. Both included letters from the hostages to Bourassa, and it was clear that he had lifted their spirits. "Tell my wife I should be seeing her very soon," Cross wrote. "Thank you for saving my life and that of Mr. Laporte." As for Laporte, he was jubilant: "I have just heard your speech. Thank you. I expected nothing less of you." And he concluded by writing, "Thank you again . . . thank you to all who have contributed to this reasonable decision. . . . I hope to be free and back at work in 24 hours."

Both cells authorized the lawyer Robert Lemieux to represent them, and the Chénier Cell gave him an open-ended mandate. "We have complete confidence in the revolutionary integrity of Robert Lemieux," Paul Rose and his accomplices wrote. "Each of his decisions will be irrevocable. He is us, we are him."

Lemieux was twenty-nine and a maverick in a conservative profession. He rode a motorcycle and had a moustache and long, curly hair that cascaded over his shirt collar and touched his shoulders. He had learned English from his mother—an anglophone—studied law at McGill and spoke the language so fluently by the time he graduated that many assumed he was an anglophone. Several prestigious law firms recruited him and he chose one led by seven English-Canadian partners. He didn't last long. In 1966, the firm accepted a legal aid case involving FLQ terrorists and handed it to Lemieux. He became preoccupied with it and neglected everything else. The partners were not pleased and dismissed him after a member of the firm observed him drafting a speech that one of the defendants would deliver in court.

Lemieux took one FLQ case after another, and his disregard for the decorum of the courtroom led to multiple reprimands from the Quebec Bar Association. He worked obsessively on the cases, and neglected his wife and their two preschool children until she said "enough" and left him. He was paid poorly, or not at all, and took a third-floor room in the century-old Hôtel Nelson on Place Jacques-Cartier in Old Montreal, a block away from the criminal courts and two blocks from police headquarters. He paid the hotel $16.20 a week, which included use of a house phone and beer in the tavern, which sometimes doubled as his office. During the first week of the kidnapping crisis, Lemieux raced around on his motorcycle visiting convicted and imprisoned terrorists to determine who would accept exile to a foreign country. And he held daily, well-attended press conferences in the dining room of the Hôtel Nelson.

The press briefings landed him in jail. He accused the police of arresting suspects on phony warrants and arbitrarily suspending civil liberties. He said government authorities were acting in bad faith. He charged at one point that "Both levels of government want to settle this problem with an armed confrontation with the kidnappers." He concluded a radio interview with encouraging words for the kidnappers: "Hang in there, boys." By then, Choquette had heard enough and had him arrested for obstruction of justice.

Bourassa turned to an old friend—his personal lawyer, Robert Demers—to represent the government. Demers was also a McGill law graduate and only four years older than Lemieux, but he had followed a much different path professionally—working for the Montreal Stock Exchange, the provincial department of education and then as a corporate lawyer with the prominent French-Canadian firm Desjardins Ducharme. Demers was also treasurer of the Quebec Liberal Party and a member of its executive committee. He had never represented anyone in a criminal case, nor had he ever set foot in a jail until that Monday evening when he met Lemieux in a dimly lit, stale-smelling holding cell at Montreal police headquarters.

Tuesday, October 13

The kidnapping of Pierre Laporte led to the biggest manhunt—up to that time—in Quebec history. Over 3,500 officers from the Montreal and provincial police forces searched private residences, conducted roadside spot checks and sorted through hundreds of tips provided by the public. Plainclothes officers watched the downtown Metro stations closest to radio stations CKLM and CKAC as well as Longueuil station on the South Shore, and those posted at Longueuil caught sight of Paul Rose three times on the same day—and they let him slip away.

The first sighting occurred at around 10 a.m. Rose boarded a Montreal-bound train, and two officers followed him—hoping he would lead them to Laporte. But when he got off at Berri station, several stops east of downtown, they lost him. The officers returned to their Longueuil post, reasoning that Rose would return and, sure enough, they spotted him getting off the train at around noon. But he saw them—two shady-looking characters, as he later told an interrogator. He walked to one of the bus stops at the station. They followed him. He chose another and they moved with him and he knew they were cops. He boarded the bus, not knowing where it was going, and they boarded too. He got off. They got off and, as he told the interrogator, "There were the three of us standing on a street corner—me and two cops. I said to myself, if they want to arrest me, they're going to arrest me."

Again, they let the opportunity pass and he hailed a taxi and told the driver to take him to 1191 Saint-Alexandre Street in Longueuil, the home of his friend Roger Venne. Rose noted that he had been followed by two men in a Volkswagen. He asked Venne's thirteen-year-old son to take a ride on his bicycle to see if the vehicle was parked nearby, and the youth returned to say that it was just down the street. Rose spent the afternoon at the Venne residence. He had dinner with the family and helped with the dishes afterward. Then he asked Roger Venne for a ride into the city. Before leaving, Rose disguised himself as an old man. He took a brick and bashed it against the arches of his eyebrows until both swelled up, and he put a few strands of cotton batten on his chin to give his own thin, wispy beard a salt-and-pepper look. He then threw an old coat over his shoulders and walked slowly and deliberately and slightly stooped to the Venne family car.

Venne drove, with his wife seated next to him, Rose in the passenger seat and the couple's son and daughter in the back. He pulled out of the driveway and onto the street, and one of the officers who had been observing the house stopped him. Venne rolled down the window and the officer leaned over and peered in. He looked at the three adults in the front seat, but did not recognize Rose or ask for identification, and waved them on. The Vennes dropped Rose in an alleyway in the east end, near the foot of the Jacques Cartier Bridge, and he made his way to the residence of another friend, Louise Verrault, who lived several miles north on St-Denis Street. She had agreed before the Cross kidnapping to act as an intermediary between the two cells and, as it happened, Rose and Jacques Cossette-Trudel were able to meet that evening.

It was the first contact between the two groups since late August, and they agreed that Cross was not responsible for the plight of the Quebec people and should not be executed. However, Laporte had been a member of the Lesage and Bourassa governments and must share the blame. Therefore, the Chénier Cell would determine Laporte's fate and that depended on whether or not the authorities were willing to negotiate.

The negotiations had begun at about 3 p.m. that day at the head office of Hydro-Québec—Lemieux having been released on bail—and they did not go well. Demers insisted that he and Lemieux had to establish a mechanism to ensure the safe release of the hostages before they could consider the demands of the kidnappers. Lemieux responded with a two-hour monologue on the origins and objectives of the FLQ, and Demers concluded that "I had before me a person who was in complete agreement with the aims and means used by the FLQ and that he was probably a member himself."

Before parting, both attorneys agreed that they would not speak to the media, but Lemieux promptly reneged. He held a press conference in the small, cramped ballroom at the Hôtel Nelson and it was a memorable spectacle. Lemieux sat at a table, flanked by Pierre Vallières, Charles Gagnon and the labour leader Michel Chartrand. "Newsmen sat along three sides of a rectangular arrangement of tables, with a welter of TV cameras within the rectangle," the *Gazette* reporters Radwanski and Windeyer wrote. "The fourth side was reserved for Lemieux and his supporting cast, grinning triumphantly in the spotlight. Unlike a normal press conference, the hall was thronged with non-journalists. All of them were supporters of Lemieux and the FLQ, most of them young, a few aging and gnarled. They cheered every statement, they hooted down hostile questions from reporters, they snarled 'en français' whenever some ventured to speak English." Years later, Demers still recalled the scene. "I was shocked," he said in an interview. "The television news comes on and the first item is a press conference by Lemieux. The worst part of it was he systematically described our discussions without any relationship to the truth."

Wednesday, October 14

Lemieux had told the media that he was withdrawing from the negotiations, but he agreed to meet Demers again after the Chénier and Liberation Cells issued Communiqué No. 9. It was dated October 14 and reached CKLM at 5 a.m. The kidnappers had renewed Lemieux's mandate, and later that morning he and Demers resumed their talks at the Hydro-Québec headquarters. The first matter on the agenda was Lemieux's press conference. The conversation, as Demers remembered it, went like this:

—What's this, Robert? We agreed there would be no press conference.
—Well, I changed my mind after I saw you.
—Robert, if you hold any more press conferences you're destroying any chance of reaching an agreement.
—That's okay. I'm not going to give any more press conferences.
—Okay, let's discuss the measures to protect the lives of the hostages.
—That's your problem. I want the political prisoners released and put on a plane and sent to either Cuba or Algeria.
—Have you got an agreement with Cuba or Algeria to take these prisoners?
—You have a Department of Foreign Affairs. I don't. It's your business to discuss this with Cuba or Algeria.

—Well, okay, now I know what is your responsibility and
what's mine. Maybe we can have a third party intervene—
the Red Cross or a representative of Algeria or Cuba. Your
terrorists are going to deliver Cross and Laporte in good
health at a place we will determine and there will be an
exchange. But I'll have to negotiate this with the Cubans or
Algerians.

—This is going to take too long. We have to do something
faster. The exchange can take place at a police station.

—C'mon, Robert. Your proposal makes no sense. I don't think
your people are going to agree to deliver themselves or the
hostages to the police.

Demers said he would contact the Department of Foreign Affairs
since the department would have to ask the Cubans and Algerians if
they were willing to accept the prisoners. That ended the negotiating
session, but as they were leaving Demers again insisted: no press
conferences.

"He wasn't out of the meeting an hour and he was giving a press
conference," Demers recalled. "I called him back and said: How can
you explain your press conference and how you're able to completely
distort the discussions we've had?

"He said: I have people advising me and they said I should do that
so I did it."

Demers decided to press on. He said they would have to meet in
Quebec City if they were to continue their discussions. Bourassa had
convened a special session of the National Assembly to deal with a
strike by medical specialists, and Demers wanted ready access to the
premier if necessary. Lemieux said he was prepared to go to Quebec
City. Demers flew to the capital aboard a government aircraft, but
Lemieux failed to show up.

Instead, he appeared before a gathering of social science students at
UQAM with Vallières and Gagnon. They read the FLQ manifesto and
encouraged the students to organize street demonstrations to support

the terrorists. Later that day, Lemieux and Gagnon addressed an assembly of students at the Université de Montréal—this time at the invitation of the faculty union. Both urged the crowd of four hundred to take to the streets, and they told the young men and women that they could unleash a parallel power—that of the people of Quebec. One young man stepped up to a microphone and proposed an immediate occupation of the hall they were in, but Gagnon encouraged him to wait until the next day. Bigger things were being planned. Upon learning of all this, Demers advised the premier that there was no possibility of reaching an agreement with Lemieux. "Bourassa was just as fed up as I was," says Demers. "He said, 'Prepare a statement saying we are willing to recommend the release of the prisoners who are eligible for parole. I'm not going to go further than that.'"

The prospects of bringing the two hostages home safely were set back even further by the actions of Claude Ryan, René Lévesque and several prominent labour leaders and academics who came to be known as the "sixteen eminent personalities." On the evening of Wednesday, October 14, Ryan, Lévesque and six other members of the group held a press conference at the Holiday Inn on Sherbrooke Street West and released a petition calling on the provincial and federal governments to exchange prisoners for hostages. Lévesque read the petition, and Ryan published it in the next morning's edition of *Le Devoir*, along with the names of 150 signatories.

Claude Castonguay, the social affairs minister in the Bourassa government, wrote many years later that "Far from worrying us, the gesture of the group of fifteen [sic] appeared to us not being something deserving lengthy consideration." But fellow cabinet minister William Tetley, in his account of the October Crisis, noted that the petition "provided the principal intellectual support that the FLQ received."

— — —

Thursday, October 15

For the first time since they had seized their hostages, the kidnappers did not issue any communiqués. They remained confined to their hide-outs—the sole exception being Paul Rose, who was fearful of returning to 5630 Armstrong after his close calls with the police and was now staying with friends in Montreal. But events beyond the *felquistes'* control were unfolding around them. Supporters and sympathizers were mobilizing for action while the authorities were preparing a decisive strike against the kidnappers and their fellow travellers.

Student leaders at Montreal's French-language colleges and universities were organizing strikes and other measures to support the FLQ, and civic authorities had every reason to be apprehensive—given all the disturbances and riots of recent years. Furthermore, Lemieux, Gagnon, Vallières and Chartrand made the rounds of the post-secondary institutions to stir things up. Vallières addressed more than a thousand students in a lecture hall at the Université de Montréal's social sciences building and captivated the crowd. "Vallières is magnificent," the political scientist Jean-Marc Piotte wrote afterward in his daily journal. "His intelligence, combined with his great passion, make him an extraordinary political leader." The celebrated *felquiste* spoke with the same unhinged intensity as he wrote, and after hearing him, the assembled students adopted a five-part resolution—with hardly a dissenting voice in the expansive lecture hall. They endorsed the FLQ manifesto and its objectives. They urged the government to meet the demands of the kidnappers. They encouraged the people of Montreal to resist police repression and the erosion of civil rights. And, they resolved to strike until the kidnappers' demands were met.

Elsewhere on the Université de Montréal campus, students of political science, theology, psychology and architecture met to discuss the crisis and express their solidarity with the FLQ. According to newspaper reports, similar assemblies were held at the École des beaux-arts, the Collège du Vieux Montréal and the École secondaire Saint-Stanislas.

Meanwhile, their peers at UQAM acted with unnerving haste and militancy. Some eight hundred students attended a noon-hour assembly at Gésu Hall and any prospect of a normal school day quickly vanished. Carole de Vault, who witnessed the event and would later become directly involved in the kidnapping crisis as a police informer, subsequently wrote that "The hall was full of smoke and students. About ten were seated on the stage. The atmosphere was solemn and there was a sense in the air that this was a momentous occasion. The organizers spoke first and asked us to support the FLQ. I don't recall a single voice urging an opposing viewpoint. After the opening speeches, the audience expressed itself. . . . Each speaker was applauded. *Bravo! Bravo! Vive le FLQ!"*

Most of the students refused to return to their classes. Some occupied the office of the rector, Léo Dorais. Others took to the street. The director of auxiliary services, André Boulet, later reported seeing students going from office to office urging faculty and staff to leave. He checked on a group occupying the Louis Joliet building and found them photocopying a document entitled *Opération débrayage* (Operation Walkout), which advocated boycotting classes, refusing to speak English and distributing the FLQ manifesto in the neighbourhoods surrounding the downtown campus. By the end of the afternoon, rector Dorais had decided to close the university.

Montreal was a city on edge and Robert Lemieux ratcheted up the tension when he strode into the Hôtel Nelson's dining room early that evening for another of his press conferences. Several radio stations carried it live, and people in every neighbourhood and suburb stopped to listen. "Dear patriots," Lemieux began, addressing the kidnappers directly. He informed them that the negotiations were stalled and there was little hope that they would resume. He warned them to prepare for an armed assault by police. "I have very, very serious information," he said gravely, "that police have found the Chénier cell and are only waiting to find the Liberation Cell, which holds James Cross, before attacking with force to free the two men. I received this information last night from a very serious businessman who had heard it from a minister of the Quebec government. While I am not absolutely certain whether the information is well founded, I take it very, very, very seriously. I demand an answer from the government as to whether this information is well-founded."

The government ignored Lemieux's demand, but issued a press release at 9 p.m. stating its final position. It would offer the kidnappers safe passage to a foreign country in exchange for the release of the hostages, and it would recommend early release for five parole-eligible terrorists. Lemieux was enraged. He held another press conference and it was not a pretty sight. He appeared before the assembled media, as Radwanski and Windeyer later wrote, his lips "taut with anger, one hand clutching a sheaf of papers, the other a fist clenched at his side. He slammed the papers down on the table and viciously tore open the buttons of his double-breasted blue blazer."

He rhymed off the names of the sixteen "eminent personalities" who had signed the petition urging the government to negotiate. They were, he declared, the voices of the people of Quebec and the authorities were ignoring them. "I urge the government to meet, not in the next few hours, but in minutes, and reconsider. Reconsider this . . . this incredible mockery. My mandate has ended. I have nothing more to say." A reporter asked if he was walking out on the negotiations. "Walking out, man?" he asked, with a mix of sarcasm and rage. "I've been thrown out on my ass." Lemieux stormed out, and then left for the Paul Sauvé Centre and a large, boisterous pro-FLQ rally. A crowd, variously estimated at 1,500, 3,000 and even 5,000, most of them students, had taken over the building even though it was already in use. The Front d'action politique (FRAP)—an amalgam of union leaders, citizens' committees and *péquistes* formed to run a slate of candidates against the Drapeau team in the municipal elections of October 25—had rented the centre and was holding an auction to raise funds for its campaign.

FRAP and its supporters graciously halted their event and turned over the stage to Lemieux, Vallières, Gagnon, Chartrand and several others who proceeded to whip the youthful audience into a feverish uproar. The actor Michel Garneau read the FLQ manifesto. He recited a litany of injustices endured by French Canadians over three centuries. Throughout his oration, those gathered before him repeatedly raised clenched fists and chanted, *"FLQ! FLQ! FLQ!"* The chants continued when Vallières told his audience, "The governments claim the FLQ is a small band of criminals. But you are the FLQ, you and all the other popular groups fighting for the liberation of Quebec." He urged the crowd "to organize the fight for liberation in each district, in each plant, in each office, everywhere." The rally ended at 11:30 p.m. and many of the young men and women went home fired up and ready to act.

WAR MEASURES

The Bourassa government had made two decisive moves that day— Thursday, October 15—aimed at maintaining public order and regaining control of a rapidly escalating crisis. First, they requested the assistance of the Canadian Army. Then they called upon the federal government to grant the police emergency powers by proclaiming the War Measures Act. The MPD had urged the premier as early as Sunday, October 11, to call in the army. The following day, senior officers with the MPD, the SQ and the army met at SQ headquarters on Parthenais Street in east-end Montreal. They drew up a list of buildings and individuals to be protected and figured out how many units would be required. Their plans were essentially complete when they adjourned. All they needed was approval from above.

They received it around 2 p.m. on Thursday, after Bourassa called Ottawa and officially requested military assistance under the National Defence Act. Troops began moving immediately. A small contingent of soldiers from the Royal 22nd Regiment, based in Valcartier, twenty-five kilometres north of the provincial capital, took up positions around the National Assembly. A company from the regiment flew in aboard a Hercules C-130 aircraft and landed at the Canadian Forces base at Saint-Hubert—no more than a kilometre or two from the shabby bungalow at 5630 Armstrong where Laporte was being held. A two-hundred-truck convoy carrying officers and men sped west toward Montreal on Highway 20, the Trans-Canada Highway, and, at the same time, a unit of the Canadian Airborne Regiment was en route from Edmonton.

Bourassa announced this dramatic development in the National Assembly, and the leaders of the Union Nationale, Ralliement créditiste du Québec and the Parti Québécois—including the PQ's parliamentary leader, Camille Laurin—supported the government. "Mr. President," Laurin said, referring to the Speaker, "the call that came from the premier was perfectly comprehensible and justified in the circumstances. I take this occasion to tell him that the members of my group deplore the unhappy fate which befell one of our colleagues [Pierre Laporte] and the blow which it strikes at the institutions of Quebec."

Upon hearing this, grassroots members of the PQ were livid, and so was party leader René Lévesque. He ordered Laurin to reverse himself, and the chastened deputy told reporters he had actually spoken approvingly of Bourassa's handling of the doctors' strike. That was far from the end of Laurin's troubles. The next day's edition of *Le Devoir* reported that "On listening to various radio stations it is clear that militant *Péquistes* have rapidly made known their displeasure with the first declaration made by their representative in the National Assembly. Presidents of approximately twenty PQ associations in the Montreal area have, at once, begun circulating a petition requesting a meeting with the National Council for Sunday in order to force the parliamentary leader to explain himself."

Péquiste opposition to the presence of troops on the streets of Montreal never wavered throughout the crisis, nor did attitudes change with the passage of time. Ever since then, in fact, sovereigntist writers and commentators have consistently referred to the army's presence as "the occupation of Quebec," as if Canadian soldiers based in the province, and many of them Quebeckers, were foreigners come to seize territory and bully the populace.

The soldiers were armed with sub-machine guns, automatic rifles and pistols. They wore helmets and full battle dress, but they were courteous with the public and generally well received. They served as an extension of the municipal and provincial police forces and received their orders from Maurice Saint-Pierre, director-general of the SQ. Their job was to guard public buildings as well as the homes of prominent federal and provincial politicians and the police were grateful for their presence.

Ten percent of the MPD—close to four hundred officers—had been pulled from regular duties to stand guard for hours on end at strategic locations. Dozens of others were consumed by the frantic search for James Cross. Some officers had been getting by on five-hour sleep breaks, according to the *Montreal Star*, and others were sleeping at various detachments throughout the city. On top of all this, the exhausted, stretched-thin police force faced the prospect of thousands of students demonstrating in the streets. Both English- and French-language newspapers supported the arrival of the troops. "The Quebec government, remembering the experiences of the last few years, considered that it had to call upon the assistance of the armed forces," Claude Ryan wrote in *Le Devoir*. "It was right to do so. They would have failed in their duty to do otherwise."

The proclamation of the War Measures Act, on the other hand, was one of the most contentious decisions ever taken by a Canadian government. The police had begun pressing their political masters for emergency powers immediately after the kidnapping of Pierre Laporte. On Sunday morning, October 11, Julien Chouinard, secretary to the Quebec Cabinet, called his federal counterpart, Gordon Robertson, at home to explain the difficulties the police were having. They had made no progress in locating Cross or his kidnappers. They had detained numerous individuals suspected of belonging to or supporting the FLQ, but the suspects had to be released after being questioned.

In his account of the conversation with Chouinard, which appears in his autobiography *Memoirs of a Very Civil Servant*, Robertson wrote, "It was impossible to hold suspicious people long enough for any effective probing of [their] stories and once released they 'disappeared.' The police did not have the resources to keep track of them. There had to be a legal way to hold suspicious individuals longer—and the only way they could find was by having the War Measures Act invoked. I told Chouinard that I thought there was no chance whatever of that being done unless the premier, Robert Bourassa, could personally convince the prime minister of the utter necessity of so unprecedented an action."

The War Measures Act was a legislative relic of World War I. It was drafted in August 1914, passed after minimal debate, and gave the federal government an astonishing array of powers. In *Rumours of War*, their 1971 account of the kidnapping crisis, journalist Ron Haggart and lawyer Aubrey Golden noted that the powers listed in the act included "censorship, arrest, detention, exclusion and deportation, control of harbours, ports and territorial waters, movement of vessels, all transportation, trading, exports, imports, production and manufacture." And that wasn't the end of the list.

The law was modelled on Britain's Defence of the Realm Act. The British government repealed its draconian wartime legislation after the armistice of November 1918, but the Canadian government left the War Measures Act on the books and Mackenzie King invoked it in September 1939 at the start of World War II. The powers granted to the government expired with the defeat of Nazi Germany in May 1945. Again, however, the act was left among the statutes of Canada rather than being repealed and replaced by legislation designed specifically for peacetime emergencies. The act could be invoked by the federal Cabinet only in a "state of war, real or apprehended, or of insurrection, real or apprehended" and Cabinet could draft regulations appropriate to the moment. In October 1970, the police wanted regulations giving them the authority to conduct searches without obtaining warrants, to arrest suspects without laying charges and to detain these individuals without bringing them before a judge within the normal twenty-four hours.

Bourassa raised the possibility of invoking the act in a conversation with Trudeau on Sunday, October 11. Further discussions and negotiations took place at both the political and official levels the next day. As well, the Quebec Cabinet instructed the police to begin drawing up plans for using emergency powers. Senior intelligence officers with the SQ and the RCMP met on Tuesday afternoon and reviewed the files of known or suspected members of the FLQ. They also began compiling a list of the individuals who would be arrested.

A final planning session was held on the evening of Wednesday, October 14, and this time intelligence officers from the Montreal department participated. Representatives of the three forces reviewed the list of suspects and classified them according to the following categories: individuals suspected of belonging to the FLQ; individuals associated with suspected *felquistes* and likely to provide transportation, shelter, money or other forms of assistance; and individuals connected to extreme left-wing movements who were likely to promote violence or incite disturbances.

"Trudeau was not keen at all about using the act," Marc Lalonde, the prime minister's special secretary at the time, recalled in an interview. "We were under pressure from the City of Montreal and the Quebec government. Drapeau was phoning Trudeau regularly, but Trudeau said 'No' for days." The critical issue was whether Quebec was on the brink of insurrection—real or apprehended. Gérard Pelletier, the secretary of state and a fellow Montrealer, provided a candid account of the thinking within the government in his 1971 book *The October Crisis*. "No one, I think, ever assumed that there was a revolutionary army poised to overthrow the Quebec government by force," Pelletier wrote. "Nevertheless, during the phase of weighing the risks that preceded the decisions of the government, one could not simply discount the possibility that the FLQ was indeed as powerful and well organized as it claimed."

The various iterations of this clandestine terrorist movement had been responsible for more than two hundred criminal acts—bombings, bank robberies, armoury heists and even murders—dating back to the spring of 1963. The movement's propagandists claimed that its militants were following a three-phase strategy of escalating revolutionary violence—bombings in the first phase, kidnappings in the second and, finally, selective assassinations of leading political figures, including the prime minister of Canada and the premier of Quebec. Only a tiny, radical core of extremists would resort to such lawlessness. "The preponderant element," Pelletier wrote, "was the presence in Quebec of a great number of conscious or unconscious FLQ sympathizers. . . . One of my sharpest fears during this part of the crisis was that a group of students, believing their great day had come, would go out into the streets and create disturbances which, with the police and army exhausted, might have ended in a shooting. . . . As to the seriousness of the threat that hung over Montreal between the 12th and 15th of October, 1970, one would have had to blind oneself deliberately not to perceive it."

Apart from all that, Pelletier argued that the rise of an underground terrorist movement represented a fundamental challenge to the established order that no government—democratic, dictatorial or otherwise—could ignore. "Every organized community is subject to a form of power," he wrote. "This power can be imposed from without by force, constraint or persuasion, or it can be the choice of a more or less significant portion of the individuals who make up the community. When certain groups go beyond the rules defined by the laws or constitution to challenge this power, *established power will defend itself.* That having been said, the forms of defence available to the authorities are not numerous." In this case, the War Measures Act was the only law on the books, but the prime minister had no intention of invoking it unilaterally. As Lalonde tells it, "Trudeau said, 'I'm not going to do anything unless the two levels of government request me to do it. Then I'll go to Cabinet with it.' He sent me to Montreal and Quebec City to get letters from Bourassa and Drapeau and he didn't want any ifs, ands or buts in them.

He said, 'When the soup gets hot, I don't want them saying, 'That's not exactly what we meant.' We didn't want anyone changing positions."

On Thursday, October 15, Lalonde flew to Quebec City and Montreal to obtain letters from Bourassa and Drapeau and both were unequivocal. "We are facing a concerted effort to intimidate and overthrow the government and democratic institutions of this province through planned and systematic illegal action, including insurrection," Bourassa wrote. Drapeau added that emergency powers had become "essential for the protection of society against the seditious plot and the apprehended insurrection in which the recent kidnappings were the first step."

Lalonde arrived back in Ottawa at around 3 a.m. and turned the letters over to Gordon Robertson. Two Cabinet orders—one to invoke the War Measures Act, the other granting the police emergency powers—were at Rideau Hall awaiting the signature of Governor General Roland Michener. "With the letters in hand," Robertson wrote in his autobiography, "I gave the clearance and at about 3:30 the governor-general signed and the act came into effect. At 4 a.m. I held a press conference in the Centre Block to explain what had happened."

YOU'RE UNDER ARREST

Shortly after 11 a.m. on Friday, October 16, Pierre Trudeau rose from his seat in the House of Commons. He tabled the letters from the premier of Quebec and the mayor of Montreal and introduced a motion asking the House to approve the proclamation of the War Measures Act. Then he spoke: "It is matter of deep regret and grave concern that the condition of our country makes necessary this proclamation," he said. "We in this House have all felt very strongly that democracy was nowhere in a healthier state than in Canada; that nowhere was there less need for frustrated men to turn to violence to attain their ends.

"Yet in recent years we have been forced to acknowledge the existence within Canada of a new and terrifying type of person, one who in earlier times would have been known as an anarchist, but who is now known as a violent revolutionary. . . . These persons allege that they are seeking social change through novel means. In fact, they are seeking the destruction of the social order through clandestine and violent means."

An armada of municipal and provincial police officers 1,200 strong had begun conducting raids and making arrests at 4 a.m. that day. They roused suspects from their sleep. They searched homes and apartments and scooped up books, pamphlets and posters—anything that seemed even slightly subversive. They seized firearms, ammunition, bayonets, knives and two-way radios, but, surprisingly, no dynamite. They had made 154 arrests by the time Trudeau spoke in Parliament. By noon, 238 people were in custody—140 in Montreal, 52 in Quebec City, 20 in Rimouski, 15 in Hull and 11 in Chicoutimi.

Robert Lemieux, Pierre Vallières, Charles Gagnon and Michel Chartrand were among the first taken into custody. Reggie Chartrand was picked up in the first wave of arrests, and so were Stanley Gray of the Opération McGill français movement, several prominent labour leaders and a number of academics and journalists, along with two municipal election candidates—Jean Roy, a printer, and Henri Bellemare, a physician—both of whom were running for FRAP. The poet and journalist Gérald Godin and his partner Pauline Julien, the singer, actress and outspoken advocate of independence, were also arrested. Julien later told the journalist Ron Haggart that she and Godin had been awakened in the third-storey bedroom of their home on Selkirk Avenue—on the southern slope of Mount Royal, not far from the Cross residence—by the sound of footsteps and male voices outside their door. Godin got up, slipped on a pair of pants and discovered three police officers in the hall.

"Why didn't you ring?" Julien asked.

"We did," one of the officers replied, "but you didn't hear us."

"You must be crazy," she snapped back. "Do you go into places and not ring the bell?"

Godin asked them for a search warrant.

"We don't need a warrant anymore, sir," an officer replied. "A special law has been voted and we can search where we want without a warrant. Listen to the radio. You'll see."

The officers spent two hours searching the home, and then one told Julien and Godin, "Come on, get your clothes on. You're coming with us." Only then did the couple realize they were being arrested.

Jean Roy received a ruder awakening. The FRAP candidate was director of a left-wing publishing co-operative located in the basement of his home in the east-end district of Saint-Louis. "The first thing I remember was being pulled out of bed," he told Haggart. "I was held up by two men and one was yelling 'Police!' They had a gun pointed at me from the end of the bed." Dr. Bellemare reported that the officers who arrested him had been polite, but then he was a prominent crusader for better public health programs for the poor and disadvantaged. "At my house they never showed their guns," he said. "Elsewhere, they broke down doors and woke people with machine guns in their ribs and all that. There still exist class distinctions, you know."

The men were herded into cramped holding cells at the Parthenais Detention Centre at SQ headquarters, and the women were held at a separate facility. The detainees, who had no access to radio, television or newspapers, were initially denied access to legal counsel and most had no idea why they had been arrested.

The police operation for that day continued until 8 p.m.—shortly before Prime Minister Trudeau made a solemn and eloquent televised address to the nation. "I am speaking to you at a moment of crisis, when violent and fanatical men are attempting to destroy the unity and freedom of Canada," he began, and then went on to remind Canadians of the demands of the kidnappers. They wanted ransom money and the release of twenty-three terrorists—seventeen of whom had been convicted of criminal offences and six who were awaiting trial. To yield to such "crude blackmail," as he put it, would only lead to further terrorism and kidnappings and ultimately the breakdown of the legal system. "If a democratic society is to continue to exist," he said, "it must be able to root out the cancer of an armed revolutionary movement that is bent on destroying the very basis of our freedom. For that reason, the government, following an analysis of the facts, including the requests from the government of Quebec and the city of Montreal for urgent action, decided to proclaim the War Measures Act."

Trudeau maintained that the terrorists hoped to provoke just such a drastic response from the state. It would be proof that they were living under an authoritarian regime and that would justify further violent attacks. This was a tried and tested trick of revolutionaries, but he warned Canadians not to be fooled. "Canada remains one of the most wholesome and humane lands on this earth," he said. "If we stand firm, this situation will soon pass. We will be able to say proudly, as we have for decades that, within Canada, there is ample room for opposition and dissent but none for intimidation and terror."

The police conducted an estimated 4,600 searches under the War Measures Act and detained nearly 500 people. Most were released within a week, and fewer than 10 percent were charged with criminal offences. The student strikes and boycotts quickly fizzled and newspapers across the country supported the government. "In a situation such as now exists in Quebec, to vacillate is worse than doing nothing," the *Winnipeg Free Press* concluded. The editors of the *Vancouver Sun*, far removed from the crisis, took a harder position than most: "At last, government has armed itself to fight fire with fire and match ruthlessness with ruthlessness."

Opinion polls, conducted later in the crisis, reflected an astonishing level of public support—89 percent among English-speaking Canadians, 86 percent among their French-speaking counterparts. Opposition Conservative and Social Credit MPs backed the government motion on the War Measures Act, and it passed by a margin of 190 to 16. Only Tommy Douglas and his tiny caucus of New Democrats dissented. "Right now there is no constitution in this country, no Bill of Rights, no provincial constitutions," Douglas said during the debate on the motion. "This government now has the power by Order in Council to do anything it wants—to intern any citizen, to deport any citizen, to arrest any person or to declare any organization subversive or illegal." Fellow New Democrat Andrew Brewin added that "the proclamation of the act jeopardizes freedom of speech and freedom of assembly for all Canadians from one end of Canada to the other."

Douglas and Brewin were lonely voices at that moment, but a curious thing happened with the passage of time. Almost everyone in Quebec and English Canada who has written about the kidnapping crisis and the War Measures Act has taken the same position. They have argued that the act led to the wholesale suspension of civil liberties, unprecedented police repression, the banning of political rallies and more. Such things have been said so often over so many years that they have become conventional wisdom. But the truth is that although the regulations accompanying the proclamation of the act were undeniably draconian, they applied only to the FLQ and any other group or association that advocated the use of force or the commission of crimes to bring about a change of government. They made such organizations and membership in them illegal. It became a criminal offence to promote the policies or principles of such groups and illegal to help individual members avoid arrest or to shelter them.

Curiously, the most sensible assessment came from a most unlikely source—Pothier Ferland, the Parti Québécois's own lawyer at the time of the kidnapping crisis. Ferland provided a legal opinion at a meeting of the PQ National Council on October 18, and it was published in the October 29 edition of the party's newsletter *Pouvoir*. "It should be well noted," Ferland wrote, "that the law itself does not target and is not aimed at other associations or political parties which do not advocate the use of violence or force, but on the contrary employ democratic methods. It is therefore evident that neither the law nor the regulations target the Parti Québécois.

"Therefore, as members of the Parti Québécois and as citizens, we have the right to attend meetings of our party, to publicly express our allegiance to the party, to express in print or speech the ideas, objectives and policies of our party . . . and to criticize the current government and the laws which they pass or promulgate, for example by demanding the withdrawal of the War Measures Act or criticizing its application."

It is, therefore, plainly obvious that if Quebeckers committed to the breakup of Canada, albeit by democratic means, retained all their democratic rights and privileges during this grave national crisis, then so did all loyal citizens.

THE ORDEAL OF PIERRE LAPORTE

The Chénier Cell held Pierre Laporte for seven days, and those seven days became an increasingly desperate ordeal for the captive and his captors. The kidnappers put Laporte in a room at the rear of the run-down bungalow at 5630 Armstrong and kept him blindfolded and bound to a bed with handcuffs and a dog chain. They looked in on him occasionally and asked him if he needed anything. Otherwise, Laporte and his abductors exchanged words only at meal time, and there wasn't much to eat or talk about. The kidnappers had acted hastily and hadn't stocked up on food, and the best they could do for lunch and dinner was canned spaghetti. At one point, Laporte asked for something else, but they didn't have anything and they didn't have any money either, so he gave them twenty dollars and they ordered barbecued chicken and club sandwiches from a takeout restaurant.

The radio and TV were on all day, and all of them—Laporte included—anxiously awaited every update on the crisis. Bourassa announced the appointment of a negotiator and the kidnappers felt relieved of a great weight. If the government was prepared to negotiate, it must be prepared to make concessions and they needed something, anything, to claim victory. Laporte was euphoric. He was sure some of their demands would be met, maybe all of them. But the negotiations went nowhere. Tuesday and Wednesday came and went and nothing happened. They knew that because they listened to Robert Lemieux's daily press conferences. The government wouldn't discuss anything except the safe release of the hostages.

Things got worse on Thursday when the Bourassa government called in the army and broke off negotiations. On Friday, they awoke to the War Measures Act and dozens of arrests. Their reckless, poorly planned kidnapping had failed completely. They had no idea what to do. They were trapped and Laporte was falling apart emotionally. "Laporte cracked," Simard wrote. "He stopped talking, he didn't react. He was lifeless, like he wasn't there. It was like all hope was gone. He was crushed."

Yet he had enough fight in him to attempt an escape. The kidnappers were watching the news in another room, and there were just three of them—Simard, Jacques Rose and Bernard Lortie—because Paul Rose hadn't returned after his brush with police three days earlier. They heard the sharp crack of glass breaking and rushed into the bedroom and found Laporte attempting to squeeze through a broken window. He had slipped free of the dog chain and handcuffs, but hadn't removed the blindfold—a scarf tied tightly and fastened with adhesive tape.

They hauled him back in. He was bleeding profusely from a deep gash to his left wrist and his thumb and a lesser injury to his chest. They applied tourniquets above his wrist and dressed the wounds as best they could with scraps of towels and bed sheets and then brought him into the living room and sat him on a chair. He pleaded with them to take him to a hospital. They refused, but tried to comfort him. "He didn't move," Simard wrote. "We took off his blindfold. He didn't even look at us. His head slumped on his chest. The tension in the house was unbearable. . . . We were on the point of bursting into tears." They considered letting him go. They thought about leaving him at the house and driving away. They couldn't think straight. They needed Paul Rose. He was their leader. He would take charge.

Lortie left for Montreal and met Rose at the apartment of Louise Verrault, where he had spent the previous two nights. Lortie pleaded with him to return, but Rose refused, fearing another encounter with the police. Lortie decided not to go back either. Verrault now had two kidnappers on her hands, but did not want either of them staying with her. She offered to take Lortie to her parents' place and he accepted, staying there for the next ten days under a false name and false pretenses. Rose contacted Colette Therrien, a friend of his younger brother, and she agreed to put him up at the apartment she shared with three others at 3720 Queen Mary Road, a three-storey walk-up near Saint Joseph's Oratory, a famous Montreal landmark, and a few blocks from the Université de Montréal.

Meanwhile, Simard and Jacques Rose were alone with Laporte. By Saturday morning, they could barely control him. And by the end of the afternoon, they had murdered him, though the precise details have remained sketchy to this day. The members of the Chénier Cell adhered to an exaggerated code of solidarity and always refused to disclose who did what.

On the night after he was arrested, Paul Rose provided a detailed account of the kidnapping, including the following account of the murder. He said he had left the apartment at 3720 Queen Mary around supper time Friday evening and returned to 5630 Armstrong, taking a taxi and public transit.

"I arrived around 7:00 or 7:30. When I got there, Jacques and Francis were with Mr. Laporte. Jacques and Francis told me what had happened and how Mr. Laporte had been injured. . . . Then we took turns guarding Mr. Laporte during the night. I watched him longer than Jacques and Francis because I wasn't as tired.

"On Saturday, October 17, we discussed the War Measures Act, Bourassa's statement the previous day, how we should execute Mr. Laporte and how we ought to dispose of the body. All three of us were present when Mr. Laporte was executed. Two of us held him down while the third tightened the chain he wore around his neck."

This was a complete fabrication. Colette Therrien and Francine Belisle, two of the four tenants who shared the apartment at 3720 Queen Mary, later testified that Rose had spent Friday and Saturday with them. Lortie was not at 5630 Armstrong either. Only Jacques Rose and Simard were there, and Simard provided the following account in his memoir: ". . . we went through a period of indecision. You don't know what to do. Actually, you do but you don't want to stare it in the face. You can't. . . . Suddenly you feel like cutting out. Opening the door and blowing the joint. . . . Escape the decision. . . . You have to decide or you'll lose your mind. . . . Kill Pierre Laporte . . . or release him. Kill him . . . release him. . . .

"I don't know how to express it. . . . We made the decision and we killed him. It wasn't an accident. . . . It all happened very fast. . . . A human life is a fragile thing. Fragile. Don't ask me how we did it. I don't know. I just don't know. I don't want to remember."

There is a third account and it comes closest to the truth. It can be found in the *Rapport sur les événements d'octobre 1970*, by Jean-François Duchaîne. Duchaîne was a lawyer in the Quebec Ministry of Justice and a member of the Parti Québécois. In May 1977, the PQ justice minister Marc-André Bédard commissioned Duchaîne to conduct an inquiry and report back to him. Duchaîne did not have the power to subpoena witnesses or hear evidence under oath, and he didn't bother to interview a number of important players, including Bourassa or anyone who had served in his government. But Duchaîne did take statements from the Cross kidnappers, who were then in exile, and Laporte's kidnappers, who were in prison.

"On the morning of October 17," Duchaîne wrote, "Pierre Laporte was so desperate that he could no longer control himself. He tried by various means, including offering his captors a lot of money, to convince them to release him. Injured and weakened by a considerable loss of blood, he was in a state of extreme agitation and they were less and less able to control him.

"At the end of the afternoon, in the midst of a particularly violent struggle, Mr. Laporte, who was wearing a thick wool sweater, which covered his neck, was grabbed from behind by one member of the Chénier cell. In attempting to quiet Mr. Laporte, whose cries threatened to attract the attention of neighbours, the one who was trying to restrain him twisted the collar of his sweater, at the same time garroting Mr. Laporte with the chain around his neck.

"When he released his grip, Mr. Laporte was dead."

Jacques Rose carried Laporte's body to the garage and placed it in the trunk of the blue Chevrolet that he had driven on the evening of the kidnapping. Rose took the wheel and drove to the end of Armstrong Street, followed by Simard in a second vehicle. He turned left onto Chemin de la Savane, which ran alongside the Canadian Armed Forces air base and a civil airport. He proceeded a short distance and then abandoned the vehicle in a parking lot outside the hangar of a small company called Won-Del Aviation Ltd.

He and Simard drove to Longueuil. They threw away the weapons used in the kidnapping, parked the car and took a bus into Montreal. They arrived at the apartment on Queen Mary Road about 7 p.m. and left it to Paul Rose to draft the communiqué announcing the death of Pierre Laporte. It was a crude note, handwritten on a scrap of paper and it read, "The arrogance of the federal government and its hireling Bourassa has forced the FLQ to act. Pierre Laporte, Minister of Unemployment and Assimilation, was executed at 6:18 this evening by the Dieppe (Royal 22nd) cell. We shall overcome. P.S. The exploiters of the Quebec people had better act properly."

INTO THE CLOSET AND OUT

Canadians from coast to coast mourned the death of Pierre Laporte, and as the country mourned, the police intensified their efforts to find his assassins and the kidnappers of James Cross. Less than twenty-four hours after Laporte was murdered, police received a tip from a neighbour that led them to the house at 5630 Armstrong. They found traces of blood, rough drafts of communiqués, names, addresses and phone numbers, and two orders of barbecued chicken as well as three club sandwiches that had hardly been touched.

By Monday, October 19, they had conducted 1,627 searches and arrested 341 people under the War Measures Act. The police were receiving 1,200 tips a day from the public, they followed up on as many as possible, conducted more raids and searches, and made additional arrests.

The police also cut off the kidnappers' access to the media. They ordered the news directors of CKLM and CKAC to surrender any future communiqués rather than broadcasting the contents. The Liberation Cell released its tenth communiqué in the early morning hours of October 18, hiding in the lobby of the Saint-Jean-Baptiste-de-la-Salle church on Pie-IX Boulevard and alerting CKLM. It contained two handwritten notes from James Cross, one to his wife and a second to the authorities assuring them that he was still alive—contrary to an erroneous news report broadcast shortly after the discovery of Laporte's body.

Meanwhile, the federal and Quebec governments each offered rewards of seventy-five thousand dollars for information leading to the arrests of the kidnappers, but weeks passed, and the investigations were still stalled.

The first break occurred following an October 26 meeting of senior representatives of the RCMP, the SQ and the MPD. The officers reviewed the names, addresses and phone numbers that had been seized in the searches. The Montreal men took all those that fell within the city, and their counterparts in the SQ took those that fell within the suburban communities surrounding the island. Among the papers littering 5630 Armstrong, officers with the SQ found the address for an apartment building at 3720 Queen Mary Road.

Two days later, MPD detectives André Bolduc and André Charette visited the complex, a once-fashionable three-storey brick apartment block built in the 1930s. The superintendent, Marcel Champagne, provided a list of tenants. There were sixteen apartments in the building and the detectives inquired about those in unit 12—Colette Therrien and Francine Belisle. Therrien was a teacher and Belisle a nurse, Champagne replied. Both were twenty-three years old and there was a young man living there as well, a student at the university, and he had seen a second, younger man coming and going.

Bolduc and Charette returned to the office and checked their files. Therrien, it turned out, had been involved in a hit-and-run accident on November 4, 1968, and she had been in the company of Jacques Rose. At the time, she was living in an apartment on Rosemont Boulevard. It took the detectives several days to confirm that the Colette Therrien in their files was the same young woman living at 3720 Queen Mary. Then Bolduc, Charette and two homicide detectives, Carlo Rossi and Laurent Guertin, returned to the complex, shortly after 7 p.m. on Friday, November 6. The detectives ascended three flights of stairs to unit 12 and Bolduc knocked loudly and insistently on the door. They heard movement inside, then a female voice urging *"patience, patience"* and then a male voice, "one minute, one minute."

There were, at the moment, eight people living in the two-bedroom apartment, including Therrien, her brother Richard, who was twenty and a law student at the Université de Montréal, and Belisle and her brother François, who was nineteen and a cabinetmaker's apprentice. The four members of the Chénier Cell were staying there as well. Paul Rose had arrived first. Simard and Jacques Rose had shown up on the evening of the murder and Lortie on November 1.

Paul Rose had written several communiqués, one of which explained how Pierre Laporte had sustained his injuries while attempting an escape. Rose relied on Colette Therrien to distribute his missives, but none were published or broadcast. He had also had Therrien deliver a note to Louise Verrault asking for money and Verrault wrote a cheque for thirty dollars.

The members of the Chénier Cell expected that the police would show up at the Queen Mary apartment sooner or later, and they were well prepared. There was a walk-in closet adjacent to the front door. It was approximately six feet deep and Simard and the Rose brothers built a false wall in it, leaving enough space behind the wall to create a hiding place. Jacques Rose designed it, and Colette Therrien and Francine Belisle purchased the materials—several planks and sheets of plywood, which cost thirty-eight dollars and which Jacques Rose covered—and they had them delivered to the home of Therrien's mother.

François Belisle cut the wood according to measurements Rose had provided, and Rose, his brother and Simard erected the false wall within forty-eight hours. The planks and rectangular plywood panels were expertly joined and the wall had a smooth, professional finish. There were two vertical rows of panels and three panels per row. Each panel was about sixteen inches wide by thirty inches high and each was decorated with bland, innocuous-looking wallpaper.

The bottom left-hand panel could be removed to allow the fugitives to crawl into the space behind the wall, and Jacques Rose had drilled a hole in the roof to ensure that they would have an ample supply of fresh air. They had also made provisions to relieve themselves, should they be required to hide for a prolonged period. They put the hiding place to the test on October 25. Friends of Colette Therrien and Francine Belisle paid a visit and Simard and the Rose brothers spent nine hours in silence in the cramped, dark space.

On the evening of November 6, the two women were alone in the apartment with the Rose brothers, Simard and Lortie. They weren't expecting visitors and were startled when there was a knock on the door. When it grew loud and insistent, they knew it was the police. Lortie and one of the women held them off while Paul and Jacques Rose and Simard slipped quietly into the hiding place. Lortie had the presence of mind not to join them. Had he done so, the police would have torn the place apart looking for the male who had told them to wait. Instead, he retreated to one of the bedrooms, ducked into the closet and hid under a heap of clothes and was quickly discovered. The officers handcuffed him and took him out. They also arrested the two women, as well as Richard Therrien, who arrived while the raid was in progress, and charged all three with harbouring the fugitives.

Before departing, the detectives padlocked the front door. The following day, identification officers arrived to dust for fingerprints and search for other incriminating evidence. They worked until 4 p.m. and then took a dinner break, at which point they left their equipment in the apartment, as well as the evidence they had collected, and secured the front door with the padlock. The officers were gone for nearly three hours, during which the fugitives crawled out of their hiding place, stood up and slowly stretched muscles stiffened by nearly twenty-four hours spent crouched and immobile. Then they put the removable panel back in place, slipped on their shoes and jackets and left by the back door.

The officers returned and found everything just as they had left it, except that the back door was unlocked. Somebody had been in the apartment while they were out. They conducted a meticulous search and discovered the false wall. Meanwhile, the Rose brothers and Simard had found another hideout with the help of a network of accommodating supporters and would remain at large for almost two months.

HOMELESS AND PREGNANT

By late October the Cross kidnappers were short of money. They had been silenced since the police started intercepting communiqués, and they had no hope of negotiating anything—other than a one-way trip into exile. Worse still, there were eight people living in the compact three-bedroom apartment at 10945 Des Récollets: Jacques Lanctôt, Jacques and Louise Cossette-Trudel, Marc Carbonneau, Yves Langlois, Nigel Hamer, *la jeune femme*—the young woman whose identity has never been revealed—and James Cross.

Cross occupied the bedroom at the rear of the apartment, adjacent to the washroom. He was allowed out only to wash in the morning and to relieve himself. He spent his days seated in an armchair. He watched TV, listened to the radio, read the newspapers or Agatha Christie mysteries in French and played solitaire. The kidnappers made him sit with his back to the door to ensure that he never saw their faces—a position he found unnatural since all the activity in the apartment took place behind him. "There were a lot of heated arguments, but I couldn't follow them" Cross told the researchers with Cambridge University's Diplomatic Oral History Programme. "They were (talking) too fast. Madame Cossette-Trudel kept on. She was a very violent bitch. She kept on shouting at the others on occasion and screaming. . . ."

Carbonneau, in particular, did not get along with the Cossette-Trudels, and they didn't like him. He was relaxed and casual when guarding Cross, and enjoyed discussing the diplomat's travels to India and elsewhere. They disapproved and insisted that everyone should remain cold and distant toward the hostage. Carbonneau found Louise Cossette-Trudel pushy and aggressive. She in turn considered him a misogynist who didn't like being challenged by a woman, and Jacques Lanctôt had to intervene and settle their disputes.

On October 22, Lanctôt's wife Suzanne showed up. She was more than a little desperate. She was pregnant. The baby was due by year's end, but she had no idea where she would be giving birth or under what circumstances. The police knew she was expecting and were looking for her, hoping she could lead them to the kidnappers. They had inquired about her at several hospitals and private clinics, but no one had any recollection of treating her. She was essentially homeless and cut off from family and friends, having been without a permanent address since April, when her husband had gone underground to avoid being arrested for conspiring to kidnap the Israeli consul Moise Golan. The Lanctôts had moved out of their apartment at 3955 St-André Street and bounced from one place to another throughout the spring and over the summer. Jacques Lanctôt had, for all intents and purposes, abandoned his wife and their eighteen-month-old son Boris to lead the Liberation Cell and the kidnapping of James Cross, and Suzanne had been relying on a network of FLQ supporters and sympathizers for food and shelter.

She had had her fill of that and wanted to remain at the group's hideout. Lanctôt objected. It was already crowded. Besides, it was dangerous. They had guns and dynamite in the apartment and none of them knew when or how the kidnapping crisis would end. This was no place for a woman who was looking after a baby and was in the late stages of a pregnancy. Suzanne left after a heated quarrel on October 25, and over the next six weeks she moved from place to place—first to Louise Verrault's apartment, then to Verrault's brother's residence in the northern suburb of Laval-des-Rapides, then to an apartment near St-Denis and Sherbrooke, and finally to another in Saint-Hubert.

POUPETTE AND THE PROFESSOR

One morning in the first week of November, a nervous young woman walked into the police station nearest her apartment on St-Joseph Boulevard and said she needed to talk to someone. She said she was a member of the FLQ's Information Viger Cell, that members of this group were planning an armed robbery to raise money for the Cross kidnappers and that she had found herself in the middle of it—albeit unwillingly. She said further that she had seen a communiqué that was about to be released and that it included a photo of James Cross. She related all this and more to Lieutenant Fernand Tanguay, who made a full report and passed it on to Lieutenant-Detective Julien Giguère, the head of the MPD anti-terror squad's intelligence section, but both officers were skeptical about the reliability of the informant.

The woman, Carole de Vault, was twenty-five and a history student at UQAM. De Vault had grown up in the village of Sainte-Anne-de-la-Pérade and had come of age during the Quiet Revolution. She had become an ardent nationalist and PQ activist and had been a volunteer during the 1970 election campaign. She had answered phones, sold party badges and distributed pamphlets for the candidate in the Montreal constituency of Ahuntsic—the distinguished economist Jacques Parizeau. De Vault discovered—as she later wrote in her memoir *The Informer: Confessions of an Ex-Terrorist*—that politics and flirtation went hand in hand. Four male volunteers made passes or asked her out, and her good looks and vivacity caught the attention of the candidate himself, then in his early forties and married. She and Parizeau became intimate. "The days we spent as lovers in Montreal, in Ottawa and in Toronto were probably part of a passing adventure for him," she wrote. "But for me, he was the first real love of my life."

De Vault became a member of the Viger Cell in mid-October, but her transition from *péquiste* to *felquiste* remains veiled in contradiction to this day. She says she was recruited by Robert Comeau, a twenty-five-year-old professor of history and Marxist theory at UQAM. In her version of events, Comeau showed up unannounced at her apartment one Saturday evening in late October—dressed smartly in a blue blazer and grey trousers and looking very professorial. They had never been formally introduced, but he said he had been referred by Noël Vallerand, another UQAM history professor and a mutual acquaintance who assured him she could be trusted.

Comeau has a very different version of these events. He contends that de Vault was working as a teaching assistant in the history department and was having an affair with Vallerand. He says that Vallerand had nothing to do with the FLQ but told de Vault that he (Comeau) was connected, and that she then began turning up at his office and pestering him to help her get involved and he finally relented.

In her memoir, de Vault says Comeau first asked her if she would be willing to hide someone in her apartment or, if necessary, store a mimeograph machine. She also relates how on another Sunday night in early November he arrived at her apartment with a copy of the communiqué that was about to be released, along with the photos of James Cross. "I was excited," she wrote. "I was holding in my hands an authentic communiqué of the FLQ. . . . Not a copy, a real one! And it had been given to me by a member of the cell that issued it."

Her enthusiasm evaporated at a subsequent meeting, when Comeau informed her that the Liberation Cell was desperately short of money and wouldn't be able to cover the next month's rent. She says he proposed an armed robbery involving her employer and planned the heist with other members of the cell. Comeau maintains that she proposed the robbery, that he thought it was a bad idea and that he refused to take part but nevertheless recommended one of his students, who agreed to participate.

In any event, there was a plot, there was a robbery and her employer was the target. De Vault was working part time in the public relations department of the Caloil Company, which operated a refinery in Montreal at the east end of the island, and she had landed the job through Parizeau, who was a consultant to Caloil. Her duties included accompanying the commissionaire on his afternoon runs to make bank deposits. He drove and always placed a large bag on the seat between them. It usually held several thousand dollars in cash and cheques, which were stowed in small canvas pouches destined for different banks. She waited in the car while the commissionaire was inside depositing the money.

According to the plan, an armed bandit would be waiting for them at the first stop. He would approach the car and she was to give him one of three signals. De Vault would light a cigarette if there was no money in the bags. She would remain motionless if she were uncertain. If there was cash, she would lower her head, in which the case the bandit would pull out a pistol, order her to open the door and grab the money. De Vault was thoroughly frightened at the prospect of being implicated in an armed robbery, and consulted Parizeau's wife Alice and Parizeau himself. Both urged her to go to the police and she heeded their advice. She revealed everything she knew about the Viger Cell to Lieutenant Tanguay—its members, its activities and the plot to rob her employer.

"[Tanguay] showed me his report," Giguère recalled many years later. "I said: What do you think? Is she a crackpot?

"He said: I can't tell. I put the report in the crackpot file."

They changed their minds a few days later. On November 7, the Viger Cell distributed the Liberation Cell's eleventh communiqué. It contained grainy images of James Cross seated on what appeared to be a case of dynamite. He was playing solitaire and there was a copy of Pierre Vallières's *Nègres blancs d'Amérique* next to the cards he had laid on a table. The kidnappers had taken the pictures with a Polaroid camera in order to prove the authenticity of the communiqué and to set it apart from all the fakes that had been issued in the preceding weeks.

Members of the Viger Cell delivered a copy of the communiqué to *Le Journal de Montréal*, but the tabloid newspaper turned it over to the police. "I looked at Tanguay's report and things matched—what she said and what happened," Giguère recalled. "I called Tanguay and said: Can I meet her?"

De Vault became informer number 945-171, though the police referred to her by the nickname "Poupette." Giguère was her handler, the officer who maintained direct contact with her, and he had an electronic listening device installed in her apartment without her knowledge. Fellow officers began shadowing her and Comeau around the clock, and through them they gradually learned the identity of the other members of the cell.

The robbery took place on November 12 at the commissionaire's first stop—a bank at the corner of Hochelaga and Bossuet streets in the east end. The big bag with the money was on the front seat as usual. The commissionaire removed one of the pouches and walked into the bank. De Vault was carrying a travel bag that held her purse and some of her school work. She scanned the street looking for the robber. "Suddenly the door opened on my left," she wrote in her memoir. "His dark brown eyes stared into mine. I saw the barrel of a gun sticking out from the trench coat draped over his arm. Not a word. His right hand pushed me back against the seat, he reached past me, grabbed my travel bag and was gone.

"For a moment I sat there stunned. It had happened. It was over. And he had taken the wrong bag. There were several thousand dollars in the bag in the middle of the seat and he had made off with my notes and a purse that contained twelve dollars."

She immediately jumped out of the car, ran into the bank and shouted to the commissionaire, "There was a hold-up. I've been robbed."

THE ROAD TO DES RÉCOLLETS

Carole de Vault went to the police nearly one month to the day after the kidnapping of James Cross, and her intervention coincided with a decisive turn in the investigation. The police had searched hundreds of homes and apartments and arrested 429 people under the War Measures Act—372 of whom had been released without being charged—but they were no closer to finding the kidnappers and their hideout.

On November 7, representatives of the three police forces held one of their periodic information-sharing sessions. They met in the third-floor offices of the MPD's anti-terror squad at Station 18 at the corner of St-Dominique Street and Shamrock Avenue. Giguère opted to keep his team focused on de Vault and Comeau, hoping that one or the other would lead them to the Cross kidnappers. He turned over a file on Suzanne Lanctôt to RCMP Detective-Sergeant Donald McLeery. "McLeery didn't have any more leads and he asked me if I had anything," Giguère recalled. "I had a few boys from the homicide squad trying to follow Jacques Lanctôt's wife, but they weren't doing so well. She was almost nine months pregnant. In my mind, I was confident she and her husband couldn't be separated too long. She was moving from place to place and we missed her four or five times. I told McLeery: you trail her. He was the guy who found out where the kidnappers were."

McLeery and his partner, Constable Rick Bennett, learned that Suzanne Lanctôt had a bank account at the Caisse populaire Sainte-Marguerite-Marie on Ontario Street. Among other things, the branch manager showed them a cheque for $450 that she had written to Louise Cossette-Trudel in early March. Cossette-Trudel had signed the back of it when she cashed it, and had written the number of an account at the Caisse populaire d'Youville on Crémazie Boulevard. The manager of that branch told the two officers that Cossette-Trudel sometimes signed cheques with her maiden name—Lanctôt—and they concluded that she was Jacques Lanctôt's sister.

McLeery and Bennett caught an unexpected break on November 17, when investigators with the SQ discovered a red Renault that had been abandoned in Longueuil. A police check on the licence plates revealed that the vehicle belonged to Jacques Cossette-Trudel and that he had been living at 3955 St-André Street in Montreal when he registered the vehicle. The two Mounties questioned the proprietor of that building and he provided three crucial pieces of information: (1) Jacques Lanctôt had leased the apartment in February. (2) Lanctôt had turned it over to Jacques and Louise Cossette-Trudel in April and the Cossette-Trudels had moved out in mid-September. (3) The proprietor also remembered a fragment of the inscription on the side of the moving van: "rue Letourneau."

McLeery checked for moving companies on that street and found la compagnie Arthur Lavoie, transport générale, at 2424 Letourneau, and the owner, Lavoie, produced a receipt signed by the Cossette-Trudels. They had moved their furniture and other belongings to 1485 Laurier Avenue East, a third-storey apartment located above a store on a commercial strip in the Plateau-Mont-Royal district. McLeery and Bennett put that address under close surveillance starting November 19. They installed an electronic listening device inside the residence, watched it from outside and followed the occupants, Denise Quesnel, who was thirty-eight, her nineteen-year-old daughter, Hélène, a student, and Robert Dupuis, who was twenty-four and a clerk in an accounting firm.

On November 25, mother and daughter inadvertently led the two RCMP detectives to Jacques and Louise Cossette-Trudel. The Quesnels left their apartment about 8 p.m., caught a northbound bus on Pie-IX Boulevard and rode it some eight kilometres to Montreal North. Quesnel and her daughter met the Cossette-Trudels at a restaurant called La Douce Marie. The four of them stayed about two hours—the detectives watching all the while. McLeery and Bennett saw them get up, say their goodbyes and go their separate ways, and they followed the Cossette-Trudels to Des Récollets but lost them near the intersection of Martial Street—a serious though short-lived setback. Detectives with the MPD's anti-terror squad had also followed a suspect to that intersection before losing him.

Claude Marcotte was a detective with the anti-terror squad and had been tracking suspects. He took part in the next phase of the investigation. Years later, he recalled laying a map of Montreal North on a table and placing the point of a compass at the corner of Des Récollets and Martial and then drawing a circle that would take in all the homes within a 1.5-kilometre radius of that intersection. Then the two Mounties and their Montreal counterparts checked street directories, which listed principal occupants at each address and their occupations. They next looked for matches in phone books and the voters list from the April 1970 election. In most cases, the names of the occupants lined up in at least two and sometimes all three sources.

There were no such matches at 10945 Des Récollets, and that residence was a few doors down from Martial Street. The detectives questioned several neighbours and learned that the apartment had been vacant most of the summer and there had been a "For Sale" sign out front. The sign had come down in mid-September and a number of young people had moved in. Neighbours who lived across the street said they had seen a woman in the late stages of a pregnancy entering and leaving, and she fit the description of Suzanne Lanctôt. Those who lived behind 10945 Des Récollets had noticed that the heavy curtains covering the bedroom window at the rear of the apartment were always drawn.

The police put the place under surveillance, setting up an observation post in the house directly across the street and a second one in the unit above 10945 Des Récollets. A civic worker and his family who lived in the Des Récollets walk-up agreed to leave temporarily and an RCMP family moved in. Officers witnessed the Cossette-Trudels leaving and returning. They also took photos of the couple meeting with Nigel Hamer, Denise Quesnel and Robert Dupuis, the young man living in Quesnel's apartment.

By December 1, the officers conducting the surveillance had convinced their superiors that Cross was being held at 10945 Des Récollets and they received orders to arrest anyone leaving the apartment. Shortly after noon the following day, detectives posted in the house across the street watched Jacques and Louise Cossette-Trudel leave and walk north toward Henri-Bourassa Boulevard. Other officers followed them to the Henri-Bourassa Metro station and nabbed the couple.

LIBERATING JAMES CROSS

The police interrogated husband and wife and managed to extract a confession. The couple admitted kidnapping the British diplomat, but not much else. They did not reveal how many accomplices remained in the apartment or how well armed they were or how much dynamite they had. Late that afternoon, Maurice Saint-Pierre, director-general of the SQ, chaired a meeting of senior officers with his own force, the RCMP and the MPD to devise a plan for freeing James Cross without bloodshed or additional casualties. The group ruled out the use of force and opted instead to convince the kidnappers to surrender and negotiate safe passage to Cuba. They moved quickly but judiciously, to avoid provoking panic.

First, they erected barricades and closed off the street. Then, in the space of two hours—between 11 p.m. Wednesday, December 2, and 1 a.m. Thursday, December 3—they evacuated the dwellings adjacent to 10945 Des Récollets. At 2 a.m., they called on Hydro-Québec to cut the power to the kidnappers' unit, though the crew chief was reluctant to do so and told an officer posted near the barricades, "It makes no sense. Usually we reconnect houses in the winter, not disconnect them." The police next summoned a public works crew to turn off the water. The crew arrived in a truck with a flashing yellow dome light, and the officers observing 10945 Des Récollets noticed that one of the kidnappers pulled a curtain back to see what was happening on the street.

Half an hour later, at 2:45 a.m., someone opened the front door just wide enough to hurl a piece of pipe onto the street. It was about a foot long and an inch in diameter and contained a final communiqué. The kidnappers said they were ready to negotiate the release of their hostage and would accept safe passage to Cuba, but warned that James Cross would be the first to die if the police used guns, gas or explosives to flush them out. They also demanded that Bernard Mergler handle the negotiations for them.

Mergler was about sixty, Jewish and spoke English and was a long-time communist who had occasionally defended fellow communists as well as union members, and he had advised the *felquiste* intellectuals Charles Gagnon and Pierre Vallières. But Mergler initially refused to represent the kidnappers and said so when he met the government negotiator Robert Demers at a police station in Montreal North at around 9 a.m. that Thursday. "I have no sympathy for the FLQ and its objectives and under no circumstances do I want to be associated with this group," he told Demers. Demers tried reasoning with him. "I cannot talk with the abductors directly," he said. "I would be taking the risk of becoming another prisoner, perhaps another victim. You are the only person who can meet with these FLQ members because they asked for you."

The two men talked for about an hour, and Mergler only relented after learning that Cuba had agreed to act as an intermediary for humanitarian reasons. He had represented the Cuban consulate in Montreal and knew the consul. "Listen," Mergler said. "I'll go see the consul. I'll offer to act for them and to represent them in this negotiation. If they accept, then I'll do what you ask." The two men went to the Cuban consulate, where Mergler met with the Cubans and Demers waited for over an hour in the reception area—an empty room with bare grey walls. When Mergler finally emerged, he told Demers, "I have obtained the mandate to act for the Cuban government so I am ready to follow you."

"What took so long?" Demers asked him.

"They had to call Cuba, the Ministry of Foreign Affairs. . . . They had to wait until Raoul Castro could be found to get his approval."

The two negotiators were driven to Des Récollets Street and Mergler later told a journalist with the *Montreal Star*, "I was amazed to see that soldiers had surrounded an area stretching for two blocks around the house. Crowds thronged outside the military barricade. Our automobile had to inch through." Police had evacuated residences up and down the street and there were some five hundred armed soldiers standing shoulder to shoulder in the streets. Snipers with high-powered rifles were posted on the roofs of nearby houses and they kept their weapons pointed at the kidnappers' hideout. The kidnappers had responded to all this by painting "FLQ" in large letters on the front window of their apartment.

Demers and Mergler parted company on the street, and Demers went to the police observation post across from 10945 Des Récollets, where the lady of the house greeted him warmly. Mergler knocked on the door at 10945 and a voice on the other side asked, "Who's there?"

"It's Mergler and I'm all alone."

The door swung open and Mergler saw two men—one armed with a machine gun, the other with a revolver.

"Are you Jacques Lanctôt?" Mergler asked.

"No. I'm Carbonneau. This is Lanctôt."

"Mr. Cross is here?"

"Yes."

"Is he all right?"

"See for yourself."

They led him down the hall to the room where Cross had been held for fifty-nine days. A third man armed with a machine gun—Yves Langlois—was guarding the British diplomat.

"Are you alright?" Mergler asked.

"Oh, I'm fine," Cross replied, then smiled and added, "Considering the circumstances."

Mergler handed the kidnappers the document he had received from Demers outlining how events were to unfold. Île Sainte-Hélène, the site of Expo 67, had been declared temporary Cuban territory. They would drive to the island with a police escort. The police would stop at the bridge leading to the island and they would continue to the Canadian pavilion. They would turn Cross over to Cuban officials and then await a military helicopter to transport them to Montreal-Dorval Airport, from where they would be flown to Cuba aboard a Canadian military aircraft.

"This means the wives and children can come along?" Lanctôt asked.

"Yes," Mergler replied.

"What about the Trudels? Are they included?"

"I have their promise," said Mergler.

The kidnappers remained skeptical. They suspected a trap. But Mergler convinced them to accept the arrangement by offering to ride with them. He left and reported to Demers and then returned as the kidnappers were preparing to leave. He told them to remove any dynamite and defuse any bombs because the police would search the place as soon as they were gone.

They had their own car—a battered, wine-red 1962 Chrysler. It was parked in an underground garage accessible by a cellar. Mergler watched as they packed the trunk, and listened with bemusement to the discussion that took place over a large portable TV resting on the floor. "We can't take it with us," one of the kidnappers said. "Think how terribly bourgeois it would be to arrive in Cuba carrying a TV set." Mergler suggested they put it in the back seat. Cross got in and sat next to it, and Lanctôt sat beside Cross. Carbonneau took the wheel. Langlois sat in the middle with a machine gun pointing upward so the barrel touched the windshield. Mergler got in last, and later recalled that Carbonneau scraped a concrete wall while backing out and that one of the doors wouldn't close properly. They also had a single stick of dynamite, wired to look as though it were a bomb.

Twenty police officers on motorcycles led the kidnappers down Pie-IX Boulevard, a broad, four-lane thoroughfare lined with thousands of people. At one point, Langlois opened the glove compartment and exclaimed, "Where's the registration?

"Do you have the registration?" he asked Lanctôt. "It's not here."

"Don't worry," Mergler interjected. "You're not going to be arrested for driving without a licence."

At the Canadian pavilion, Cuban officials escorted Cross to one room, while the kidnappers surrendered their weapons and went to another. The Cossette-Trudels arrived, and then Suzanne Lanctôt with her eighteen-month-old son Boris. "The reunion between Jacques Lanctôt and his child . . . was touching," Mergler later recounted. "His face lit up as he raised the child in his arms."

The flight to Cuba was considerably less joyous. The group flew aboard a four-engine CC-130 Yukon, which was little more than "an old metal crate," as Jacques Lanctôt wrote many years later. He, Carbonneau and Langlois had forgotten to bring the TV and they were unable to open the trunk of the Chrysler to retrieve their possessions. The plane housed two or three rows of seats and the rest of the fuselage was empty. "There was a lot of crying during the flight," Lanctôt wrote. "Everyone had a heavy heart. It was the first time we had left our beloved Quebec, which we had plunged into a grave crisis. . . ."

The kidnappers arrived in Cuba in the early hours of December 4. A few Cuban journalists met them at the airport and interviewed them briefly, and then they boarded a minibus for the trip into Havana and the Hotel Deauville. The thirteenth floor of the hotel had been cleared of other guests and reserved for the exiles. They had scarcely settled into their rooms when Suzanne Lanctôt went into labour. A French-speaking Cuban official had accompanied them, but for some considerable time he could not grasp the meaning of the phrase "*les eaux sont crevées*" (her waters have broken). When he finally comprehended, he called an ambulance and attendants rushed her to hospital where she gave birth to a baby girl, Olga, with her husband at her side.

THE FLIGHT OF THE ROSE BROTHERS

No such soft landing awaited the Rose brothers and their devoted accomplice Francis Simard. The trio had cleverly evaded the police in early November, then fled the apartment on Queen Mary Road and found refuge in two places—first in a cold, empty barn near the village of Saint-Bonaventure, some eighty kilometres east of Montreal, and then in an isolated century-old farmhouse located on a country road outside the South Shore community of Saint-Luc.

A network of supporters had assisted them. Denise Quesnel put them up on successive nights at her apartment on Laurier Avenue East. And on the third evening, November 9, two members of the network—Claude Larivière and Yves Roy—drove the brothers and Simard to Saint-Bonaventure. Larivière led the way in one vehicle while Roy and the fugitives followed in a second. They dropped the wanted men on a rural road outside the village, told them where the barn was supposed to be and then headed back to Montreal.

It was pitch black and chilly when Simard and the Rose brothers set off along a trail, wearing summer clothing and carrying a week's supply of canned food and their weapons—a light machine gun and two sawed-off shotguns. They got lost, slept in a ditch and awoke dusted in snow, and fared little better when they found the barn. They slept in the crawl space under the floor and hid there all day. "With some straw we picked up from a neighbouring farm, we made ourselves a kind of nest," Simard wrote in his memoir, *Talking It Out*. "Since our basement was only two feet high, we had to lie down the whole time. At night we went out to stretch our legs. We spent two weeks in Saint-Bonaventure. It was starting to get cold. To keep warm we lay down together. A Rose brother on each side [of me]. They told me I was the lucky one."

Larivière, Quesnel and Robert Dupuis brought the fugitives a supply of food on November 17, and Paul Rose asked them to find another hideout. Dupuis made discreet inquiries over the next week, and these led him to Michel Viger. Viger was a thirty-three-year-old accountant who worked in Longueuil and lived alone in a farmhouse outside the village of Saint-Luc. The isolated dwelling was set well back from the road and a good distance from the nearest neighbours. Viger knew the Rose brothers and liked them, having met them through the independence movement. He visited the fugitives in their hideout on the evening of November 23 and was moved by their pitiable state. The following day, he returned and, as he later told an interviewer with the Radio-Canada program *Format 60*, "There was a heavy snowfall—unimaginable for the twenty-fourth of November. Already there was an accumulation of three to four inches, plus ice and everything else. I decided I couldn't leave them there."

Simard and the Rose brothers knew the police would trace them to Viger's house, and they would need a hiding place. A false wall wouldn't fool anyone again so they began burrowing in the cellar. They started behind the furnace, which rested on a bed of concrete blocks a few feet from one wall. After lifting several blocks and breaking through the concrete floor, they dug a shaft straight down that measured fifteen by eighteen inches. Then they dug a tunnel eighteen feet long by three feet high and three feet wide. Lastly, they created a small chamber that was six feet square and three feet high. "Two of us carried out the work while the third kept watch from the living room window," Simard wrote. "It had to be done at night. As we dug, water came filtering into the tunnel. We worked without a break, digging, carrying out the dirt, spreading it evenly. It was cold and we were down on all fours in the mud. We started as soon as darkness fell and didn't stop till sun-up. It took us days to finish. Once the hideout and tunnel were dug and the floor opened up, we made the whole thing functional. We lined the inside with wood. We installed electricity and a heater."

The RCMP had been watching the house all the while. Viger had come to their attention on November 24—the same day that he rescued the Rose brothers and Simard. He had called Dupuis after returning from Saint-Bonaventure. The two men had discussed "their cousins" and the police had listened in through a wiretap on Quesnel's phone. The RCMP set up an observation post in a neighbouring cottage, but it was too far removed for effective surveillance. Furthermore, they waited three weeks before alerting the SQ, who were responsible for policing the South Shore. The RCMP only disclosed their suspicions about Viger at a meeting with SQ and Montreal intelligence officers on

December 15. Over the next few days, the police began arresting and interrogating those who had been assisting the fugitives. According to Marcel Sainte-Marie, a former homicide detective with the provincial force, two of his fellow detectives went to Viger's house and questioned him. "They didn't like his answers so they decided to watch the house," Sainte-Marie said. "As soon as they left, he left. While he was gone, the detectives saw lights go on and off and knew somebody else was there. So they called in five or six of us and we searched the entire house."

There were, in fact, two unsuccessful searches at the modest one-storey dwelling—on December 22 and Christmas Day—and Simard recounted both in his book. "The first had been a routine raid," he wrote. "We were in the living room. We saw four or five cars come driving up and we knew right away who was behind the wheel. By the time we grabbed our sleeping bags and picked everything off the floor, went down to the basement and climbed into our hiding place the police were in the house.

"The second time we almost got caught. Jacques had left something, an item of clothing, I think, in the kitchen. We got down to the basement in a hurry. Realizing what he had forgotten, he ran upstairs to grab the evidence. The police were coming through the door. By the time he replaced the cement blocks that camouflaged the tunnel entrance, the police were searching the basement."

Two officers, Corporal Jacques Gaboury and Constable Marcel Vigneault, returned to the house at around 5 p.m. on December 27. Viger wasn't home, but there were copies of the most recent editions of *Québec-Presse* and *Dimanche-Matin* on the kitchen table, as well as a pile of freshly laundered shirts. Gaboury and Vigneault went down to the basement, looked around and heard a strange noise that seemed to come from nowhere. They left at about 5:30, feeling troubled by that noise they'd heard, and returned at about 9. An outside light had been turned on. Viger was home. They questioned him and he relented and told them where the fugitives were. Gaboury and Vigneault called in reinforcements and a number of their fellow officers arrived, including Sainte-Marie.

"Viger took us downstairs near the furnace where they had their hide-out," Sainte-Marie recalled. "He said: Paul, they know you're in there.

"Rose said: Okay. Who's in charge? I want to talk to the one in charge."

Captain Denis Viau, the senior officer, identified himself.

"Paul said: Okay. We're ready to come out, but we want a negotiator present so nothing's going to happen to us.

"We said: Who do you want?

"He said: Dr. Ferron."

Jacques Ferron was a Longueuil physician who devoted much of his practice to treating the poor. He had also run unsuccessfully for the Co-operative Commonwealth Federation (forerunner of the NDP) and the RIN and was a prolific author who wrote novels, plays and essays. The police sent a car to pick him up at his home, but Ferron's arrival was not enough to convince the fugitives to give up, according to Sainte-Marie.

"Paul said: Before I come out I want to know who's there. Is Lisacek there?

"Dr. Ferron asked me and I said: Yeah, Lisacek is here.

"Paul said: We don't want to see him. We want him out of the house."

Rose was referring to Albert Lisacek, a tall, broad-shouldered detective with the holdup squad. He kept his head shaved bald to complement his imposing physique and intimidating demeanour, and he carried a sub-machine gun rather than a standard police revolver. He was known for kicking down doors during raids and roughing up suspects in interrogation rooms, and a national magazine once called him "the toughest cop in Canada." Lisacek had employed his usual tactics during a search of the Rose family home in Longueuil. "Instead of knocking on the door he took a battering ram and battered in the door," said Sainte-Marie. "He nearly hit their little girl. He walked in and took Mrs. Rose by the hair and put a gun to her head and said: If they're here, and anything happens to any of my men, I'll kill you, you bitch. And she screamed: They're not here! They're not here!"

Lisacek left, as Paul Rose demanded, and waited in a cruiser, and Rose and his brother and Simard surrendered. It was 5 a.m. on December 28, and one of the biggest manhunts in Canadian history was over. So was the October Crisis, as these events have come to be known. In the first days of January, the army withdrew most of its seven-thousand-odd troops from the streets—ending what sovereigntists call the "occupation of Quebec"—and life in Montreal and elsewhere in the province returned to normal.

But the October Crisis was destined to cast a long shadow over the lives of the victims, the perpetrators and those who had assisted them. James Cross never forgot the ordeal he had endured and never forgave his abductors. Pierre Laporte's immediate and extended family experienced years of grief and sorrow.

The police had arrested and detained 497 people under the War Measures Act or the Public Order Temporary Measures Act, which Parliament had passed in a hurry on November 2, 1970, to replace the WMA. Of these, 435 were questioned and released, most of them within a few days, and the Quebec government later compensated many of them for lost earnings, property damage and the disruption to their lives. Sixty-two of those arrested were charged with offences, but only thirty-two remained in custody when the crisis ended. Robert Lemieux, Michel Chartrand, Pierre Vallières and Charles Gagnon were among those held without bail, and they faced charges of seditious conspiracy, membership in the FLQ and various Criminal Code offences.

Those who had aided the Laporte kidnappers were charged and convicted, and served time. Michel Viger was sentenced to eight years in prison. Robert Dupuis and Claude Larivière both received two years. Four others—Louise Verrault, Denise Quesnel, Colette Therrien and Richard Therrien—each got a year. Francine Belisle went to jail for nine months, while her brother François, as well as Hélène Quesnel and Yves Roy, all got six months. One member of this group—Richard Therrien—paid a price in his professional life decades later. Therrien completed a law degree after he was released from prison. In the mid-1990s, he was appointed to the bench, but the appointment was revoked because he had failed to reveal his criminal conviction.

The Cross kidnappers endured several years of mostly unhappy exile—first in Cuba and then in France—before returning to Quebec, and the Laporte kidnappers served lengthy prison sentences.

Fourteen

EXILES AND INMATES

UPON LEARNING THAT THE KIDNAPPERS of James Cross would accept safe passage to Cuba, Pierre Trudeau reportedly said, "Well, let them go. They'll be back." And time would prove him correct. The Cross kidnappers and their party learned very quickly that exile in Cuba was something to be endured rather than enjoyed.

There were seven adults in the party—Jacques Lanctôt and his wife Suzanne, Jacques Cossette-Trudel and his wife Louise, Yves Langlois, Marc Carbonneau and a young woman who had accompanied him. There were, as well, the two children of Jacques and Suzanne Lanctôt—the toddler Boris and the infant Olga. Initially, Cuban officials watched them closely and controlled their every move. Their first stop was the Hotel Deauville in central Havana, and their handlers instructed them to check in under pseudonyms. The Deauville was a fourteen-storey establishment, located a few blocks west of the harbour and a popular destination for international travellers and tourists. It overlooked the Malecón, a seaside boulevard that hugged the broad arc of the coastline. There was a promenade and seawall alongside the Malecón, and the promenade was a gathering place for fishermen, for lovers, for families out for a stroll, and for daring young men who could find places to dive into the sea.

The exiles could observe all this but could not partake of any of it, as they were prohibited from leaving the hotel. They were scarcely allowed out of their rooms and their guardians kept close watch on them, a fact that Jacques Lanctôt learned in embarrassing fashion. He met an attractive young Englishwoman at the hotel bar and managed to arrange a tryst, but one of the guardians caught them—*in flagrante delicto*—and hauled Lanctôt down to the hotel manager's office for a reprimand.

In mid-December, the Cuban authorities moved the group to a large, modern split-level home in the coastal village of Guanabo, thirty kilometres east of Havana, and provided a live-in cook and an interpreter. The exiles could view the sea from a small terrace, but they could not leave the property. They had been moved in anticipation of a visit from one of the leading figures in the Cuban Revolution, Manuel Piñeiro, the then deputy minister of the interior. Piñeiro ran the state security apparatus that protected Fidel Castro, monitored dissidents and quashed any hint of opposition to the regime. But things didn't happen overnight in Cuba. The Quebeckers waited weeks for this distinguished visitor and soon suffered from excruciating boredom, according to Louise Cossette-Trudel, who later wrote a memoir, *Une Sorcière comme les autres*. "The days are long," she wrote. "We have no pens, no paper, no books. The journal *Granma* arrives once every three weeks when our guardians think of it and we have no communication with the outside world."

Jacques Lanctôt had managed to bring a shortwave radio with him, and one day he picked up a Radio-Canada broadcast. They listened closely and learned that the Rose brothers and Francis Simard had just been arrested. Foreign Affairs Minister Mitchell Sharp gave an interview and they were astonished to hear him say that their own group remained under the jurisdiction of the Canadian government according to the terms of a special agreement between the two countries. Then the radio ceased to function—severing their one link with the world.

One Sunday their guardians arranged a visit to the zoo. Five cars full of overseers accompanied the small party of seven adults and two children and formed a cordon around them as they walked the grounds. "During that first year," Louise Cossette-Trudel wrote, "each time we went out it was like there was a strange cloud around us, which followed us and kept us isolated. We were very well surrounded and contacts with the people were denied us."

Piñeiro eventually arrived and it proved a happy occasion, according to Jacques Lanctôt. "The commandant arrived in mid-afternoon, dressed in his olive-green uniform, a pistol at his belt, black boots gleaming and laced tightly beneath his pant legs," he wrote in *Les Plages de l'exil*, his 2010 memoir. "An immense meal was quickly prepared and everyone sat around the table. The discussion lasted several hours, interrupted by stories and laughter, serious and light moments." Louise Cossette-Trudel saw things differently. "We had a short conversation with a series of questions where we showed ourselves in all our splendour," she wrote. "One took the floor precisely to interrupt or contradict the other. . . . Each time I tried to speak, someone was there to cut me off. It seemed to be necessary for the men, in such circumstances at least, not to let themselves be dominated by the women."

The isolation and boredom had taken a toll on them. They had begun to fight and argue. Their disputes became increasingly heated and bitter, and Louise Cossette-Trudel learned from reading the works of Lenin and a biography of Marx that dissension was common among exiled revolutionaries. However, their guardians were perplexed. They could not understand how these youthful Quebeckers, who had planned and carried out the kidnapping of a diplomat and held him hostage for two months, could not sit around a table and resolve their differences. In order to "puncture the abscess which was poisoning the air," as Louise Cossette-Trudel put it, their guardians organized a week-long expedition. She naively hoped that they might be off to receive some training in the techniques of guerilla warfare, but it was a mere sightseeing tour. They travelled under assumed names—she and her husband Jacques Cossette-Trudel as Mr. and Mrs. Alfred Cauteau from France. They dined on crocodile and turtle and visited historic sites, a rum distillery, a cigar factory, and coffee and banana plantations.

Afterward, they were taken back to the Hotel Deauville and assigned to rooms, and by then they had learned much about the system and found much they disliked. They also realized, according to Louise Cossette-Trudel, that all the planning and preparation for the kidnapping of James Cross had merely camouflaged the deep personal differences among the members of the group.

Legal proceedings against the Laporte kidnappers and their network of supporters began in the first days of January 1971, and they moved with extraordinary haste. Michel Viger, Robert Dupuis, Louise Verrault, Francine Belisle, Colette Therrien and her brother Richard, as well as Denise Quesnel and her daughter Hélène, all appeared in court charged with being accessories after the fact to murder and kidnapping. The Rose brothers, Francis Simard and Bernard Lortie faced charges of murder and kidnapping, and the murder trial of Paul Rose opened on January 25.

It was held in a windowless, wood-panelled courtroom on the sixth floor of the SQ headquarters. Throughout the trial, Rose wore the same shabby clothes that he was wearing on the night of his arrest—a blue shirt that he left untucked and a brown crewneck sweater that was too small for his large, strapping frame and had a hole in the left elbow.

He wanted Robert Lemieux to defend him, but Lemieux was being held on the eleventh floor of the SQ building, facing charges of obstructing justice, seditious conspiracy and being a member of the outlawed FLQ. The presiding judge, Mr. Justice Marcel Nichols, had no authority to order Lemieux's release. Rose refused to accept a court-appointed lawyer. Instead, he represented himself and his swagger impressed some observers. "When he stood and leaned forward with his hands on the wall of the prisoner's dock and his powerful shoulders hunched, it was with confidence," *Gazette* columnist Chris Allan wrote. "When he sat back with his chin in his hand or stroking his reddish moustache, it was with calculated arrogance."

Rose filed two pretrial motions asking that the charges against him be withdrawn. First, he contended that publicity surrounding the case made it impossible for him to receive a fair hearing. Second, he would not be judged by a jury of his peers—the workers, women and students of Montreal's poorer neighbourhoods. Quebec law at the time stipulated that only men could serve as jurors, and they had to own at least five thousand dollars' worth of property or pay more than five hundred dollars a year in rent. "How can a law be fair if it excludes women—fifty percent of the population?" Rose asked. "And I don't know what percentage is cut off by other restrictions. Just as men were once tried by the king or the aristocracy, so I will be judged by the establishment." Arguments over these motions lasted for two days, and Rose continually baited the judge—eliciting laughter from the public galleries and warnings from the bench. But Rose kept it up.

"Don't abuse my patience," the judge snapped at one point.

"Mine is even more abused," Rose replied.

"I repeat the warning I gave this morning," Nichols said. "I can have you ejected from the courtroom for the rest of your trial."

"And I repeat my warning," Rose said.

"This is directed at me personally and I can cite you for contempt of court," Nichols said.

"Oh yes," replied Rose. "What I have said is very contemptuous for a member of the establishment."

"And for me personally," Nichols said.

"And for you personally as a member and lackey of the establishment," Rose said.

That was merely the start of the sparring. Rose accused Nichols of collaborating with the prosecutor after seeing both men leave the courtroom by the same door. He called the judge a "gadget of the Liberal party" and repeatedly described the trial as "a monumental farce." Twice during jury selection, Nichols ordered police officers to remove Rose from the courtroom. Finally, on February 8, the judge expelled him for good following one particularly ugly exchange.

"You're a whore of the establishment," Rose shouted after being admonished by Nichols. "No, you're worse. At least whores earn their money. They work for it."

"I cannot permit the further degradation of the court under which I have been called to preside," Nichols replied.

Two officers seized the defendant and hauled him out of the courtroom, with Rose shouting, "The comic opera continues! We shall overcome!"

By then, Rose had insulted or berated the judge twenty-nine times. But expelling him created a thorny legal problem: the trial could not continue with the defendant absent and without counsel to represent him. Nichols got around the issue by asking the Montreal Bar Association to appoint a lawyer who would serve as an *amicus curia*, or friend of the court. The lawyer in question, Claude Boisvert, could intervene on behalf of Rose on points of law, but could not call witnesses for the defence or cross-examine Crown witnesses.

Prosecutor Jacques Ducros began presenting the Crown's case on Thursday, February 19. Over the next three weeks, he called 206 witnesses and submitted over 200 exhibits. Bernard Lortie was summoned to testify but refused to co-operate. At his swearing in, he told Nichols, "I swear I will not testify against my comrades." Asked his age, he replied, "Nineteen years of slavery under the economic and financial domination of the establishment." Asked his occupation, he replied, "*Felquiste.*" Ducros began his examination and Lortie interrupted and said, "I'm fed up with this nonsense." When Nichols threatened to cite him for contempt, Lortie snapped, "What are you going to give me? Ten years, fourteen years, twenty years?"

Lise Balcer, another Rose associate, was equally uncooperative. She was twenty-one, unemployed and had posed as Rose's wife in March 1970 when he rented the Armstrong Street house where Laporte was later held hostage. Balcer took the oath, then asked, "Why are there no women on the jury? If you cannot accept a woman as a juror, how can you accept one as a witness?"

The Crown presented a substantial amount of evidence linking Rose to the kidnapping of Pierre Laporte. His fingerprints were found at 5630 Armstrong and he had visited the landlord on October 13—three days after seizing Laporte—to pay the overdue October rent. His finger-prints were found on several communiqués, and handwriting experts testified that his writing matched that found on the communiqués. There was only one piece of evidence linking him to the murder—a statement he made while being interrogated by Constable Claude Boillard on December 29, the day after his arrest. Rose had told the detective, "All three of us [he, his brother and Francis Simard] were present in the house at 5630 Armstrong Street in Saint-Hubert when Mr. Laporte was executed. Two of us held him while the third tightened the chain around his neck."

Rose remained locked up in his cell while the Crown presented its case, but he received a transcript of the day's proceedings the follow-ing morning. The judge offered on three occasions to readmit him if he would apologize and promise to behave. But Rose steadfastly refused. However, he had to be readmitted to mount his defence. The public gal-lery was packed when he rose from the prisoner's box, flanked by two burly police officers. His mother and one of his sisters were among the spectators. But it quickly became evident that Rose didn't have a defence. He maintained he hadn't been allowed to consult a lawyer until the day before the trial opened, a claim that was easily disproven. He asked the judge to adjourn the trial and allow him to subpoena two witnesses. The judge ordered the jury out and gave Rose the opportunity to argue the relevance of the witnesses' testimony, but he refused and called Nichols a hypocrite.

"I don't accept the term hypocrite," the judge replied. "You are expelled from the court."

At that point Nichols accused Rose of "systematic obstruction" and declared, "I consider the defence terminated."

Rose returned the following day to address the jury. He spoke for eighty minutes, ignoring several warnings from the bench to restrict his remarks to a summation of the defence. Nichols finally ordered him to sit down and began his own address to the jury, but Rose repeatedly interrupted and was expelled again.

The case finally went to the twelve male jurors late on the afternoon of Friday, March 12. The jury deliberated for twenty-five minutes and then broke for the day. Court resumed at 10 a.m. on Saturday, and everyone expected that the jury would resume deliberations. Instead, the foreman, Romuald Côté, a forty-nine-year-old city employee, rose from the box and declared that the jury had reached a verdict: "We find the accused guilty of murder."

Nichols immediately sentenced Rose to life in prison, with no eligibility for parole for ten years, and the convicted terrorist left the courtroom with one arm raised and his fist clenched while shouting, "*Vive le Québec libre! Vive le pouvoir du peuple! Nous vaincrons!*"

The arrival of the Cross kidnappers in Havana merited a three-paragraph story in *Granma*, the official newspaper of the Cuban Communist Party, and an equally short item in a youth newspaper called *Juventud Rebelde*, and Pierre Charette and Alain Allard read both pieces with considerable interest. They too were terrorists enduring exile in Cuba and they were eager to meet their compatriots. However, they required state approval and they applied to the appropriate ministry. Then they waited. Weeks passed, then months—and still they waited.

Charette was twenty-four, Allard twenty-three, and they were accomplices of Pierre-Paul Geoffroy, the prolific FLQ bomber then serving 124 concurrent life sentences in a Quebec prison. Charette and Allard had fled Montreal after Geoffroy's arrest on March 4, 1969. They had hidden out briefly in New York with the Black Panthers, the radical African-American organization, and then found refuge with a leader of the equally radical Students for a Democratic Society. Along the way, they had acquired false identification papers and enough money to purchase tickets for a flight to Miami. At 4:10 p.m. on May 5, 1969, they boarded a National Airlines Boeing 707 at La Guardia Airport in New York. There were sixty-eight passengers and seven crew aboard the aircraft. Charette and Allard sat quietly and inconspicuously until 5:45 p.m. when the pilot, Captain Ed Hodgson, began his descent into Miami International Airport.

At that point, Charette summoned a flight attendant. Pulling a .38-calibre revolver from inside his jacket, he marched the terrified attendant to the front of the aircraft and told her, "Open the door to the cockpit or I'll shoot you in the head." He ordered Hodgson to cease all communication with the ground and to turn the aircraft toward Cuba. Forty minutes later, the plane landed in Havana, where soldiers lined the runway. They apprehended the two Québécois terrorists and hustled them off to La Cabanna fortress, an imposing, two-centuries-old edifice that overlooked Havana harbour. It had served as a revolutionary prison, and Charette and Allard were held there for a month and interrogated repeatedly.

The Cuban authorities then moved them to a rundown, older establishment called the Hotel Vedado, and assigned a guardian who prohibited them from leaving the premises. Charette and Allard spent long days sitting in their room or hanging around the lobby. They perused the Cuban newspapers, although neither of them understood Spanish. The Ministry of the Interior paid for their meals and their dry cleaning, but the guardian was supposed to pick up the tab for drinks and cigarettes at the bar. He neglected to pay, so the bar cut them off and they had to scavenge butts from ashtrays in the lobby.

After two dreary months, Charette and Allard felt like they were in prison. But then their guardian allowed them to leave the hotel and explore the city. They set out for the Havana Libre, one of the largest hotels in the country. Three fellow Quebec terrorists—Raymond Villeneuve, Mario Bachand and André Garand—were staying there. Villeneuve was one of the founders of the FLQ and had been sentenced to twelve years for his part in the bombing campaign during the spring of 1963. He had been paroled in the fall of 1967 and resumed his underground activities. Bachand was also involved in that first wave of *felquiste* violence and received a four-year sentence, and he too rejoined the movement after his release. Garand had played a marginal role in the 1963 violence and got off with a suspended sentence.

Villeneuve and Garand left Quebec in the fall of 1968, drove to Mexico and caught a flight from there to Cuba. Bachand departed for France in the spring of 1969, moved on to Spain and finally Cuba. All three exiles hoped the Cubans would train them in the finer points of waging guerilla warfare in rural and urban areas, but that didn't happen. By the time Charette and Allard caught up to them, they were anxious to leave Cuba, as Charette noted in his 1979 memoir *Mes Dix Années d'Exil à Cuba*. "We undertook visits to various embassies, such as those of China, of North Korea and Algeria, with the very utopian goal of establishing relations that would eventually lead to our departure from Cuba," he wrote.

Charette and Allard had become comfortable at the Vedado, but their stay ended abruptly one day in October 1969 when a member of a state security agency, the Seguridad, visited them.

"Pack your bags," the agent said. "You're leaving the hotel."

"To go where?" Charette asked meekly.

"You'll see when you get there," the agent replied.

A driver waited outside in a 1956 Chevrolet. He took them through the embassy district and past the grand homes and mansions of the pre-revolutionary elite and pulled up at one such residence. Now it was a detention centre for foreigners. The dining room had become a cafeteria, the upstairs bedrooms had been converted to dormitories crammed with bunks and the swimming pool was being used as a garbage dump.

There were people from all over Central and South America, some of them members of guerilla movements, others refugees fleeing military juntas. There were a number of Americans, most of them black, some of whom had been charged with crimes and others who had hijacked aircraft. Charette was appalled by the sanitary conditions and lack of personal hygiene, particularly among the Peruvians, Bolivians and Colombians. The water was turned off for twenty hours a day, lice and other parasites were rampant, and the security agents who ran the house eventually called in the Ministry of Public Health to disinfect the premises.

For two months, the Quebeckers were not allowed to make a phone call or leave the residence. In exasperation, Charette wrote to Fidel Castro himself. He complained that their treatment was contrary to "the ideals proclaimed by the fathers of Marxism." He contended that their rights under the charter of the United Nations were being violated. Furthermore, he threatened to go on a hunger strike until he was allowed to meet a representative of the government. The letter prompted a quick response. A delegation of men in olive-green uniforms arrived, led by Enio Leyva, head of the Seguridad. Charette was terrified. His legs shook. He imagined that he and Allard would be hurled into prison. But Leyva merely questioned them, and after determining that they posed no threat to state security, he granted them a limited amount of freedom. But they had to make a formal request each time they wanted to leave the premises, and the agent in charge would forward all requests to the chief of immigration services. Some were not sent on, and soldiers guarding the entrances sometimes refused to let them leave.

Deliverance arrived unexpectedly in January 1970. The government—which was desperate to improve the country's balance of trade and to earn foreign currency—launched a massive public mobilization campaign for the sugar harvest. Cubans from all walks of life—students, housewives and office workers, among others—were urged to take part for the good of the nation and an estimated one million did so. The objective was ten million tons, although the previous record of 7,298,023 tons was set in 1952 and the harvests of the revolutionary era had come nowhere close to that mark.

Charette and Allard volunteered their services as *macheteros*—working on a plantation as cane cutters. It was hard, dirty work. The Cubans burned a cane field the day before the *macheteros* arrived, to strip the plants of the foliage and to kill the scorpions and poisonous spiders that inhabited the plants. The *macheteros* had to endure the heat of the sun. They had to walk on hot, charred ground. They had to stoop all day and cut the cane as close to the ground as possible, and the cane was black and sticky, but as Charette later wrote, "It was that or die of boredom and anguish at the house." The duo lasted a month—until Charette developed a dental infection and injured himself with a machete.

More idle days at the house ensued, but by then Charette and Allard and their compatriots—Villeneuve, Bachand and Garand—had applied to leave Cuba for France. They learned on the afternoon of April 5, 1970, that the authorities had approved their request, and they sailed that evening on a Cuban merchant ship. They were surprised to learn upon boarding that the vessel was destined for Genoa, Italy, and a nasty surprise awaited Charette and Allard upon arrival. The other three Quebeckers had Canadian passports and Cuban travel documents, so they walked off the ship as free men and flew to Paris. Charette and Allard, however, did not have passports and the Italian customs officers would not admit them on the basis of their Cuban documents. Furthermore, the Italians contacted Canadian consular officials who informed them that the two Quebeckers were wanted in both Canada and the United States and should be arrested if they stepped off the ship.

Charette and Allard returned to Cuba, where they found jobs—Charette teaching French at l'École de langues Maximo Gorki, and Allard repairing televisions at an electronics shop. The Cubans put the two men at the Vedado, and they were staying there when the kidnappers of James Cross arrived on December 4. They sent letters to the Minister of the Interior and the Central Committee of the Cuban Communist Party requesting permission to meet their fellow Quebeckers, but by the year's end they hadn't received so much as an acknowledgment of their request.

Another month passed and they still hadn't had a response. One morning in February, Charette and Allard showed up at the Ministry of the Interior determined to secure an answer. They sat in a reception area, without food or water, until 5:30 p.m. Finally, Manuel Piñeiro came out. "He declared that our comrades were in perfectly good health and had demonstrated no interest in seeing us, even after having learned that we were looking for them," Charette wrote. "He was not too convincing, but we had to leave without having advanced our cause." Another three months elapsed and they heard nothing. Then one afternoon in May 1971 a soldier came to the Vedado to get them. "We next found ourselves in a room at the luxurious Habana Riviera Hotel on the Malecón where we were to meet the members of the Liberation Cell," Charette later recounted. "We learned that no one had been informed of our presence, nor of our requests to meet them until that day."

The exiles spent the afternoon and the evening together and continued to talk into the night. Charette and Allard were eager to hear about the kidnappings, as well as other news of Quebec since they had been away for over two years. Charette noted that Marc Carbonneau did not participate much at all and appeared to have been ostracized by the others. He had brought a younger woman with him—contrary to the wishes of the group. She had taken no part in the kidnapping and apparently for that reason was not accepted.

The distance between Carbonneau and the others made for some awkwardness, but otherwise everyone had a pleasant time until the conversation turned to Mario Bachand. Two months earlier, on March 29, 1971, Bachand had been gunned down in the apartment where he was staying in the Paris suburb of Saint-Ouen. The murder took place at midday. He was alone and responded to a knock at the door. By all accounts, two people were there, a man and a woman. They shot him twice in the back of the head with a .22-calibre revolver and fled the scene with the help of a third person who was waiting outside the building.

The identity of the killers and their motive was a mystery then and has remained so to this day, since no one was ever arrested for the crime. But it was much on the minds of the exiles as they talked that night, and Charette spoke freely about Bachand. He told the group that "If Bachand continued to behave in France the way he did in Cuba he would inevitably have made enemies." He was a braggart and a pathological liar, according to Charette, an instigator who delighted in sowing discord, and everyone who encountered him sooner or later avoided him like a pest. Jacques Lanctôt remembered the evening differently in his 2010 memoir *Les Plages de l'exil*. "At a certain moment, well into the night," he wrote, "Charette was chatting freely and admitted proudly that he was the *auteur spirituel* of the death of Bachand. This admission struck me like a dagger in the heart."

Lanctôt and Bachand had been close friends since the earliest days of the FLQ. Bachand had been one of the organizers of the massive Opération McGill français demonstration in March 1969, had never wavered in his commitment to an independent Quebec, and had been imprisoned for his actions. Lanctôt believed that Charette had arranged Bachand's murder through some of his *felquiste* associates who were in exile in Algeria.

Lanctôt resolved never to speak to Charette again. But Charette maintained cordial relations with Lanctôt's sister Louise and her husband Jacques Cossette-Trudel. "Our group definitely split in two over the issue," Lanctôt wrote. "It was sad and ridiculous and did nothing to advance the cause of Quebec's independence. But I learned over time that we were not the only ones experiencing discord. Exile is fertile ground for division."

On the opening day of his trial, and again on the second day, Jacques Rose showed up in court wearing blue pyjamas, a maroon bathrobe and slippers. It was a protest of sorts. Rose was being held in a cell on the twelfth floor at the Parthenais Street headquarters of the SQ. The courtroom was on the sixth. Guards at the facility were on strike and picketing on the street. Rose initially refused to leave his cell, arguing that he would be crossing the guards' picket line. But several burly police officers ignored his objections and hauled him off to court— dressed as he was.

Rose was the last member of the Chénier Cell to be tried for the kidnapping and murder of Pierre Laporte. His older brother Paul had been convicted of murder in March 1971, and of kidnapping in the fall of that year. Francis Simard was convicted of murder in June, and Bernard Lortie of kidnapping in October. All three had been disruptive defendants. They were repeatedly cited for contempt of court and refused to allow defence lawyers to represent them.

Jacques Rose's trial on a charge of kidnapping opened on Monday, February 7, 1972, and Robert Lemieux defended him. Lemieux—who had spent part of 1971 in jail but had been released by the time of Rose's trial—began by introducing a thirteen-page motion that challenged the legitimacy of the court. He maintained that the Court of Queen's Bench was "a colonial court which cannot by law judge Rose, who is fighting against colonialism and for the installation of an authentic, popular and democratic regime in Quebec."

Five court stenographers had to work as a relay team to record Lemieux's rapid-fire four-hour argument. The presiding judge, Eugène Marquis, who was seventy years old and a twenty-three-year veteran of the bench, listened patiently, but finally dismissed Lemieux's motion as mere propaganda devoid of any merit. He also threw out the lawyer's second motion—for the dismissal of the all-male jury pool— prompting an angry retort from the defendant. "You reject our motion and I reject your decision!" Rose shouted from the prisoner's box. "This is what I think of your constitution and your decision." Rose had an abridged version of the British North America Act. He ripped it in two and hurled a portion of it at the bench. It sailed over the judge's head, but Marquis ignored the provocation and calmly declared, "I'm an old pacifist."

The trial lasted eleven weeks. Lemieux held up the proceedings at every turn, filing a motion for a mistrial on the grounds that the Crown should have proceeded first with the more serious charge of murder, and then filing a ten-page bail application on behalf of his client. "The primary purpose of the FLQ cell was to detain Laporte until an agreement was negotiated in good faith," Lemieux told the court. "This stated aim excludes any intent to murder. This leaves us with the kidnapping charge—a bailable offence." The judge dismissed the argument and Rose remained locked up.

Prosecutor Marcel Beauchemin called 150 witnesses and entered 174 exhibits. The evidence against Rose appeared overwhelming. One witness, SQ Corporal Jacques Gaboury, testified that on the night of the arrest he overheard a conversation between the Rose brothers and Dr. Jacques Ferron in which the accused man said, "We have not kidnapped a minister for nothing." And a fellow officer, Captain Raymond Bellemarre, told the court that during the trip from the Saint-Luc farmhouse to SQ headquarters, Rose had said, "Laporte was kidnapped and he got what he deserved."

Beauchemin appeared to have presented an airtight case, whereas Lemieux had not called a single witness or mounted any defence. In his address to the jury, Beauchemin said, "You cannot ignore the evidence. . . . The Crown has, without doubt, presented evidence which shows Rose's guilt." Or so it seemed when the all-male jury left the courtroom to begin their deliberations. They spent nearly twelve hours weighing the evidence, only to return and announce that they were hopelessly deadlocked. Rose's family, friends and supporters were jubilant and celebrated noisily in the public gallery.

But that long, arduous trial was only the start of the legal proceedings against the defendant. Rose remained behind bars at SQ headquarters. In late June, his mother, Lemieux, the singer Pauline Julien, the sculptor Armand Vaillancourt and several prominent labour leaders formed the Comité Jacques Rose to pressure the authorities for his release—a futile effort. Rose was tried again on the kidnapping charge in the fall of 1972. This time the jury acquitted him and a triumphant Lemieux told the jurors, "This verdict is not the verdict of the establishment, but a popular verdict, an authentic Québécois verdict. You will be proud of it for a long time." Shortly afterward, the Crown charged Rose with being an accessory after the fact of kidnapping and forcible confinement in the detention of Pierre Laporte. Meanwhile, Rose was still charged with the murder of the former cabinet minister. His murder trial began January 9, 1973, and the jury panel included three women—the law having been amended to eliminate the all-male rule.

Lemieux introduced a number of motions at the outset, all of which were thrown out. The Crown called its first witnesses on January 16 and spent a month presenting the evidence against the accused. The nine male and three female jurors began their deliberations at noon on Tuesday, February 20. At 11 a.m. on Thursday, February 22, they returned to the courtroom. The public gallery was packed. "Silence hung over the courtroom," the *Gazette*'s Eddie Collister wrote, "as the foreman stood and in a loud clear voice said: 'After studying the evidence, we have arrived at the unanimous conclusion that the accused is not guilty.' There was a moment of silence then someone started clapping and within seconds most of the people in the courtroom were on their feet clapping." Rose broke into tears. His mother, father and three sisters rushed forward to embrace him, but guards stopped them. "Robert Lemieux all but jumped into the prisoner's box wrapping his arms around Rose," Collister reported.

That afternoon Rose walked out of the Parthenais Street jail a free man for the first time in over two years. The following day, he and Lemieux held a press conference. "I am going to fight for the liberation of my brother Paul and all the political prisoners, who have been tried by the iniquitous and scandalous justice of the establishment," Rose told the assembled media.

But Rose had one more legal battle to fight. His trial on the charges of being an accessory after the fact of kidnapping and forcible confinement began on June 13, 1973. Again, the Crown presented an exhaustive case. Prosecutor Fernand Côté called fifty-four witnesses and submitted 213 exhibits. Lemieux, on the other hand, did not call any witnesses, but objected and obstructed at every opportunity. He made a motion for a mistrial on the grounds of double jeopardy, which he termed a principle of British common law that prevents an individual from being tried as an accessory to a crime of which he has been acquitted. Côté called Paul Rose and Francis Simard as witnesses. Each man was led into the courtroom and to the witness box handcuffed to an officer. Rose refused to be sworn in and the judge, Mr. Justice Guy Mathieu, sentenced him to a year in jail for contempt.

Lemieux advised Simard not to testify and Simard happily obliged. He called Justice Mathieu "a puppet in a red bib." Mathieu asked the jury to leave the courtroom and immediately sentenced Simard to a year in jail for contempt. "I'm proud to be held in contempt," Simard said. "Thank you. It's my pleasure." Another witness, François Belisle, who was living in the apartment on Queen Mary Road in November 1970 and had helped construct the secret hiding place, was also uncooperative. To each of Côté's questions, he responded, "It's possible." Or "It could be." Or "Perhaps." Finally, an exasperated Mathieu said, "It appears your memory is blank so I'm giving you a night in jail to refresh it."

The Crown concluded its case on July 10. Côté made his address to the jury, then it was Lemieux's turn. He contended that the police had framed Rose and that they had coached a key witness, a woman who lived on Armstrong Street in Saint-Hubert and had seen Rose on the street during the week in which Pierre Laporte was held hostage. Then he began reading extracts from the FLQ manifesto.

Justice Mathieu interjected, "You're not going to make a political speech here."

Lemieux ignored him and continued, and Mathieu interrupted him again. "Stop talking politics and stick to the boundaries of the case," Mathieu said.

Lemieux changed course and launched into a lengthy discourse on the struggle for Quebec independence. By then, Côté was exasperated and stood and snapped, "Call him to order or let me leave this room. I don't want to listen to Lemieux's version of the history of Quebec." Justice Mathieu ordered the jury to leave the room and reprimanded Lemieux, but when the jurors returned, the defence lawyer was back on his feet and contending that Paul Rose's trial had been a farce. Mathieu intervened once more. "The jury is not here as an appeal court for Paul

Rose," he said. Lemieux replied that Paul Rose had been referred to throughout the trial, and this time Mathieu angrily cut him off. "I don't have any intention of arguing with you," he said. "Plead the case of Jacques Rose." Lemieux concluded by saying he hoped the trial "would bring an end to this enterprise of repression."

Then Justice Mathieu addressed the jury. "In all my experience as a lawyer and a judge, I have never seen a trial like this one," he said. "But I ask you to forget the numerous altercations between the two lawyers and between Mr. Lemieux and myself. You are not here to judge Justice Mathieu or lawyer Robert Lemieux. You are here to judge Jacques Rose." He told the jurors that being an accessory after the fact of kidnapping required proof beyond a reasonable doubt that the accused knew that his brother, as well as Francis Simard and Bernard Lortie, were wanted for the crime and that he had helped them evade the police. The forcible confinement charge required proof that Rose was involved in detaining Laporte.

The jury deliberated for less than five hours before returning with a verdict of guilty on all charges. Justice Mathieu immediately sentenced Lemieux to two years in prison for advising Francis Simard not to testify and an additional ten months on eight other counts of contempt, and police officers escorted the lawyer out of the courtroom shouting, "*Vive le Québec libre!*" Jacques Rose returned on July 28 and Judge Mathieu sentenced him to eight years for his role in the kidnapping and death of Pierre Laporte.

Jacques Lanctôt was conflicted during his years of Cuban exile. He missed Quebec, yet there was much that he loved about Cuba. He came to admire the people. He adapted to their slower, more casual pace of life. He wore the same clothes as Cuban men and cut his hair very short like them, and his pallid northern complexion acquired a rich, bronze hue. He spoke Spanish so fluently that he could pass unnoticed in the streets of Havana. He took his son for early morning walks in the historic Vedado district and together they enjoyed the warmth, the humid air and the smell of the sea.

Lanctôt met Latin American revolutionaries of all stripes—men who were lodged in the same hotels as Lanctôt and his fellow Quebeckers. Some had fled prison or death sentences in their homelands, while others were gathering resources and plotting their return to topple hated dictators. The exiles led a privileged existence. They carried small, white, government-issued cards, which signified that they were special guests and enjoyed unlimited credit in the hotel restaurants and bars. "We were entitled to the best meals—fresh fish, shrimp, calamari, crayfish, frog legs. . . . The best cafés, the best rum, the best cigars, the most beautiful beaches, the best music, all these exotic pleasures were ours to discover. And all the women that I saw day after day made me swoon. I must admit, I secretly dreamed of approaching them one by one, singing to them in my best Spanish . . . and more than once I thought of divorcing immediately to make a new life in Cuba and forgetting Quebec forever."

But this life of perpetual leisure had its pitfalls. Lanctôt had nothing to do for weeks and months on end. He became depressed, contemplated suicide, sought solace in drink. He and some of the men in the Quebec contingent spent endless evenings at the hotel bars. They drank rum—straight or in cocktails—and listened to whatever orchestra happened to be providing the entertainment. The prolonged, excessive drinking brought down a member of the group who one day had to be rushed to hospital in an ambulance suffering from cirrhosis of the liver. "Before lapsing into alcoholism," Lanctôt later wrote, "I asked our Cuban guardians if I could do something to cover the cost of putting us up and they proposed cutting cane for several weeks on a sugar plantation."

He was sent to an all-male camp about an hour or two outside the capital. The men were assigned to twelve-member brigades. They worked six days a week, starting at 5 a.m. and cutting until about 11. It was too hot to work at midday, so they broke until about 2:30 p.m., then worked till early evening. Lanctôt had never performed manual labour and his back ached at the end of each day and was stiff and sore the following morning. The palms of his hands were covered in painful blisters, even though he wore gloves, but the Cubans had a solution. They told him to piss on the blisters to harden the skin and prevent infections.

The harvest lasted ten to twelve weeks—from early November until late February. Then Lanctôt returned to Havana and the same idle life. He pressed the guardians to find him some meaningful work and he landed a position as a translator with a weekly newspaper called *Resumen semanal de Granma*. The newspaper published English and French editions and was distributed abroad to groups and organizations sympathetic to the Cuban Revolution. Pierre Charette and Yves Langlois also worked there, and the three of them translated speeches by Castro, official declarations and stories about political, cultural and social events and developments.

But there was no remedy for the melancholy that dampened Lanctôt's spirit. "Quebec seemed . . . light years from where we were living," he wrote in his memoir. "Gazing out the French window in my hotel room at night, I would scrutinize the northern horizon. I knew that the Big Dipper was equally visible there, at the other end of the world, and it brought back images of my youth at a scout camp deep in the forest, organized by the Jesuit college I attended." Elsewhere he wrote, "I cannot deny my origins, my culture, my fight for a free and socialist Quebec and my comrades living there."

Jacques Cossette-Trudel and his wife Louise were the first to inquire about leaving Cuba. In the summer of 1972, they visited the French embassy in Havana, hoping to be granted political asylum and a quick exit. But their efforts came to nothing and they left disappointed. Exile, for them, had become a miserable ordeal. "It was necessary to fight in order to work a little, fight for the right to have some books, fight to go further than our hotel," Louise wrote in her memoir. "And where could we go on this island without money, without contacts, without approval?

How could we ever leave the island?" The infighting between the couple and the others had continued. She had withdrawn from what she termed "the battles of the roosters" and had become "an exile among exiles, banished among the banished."

The Cossette-Trudels had reflected on the path that they and many of their radical contemporaries had chosen. They concluded that the kidnappings, the bombing campaigns and other *felquiste* acts of terror had been a terrible mistake. They revealed their change of heart in a letter dated August 24, 1972, which they wrote and sent to Louise Vandelac, a former college classmate then working as a journalist in Montreal. "There is a time for everything and the FLQ is a thing of the past," they wrote. "The critical analysis of the so called 'October Crisis' has taught us that armed agitation must stop. FLQ terrorism is a two-edged sword which has begun to cut off the heads of the Québécois themselves. . . . We have come to the conclusion that it is necessary to do away with the FLQ and especially 'felquisme' as a strategy, a way of thinking and acting and even simply as a political presence. . . ." The couple also drafted a long letter to the rest of their party explaining their rejection of terrorism and they made copies for each member. They received written responses accusing them of opportunism, *arrivisme* and weakness, among other things, and the acrimonious fallout led to a complete rupture between the Cossette-Trudels and the others.

Both husband and wife were eager to work, and their Cuban guardians offered them positions as translators with *Granma*. They turned down the opportunity, Jacques explaining that they couldn't work alongside the other Quebeckers without risking conflicts, which greatly surprised the Cubans. The couple worked briefly as translators with *Prensa Latina*, the Cuban press agency, and later received permission from the authorities to file dispatches to L'Agence de presse libre du Québec (APLQ), a Montreal-based, left-wing collective that published a weekly newsletter. They had to mail their reports, but only one of the first three packages arrived and the couple's relationship with the APLQ withered.

Louise Cossette-Trudel gave birth to a baby boy in October 1972, and she and her husband were as happy as any first-time parents, but there was no escaping their shabby surroundings or meagre social lives. A week after the baby was born, the authorities moved all the Quebeckers from the Hotel Deauville to Hotel Nacional, which was full of Latin American exiles. The Nacional had a large, lovely garden and faced the sea, but the Cossette-Trudels' room was small and cramped. On their first night, they discovered cockroaches and they had to learn to live with these unpleasant creatures. They spent many days pacing in the lobby or strolling in the garden, they exchanged pleasantries with the other exiles and made friends with a woman from France and her Colombian husband—Guitemie and Oscar—and the two couples enjoyed pleasant evenings together. They created "the illusion of a normal social life," but there was nothing normal about their lives. "Spending nearly four years on a tropical island, close to the sea, moving from hotel to hotel with nothing to do represents, for many people, *la dolce vita*: the dream," Louise wrote. "But who can, in reality, remain inactive for such a long time with no social or material independence?"

In September 1973, the Chilean military overthrew the democratically elected socialist government of Salvador Allende and arrested thousands of Allende supporters, many of whom were tortured or executed. Thousands of others fled, and Cuba granted political asylum to as many as it could accommodate. France was prepared to open its doors as well, according to a report that appeared in *Le Monde*, and the newspaper quoted the French president Valéry Giscard d'Estaing as saying, "France will be a land of asylum as she has always been."

Jacques Lanctôt routinely read *Le Monde* while working at *Granma*, and he read this report with keen interest. "I said to myself: 'If France is ready to welcome Chileans she should be ready to accept some of her little cousins from Quebec,'" as he put it in his memoir. "It was up to me to convince the Cuban officials as well as those in our party who were ready to take this risk and leave." He and his wife, as well as Marc Carbonneau and Yves Langlois, visited the Canadian embassy to inquire about obtaining passports. They met a low-level official who was astonished to see them. Didn't they know that the embassy was Canadian territory? he asked. Didn't they realize they could be detained? Surely Lanctôt, Carbonneau and Langlois knew that there were still warrants outstanding for their arrests. And, no, the government would not issue passports to wanted men. But Suzanne Lanctôt did receive a passport, under which her children could travel, and Carbonneau's partner received one as well.

Later that fall, they met with Manuel Piñeiro from the Cuban Ministry of the Interior. "Since our group was split in two, the commandant respected this humiliating, petty dispute and met us separately," Lanctôt wrote. Piñeiro questioned them at length and was satisfied that they had no intention of returning to Canada surreptitiously, via France, in order to resume their terrorist activities. He told them the government would prepare travel documents for those without passports and his officials would arrange their departure. In the meantime, they should stay close to the hotel and await further word. Lanctôt and Langlois resigned their positions at *Granma* and then the exiles waited—for months as it turned out.

At last, Lanctôt and his family, Marc Carbonneau and his partner, who was pregnant, and Yves Langlois left Havana on June 18, 1974. The Cubans had provided documents, as promised, for those without passports and had given each of them the equivalent of two hundred to three hundred dollars to cover initial expenses. They flew to Prague with the Cuban national airline, spent a night in the Czech capital and then transferred to Air France for the flight to Paris. Arriving on the evening of June 20, the group cleared customs and, as Lanctôt later put it, they walked out of Charles de Gaulle Airport "free as the air in the Parisian night."

Six weeks later, on July 30, the Cossette-Trudels left Cuba as well. They had their young son with them, a second child on the way and $150 with which to start afresh in France.

———

Shortly after arriving, the Cossette-Trudels applied for political asylum. They sent their request to the Office français de protection des réfugiés et apatrides (French Office for the Protection of Refugees and Stateless Persons). The other exiles had applied as well, but they were all turned down, which came as an unpleasant surprise. Everyone accepted the decision, except Jacques Lanctôt. He appealed in writing and was granted a hearing. He sat at an oval table with a lawyer at his side and faced a panel of seven or eight officials. Each had a copy of his appeal and some had underlined passages here and there. One of the officials asked Lanctôt what his profession was in Quebec and he blurted out, "A drawer of water."

His inquisitors were perplexed, but recorded his response. Then one said, "Yes, but did you have another profession besides drawer of water?"

And he replied, "Hewer of wood."

One of the presiding officials asked gruffly, "How is it, Mr. Lanctôt, that you affirmed in writing that you had been a French teacher in Quebec then you tell us today that you were at the same time a drawer of water and a hewer of wood?"

"But you don't understand," he replied, "it's a metaphor. . . . I mean to say that I belong to a people who are drawers of water and hewers of wood, a people who do not control their own destiny."

By then, some on the panel were clearly angry and ordered him to answer truthfully. Had he personally experienced discrimination due to his language or opinions? "No," he replied. Had he been prevented from working? To this, he could only respond, "No." The hearing ended and the panel's written decision arrived in the mail several weeks later. His appeal was rejected unanimously and the decision was final. He and the others were allowed to remain in France on visitor's permits, though they had to renew them every three months. They were able to work and rent apartments, but the jobs they found were mostly menial and low-paying and they could not afford to live in desirable neighbourhoods.

Lanctôt and his wife and children spent their first Parisian winter in a small second-floor apartment located in a working-class district, where they shared a washroom and its squat toilet with another family. They used public baths until they purchased a portable shower stall that could be mounted and attached to the faucet in the kitchen sink and afterward folded and put away. The Cossette-Trudels and their two-year-old son and newborn daughter landed in a cold, drafty, two-room attic apartment. The power frequently went out, the landlord turned on the heat only two or three times a day and then only for half an hour at a time, and the temperature at night sometimes dropped to ten degrees Celsius.

In the summer of 1975, both families found better lodgings, relatively speaking, in La Cité des 4000—a massive complex of low- and high-rise apartment blocks with all the elegance of Stalinist architecture. La Cité des 4000 was located in the northern suburb of La Corneuve, some ten kilometres from the centre of Paris. Jacques Cossette-Trudel worked as a desk clerk at a low-end hotel that catered to North African migrant workers, and later as a milling machine operator in a small workshop.

Lanctôt also started as a clerk at a nondescript hotel, but loathed the owners, a wealthy couple who treated their employees poorly and paid paltry wages. He took a government-sponsored bookkeeping course while working at the hotel and afterward landed a job with an employment agency. But Lanctôt remained a militant at heart. He immersed himself in the Latin American liberation movements that were waging their struggles from Paris. He attended meetings, translated documents from Spanish to French, printed and produced them in the living room of the family apartment and travelled all over the city to distribute such literature.

Louise Cossette-Trudel worked in the records department at the same employment agency as her brother. She became a union representative and was compelled to listen to the endless, mostly petty complaints of her fellow employees. She joined a Marxist-Leninist organization, served on several committees and pursued the cause with vigour.

They could keep themselves busy—holding down day jobs, raising their children and supporting their causes—but the Quebeckers remained outsiders. "What instability we experienced in France," Louise Cossette-Trudel wrote. "One foot in the day-to-day reality and the rest lost in a thick, nebulous cloud. . . . Exile was like a life sentence that reduced your vision and prevented you from advancing. . . . Not a day went by, not a minute without my thinking that tomorrow I would bid it adieu." She could see the Eiffel Tower from the balcony of their fifteenth-floor apartment, but the view only reminded her of the drabness of their surroundings. The buildings of La Cité des 4000 were poorly maintained. Elevators sometimes reeked of urine. Lobbies and corridors were dirty and the dirtiness seemed to seep into their apartment, which they had furnished, in part, with goods left behind by tenants who were moving out.

By the fall of 1977, Louise wanted to go home, but the couple's departure did not happen quickly. Jacques and Louise fought over the issue, he fearing they could be sent to prison—perhaps for ten years, maybe life. Maybe, he reasoned, they'd be better off staying in France. She was adamant. Times had changed. The FLQ was dead and they had renounced terrorism. The Parti Québécois was now in power, having won the provincial election of November 15, 1976. She wrote to Premier René Lévesque and his justice minister, Marc-André Bédard, and pleaded with them to stay the charges against them. Neither promised anything.

In December 1977, the Cossette-Trudels sent a long letter to *Le Devoir*, which the newspaper published on January 3, 1978. The couple maintained that they had paid dearly for their actions. They had endured seven years of exile. Furthermore, the press had defamed them and public figures had smeared them. "The trial with which we are threatened, sometimes from Ottawa, sometimes from Quebec we have already endured a hundred times since December 3, 1970, when the federal Cabinet expelled us," they wrote. "One hundred times accused, one hundred times summarily judged, one hundred times condemned by the political powers that be."

Early in April 1978, they granted an interview to Denise Bombardier of Radio-Canada, who was in France covering an election. They told her that they had paid their debt to society and repeated their appeal for clemency. The interview was broadcast across Quebec, but it won them little or no favour. There was no chance that they could avoid being prosecuted, Justice Minister Bédard declared. Left-wing militants and activists had no interest in taking up their cause. Such groups were focused on winning the release of the ex-*felquistes* doing hard time in federal penitentiaries.

Eleven former FLQ terrorists were behind bars in the spring of 1978, including François Schirm, who was convicted of murder in the August 1964 shootout at International Firearms and was serving a life sentence; Pierre-Paul Geoffroy, the Silver Bell bomber, who was arrested in March 1969 and was serving 124 concurrent life sentences; Robert Hudon, who was serving twenty years for armed robbery; Paul Rose, who was serving life sentences for the kidnapping and murder of Pierre Laporte; Francis Simard, who was serving life sentences for the same offences; Bernard Lortie, who was serving a twenty-year sentence for kidnapping; and Jacques Rose, who was completing an eight-year sentence for being an accessory after the fact of kidnapping.

Schirm, Geoffroy, Lortie and Jacques Rose had all been denied parole. They and others had been denied transfers from maximum to medium security prisons. Most had spent time in solitary confinement. Paul Rose had done more than one stint in solitary and he began another on March 25, 1976, along with four other ex-*felquistes*—all of them locked up in the segregation unit at St-Vincent-de-Paul Penitentiary for refusing work assignments and protesting conditions in the prison.

St-Vincent-de-Paul was an old and forbidding place, built in the 1870s, with high stone walls around the yard and grim cell blocks that reflected a nineteenth-century approach to crime and punishment. The tomb-like segregation cells were five feet wide by eight feet long and windowless. The doors were solid iron except for a four-inch porthole with a sliding cover that could only be lifted from the outside. Inmates were allowed an hour of exercise a day in a courtyard where they could pace twenty-five feet from side to side or fifty feet end to end. Otherwise, they were locked up in maddening isolation, though they could communicate with one another by shouting through the narrow, rectangular vents above the doors.

Rose and the others remained in solitary until March 4, 1977—a few days short of a year—but they were not forgotten. Lawyers Robert Lemieux and Pierre Cloutier, comedian Yvon Deschamps and Mrs. Rose Rose had formed the Comité d'information sur les prisonniers politiques (CIPP) to rally support. In their first communiqué, the committee demanded that the "federal-colonial" authorities end "their constant and vexatious discrimination against the Quebec political prisoners . . . who have rotted too long in the foul Canadian prisons which are polluting the territory of Quebec." Labour leaders, artists and intellectuals as well as rank and file members of the Parti Québécois heeded this call to arms. Unions contributed to a legal defence fund. Sculptors, painters and writers donated works for fundraising auctions. And Parti Québécois riding associations in the counties of Prévost and Roberval passed resolutions demanding the immediate release of all those ex-*felquistes* who were eligible for parole.

The CIPP launched Opération Libération in March 1977 and circulated a petition calling for "the immediate liberation without conditions of all political prisoners detained in federal penitentiaries." Fifty thousand Quebeckers signed it, including two PQ members of the National Assembly, Gérald Godin and Guy Bisaillon. In March 1978, *Le Devoir* published a full-page petition signed by four hundred people—professors, union leaders, lawyers, singers and writers, among others. They too demanded the release of the prisoners "in the name of justice and history."

Bernard Lortie was freed in January 1978, Jacques Rose in July and François Schirm by the year's end. Paul Rose applied for day parole in

November 1978. Having been admitted to a third-year sociology program at UQAM, he planned to live in a halfway house and had the support of friends and family. But he was turned down and would spend four more years behind bars, along with Francis Simard and Pierre-Paul Geoffroy.

Jacques and Louise Cossette-Trudel returned to Montreal on Wednesday, December 13, 1978, amid a blaze of publicity. Both were thirty-one years old. Their son Alexis was six, their daughter Marie-Ange four. The couple flew home aboard an Air Canada Boeing 747. There were fifteen journalists among the 110 passengers. The Cossette-Trudels and their children had a whole section to themselves and two officers from the Sûreté du Québec kept the media representatives well away. The flight landed shortly after noon at Mirabel Airport amid a heavy early-winter snowstorm. The other passengers exited, after which two members of the Montreal Police Department boarded and arrested the couple and charged them with kidnapping, forcible confinement, assault and possession of an illegal firearm.

A throng of reporters, photographers and TV cameramen waited anxiously in the terminal. Three members of the Rhinoceros Party, one with a snare drum, another with an accordion and a third with a trombone, hovered alongside the media, hoping to serenade the couple when they entered. But police escorted the Cossette-Trudels straight from the aircraft to an unmarked RCMP vehicle parked on the tarmac. Their journey ended at a Montreal police station, where they were interrogated briefly and then allowed to meet their families and have lunch. "They ate their first club sandwich in eight years and they asked for lots of gravy on the fries," their lawyer Serge Ménard told reporters as he left the station. The Cossette-Trudels dined on jailhouse food over the weekend but were released on fifty thousand dollars' bail apiece in time to spend Christmas with their families.

Jacques Lanctôt, his wife Suzanne and their three children—Boris,

ten, Olga, eight, and eleven-month-old Agathe—returned to Montreal
on January 6, 1979, and an even bigger media mob awaited them at
Mirabel. But the journalists caught only a glimpse of the thirty-three-
year-old Lanctôt and some were struck by how much he had changed.
"Most Quebeckers remember Lanctôt as a young man whose picture
appeared on a police-wanted poster that hung in post offices across
the province in the fall of 1970," Steve Kowch of the *Gazette* wrote. "The
boyish image of the 1970 picture no longer exists. Instead, he looks
drawn. There are bags under his eyes, and a thick bushy moustache and
a different hairstyle have changed his appearance drastically." Lanctôt
was released under the same terms as his sister and brother-in-law, and
he went to work as an editorial assistant at VLB éditeur, the publishing
house of writer and editor Victor Lévy-Beaulieu.

The Cossette-Trudels appeared in court on May 31 and pleaded guilty
to all the charges against them. Defence attorney Ménard addressed
Judge Yves Mayrand for four hours. He argued against sending the
couple to jail and suggested that they should be ordered to perform
community service. Prosecutor Jean-Pierre Bonin called for stiff prison
terms so that "the people of Quebec and other countries will know that
in Canada we protect diplomats." Mayrand reserved his decision, noting
that he needed time to reflect. There were few precedents to guide him
and, besides, this was a closely watched trial. "History looks down on
us," he told those present in the court, "and we cannot disappoint it."

He rendered his decision on August 7. The hearing was held in the
largest courtroom at the Palais de Justice, where some two hundred
onlookers and fifty journalists filled the public galleries. The Cossette-
Trudels were photographed entering the courthouse, and they were
well dressed and neatly groomed and could have passed for a young
middle-class couple on their way to the office. Mayrand reminded all in
attendance that the two former *felquistes* had committed "particularly
heinous crimes." Had they been arrested in 1970, they would have been
sent to prison for eight to ten years. "It should not be forgotten," he continued, "that it was under the threat of killing their hostage that they

obtained their freedom and safe conduct to another country." Any kidnapping was a grave crime, the judge said, but the abduction of a foreign diplomat was even worse. "Their crime amounted to a violation of international law," he said. "Terrorist activities are crimes detrimental to human rights and fundamental freedoms and when committed against diplomats are detrimental to the good relations between states."

On the other hand, the Cossette-Trudels had spent eight years in exile and that was a form of punishment. They had endured "insecurity, anguish, sorrow and anxiety as to their future and that of their children." And there were other mitigating factors. "We must admit," Mayrand noted, "that within Jacques Lanctôt's group, the two accused played a less important role than the other members and that they were the first to disavow publicly their actions and to renounce all violence as a means of action." He sentenced the couple to two years less a day in jail, followed by three years' probation—a decision deemed wise and prudent by Jean-Claude Leclerc, an editorial writer for *Le Devoir*, who concluded that "Between an excessively severe sentence and a pardon, which would have been scandalous, Judge Mayrand has—with clarity and consideration—found a solution that was equitable for the accused and credible to the public."

Mayrand presided over Jacques Lanctôt's trial as well, on November 7, 1979. Lanctôt was charged with four offences—conspiracy, kidnapping, forcible confinement and attempted extortion—and pleaded guilty to all of them. His lawyers, Robert Lemieux and Claude Lebeau, argued for a suspended sentence, but the Cossette-Trudel precedent, Lanctôt's record and his defiance before the court precluded such a favourable outcome. "I am not a criminal," Lanctôt told Mayrand. "I never derived any benefit from my political involvement. On the contrary. But what is expected of me? That I acknowledge my so-called error, that I admit I am repentant and that I state loud and clear without lowering my eyes that I regret everything, as others have done before me? If I did so, I would be betraying the noble cause for which I sacrificed everything."

Then the judge spoke. The evidence showed that Lanctôt had been the leader of the Liberation Cell. The record showed that he had a criminal record for three firebombings in the summer of 1963, when he was only seventeen, and that he had spent several months behind bars. Furthermore, he had been a participant in one violent disturbance— the 1968 St. Jean Baptiste Day riot—and had been a lead organizer and agitator in the October 1969 taxi riot. And he had shown by his words and his courtroom conduct that he was unrepentant. "A crime remains a crime regardless of the nobility of the cause invoked to justify it," Mayrand said, and he sentenced Lanctôt to three years in prison followed by three years' probation.

The CIPP and its supporters came to loathe the National Parole Board, and they denounced it at every opportunity. In one of their publications, they referred to this federal institution as "a despotic and tyrannical organization" and went on to explain how unfairly it treated imprisoned *felquistes*. "When the political prisoners become eligible for unescorted temporary absences, the board—in order to justify its refusal—invokes the fact that they haven't benefitted from escorted temporary absences.

"Then, at the moment when they become eligible for day parole, the board tells them they have spent too much time in maximum security penitentiaries and that they will have to spend time in medium or minimum security institutions.

"Finally, when they become eligible for full parole, they tell them that they must first be released on day parole. And after each refusal, the board says that the *felquistes* are not the object of more severe treatment than other inmates and that they are subject to the same criterion as others serving identical sentences."

The parole board's power over an inmate serving a fixed sentence was limited. Such an inmate could do his or her time and leave without applying for parole. But the board wielded absolute power over those who were in for life. Those inmates could be released only with the blessing of the parole board, and that applied to Paul Rose, Francis Simard and Pierre-Paul Geoffroy. In the spring of 1980, the CIPP launched a fresh campaign to win public support for the three prisoners and to pressure the board. The campaign began with back-to-back Evenings of Solidarity, the first held on April 14 at the Théatre Outremont in Montreal and the second two nights later at the Palais Montcalm in Quebec City. Gilles Vigneault, Pauline Julien, Paul Piché and nearly a dozen other prominent Quebec singers and musicians performed on behalf of the imprisoned *felquistes*.

Many of the same artists, as well as a number of prominent activists, appeared at a third evening of speeches and song on October 18, 1980, marking the tenth anniversary of the proclamation of the War Measures Act. This commemorative event was held in the gymnasium of the CEGEP Vieux Montréal, and the crowd of three thousand repeatedly chanted the FLQ slogan *"Nous Vaincrons!"* (We Will Win!) Jacques Rose announced that he had just returned from a trip to communities along the North Shore and the Saguenay–Lac-Saint-Jean region, where he had collected sixty-five thousand signatures on another CIPP petition calling for "the immediate release without conditions of all the Québécois political prisoners and a general amnesty for all those who remain in prison, on parole or burdened with a record and amnesty for those who remain in exile."

Geoffroy had appeared before the board in the summer of 1980. He was, by then, detained in the medium security Cowansville Institution and convinced his inquisitors that he was no longer a danger to society, and the board granted day parole. Rose, who was also incarcerated at Cowansville, made another appearance before the board that fall, but the board refused to grant him either full or day parole. "We have not detected any significant change in his attitude," the commissioners stated in their written decision. "His perception of his actions remains nearly unchanged after ten years. His analysis is marked by rationalization and intellectualization. His introspection is limited . . . and, finally, he demonstrates great difficulty assuming individual responsibility. The absence of change leads us to believe that the inmate is the same man and has shown himself capable of committing the same offences for which he has been convicted."

The board informed Rose that he would be eligible for day parole on December 15, 1981, and for full parole one year later. His supporters were outraged. Lawyers Robert Lemieux and Claude Lebeau held a press conference to denounce the commissioners. Lemieux appeared before the Federal Court of Canada twice in February 1981, first to argue that the board's decision should be overturned. Then he appealed for the release of reports prepared by two parole officers supporting Rose's bid for freedom.

Two dozen prominent labour leaders, defence lawyers, academics and artists formed the Comité pour la libération de Paul Rose. Jacques Rose was the most persistent advocate. In early December 1981, one week before his brother's next parole hearing, he appeared at a national convention of the Parti Québécois. He stood in a crowded hall and presented a motion urging the PQ government to pressure federal authorities to free his brother and the other imprisoned FLQ terrorists. "Not only did Mr. Rose get the vote of support for which he had long lobbied," Lise Bissonnette wrote in *Le Devoir*, ". . . but he was enthusiastically applauded by the crowd during his appearance at the microphone."

Rose was released on day parole in early 1982. He was thirty-eight years old and his father and mother had died while he was in prison. He enrolled in a third-year sociology program at UQAM and taught part. time at a small alternative school in Longueuil. Upon being granted full parole in December 1982, he left immediately with a group of friends for the Beauce region, south of Quebec City, without issuing any public statements. However, his girlfriend Andrée Bergeron, whom he had met through a prison volunteer program, told a journalist, "After twelve years in prison, he wants to get away from it all and celebrate a Québécois Christmas."

Francis Simard had been released on parole in March 1982 and he too left without granting interviews. That fall, however, his unapologetic account of the kidnapping and murder of Pierre Laporte—*Pour en finir avec octobre*—was published. An English version appeared later under the title *Talking It Out: The October Crisis from Inside*. Simard dedicated the book to Michel Viger, who had harboured him and the Rose brothers in December 1970, and for that was sentenced to eight years in prison. In the final pages of his book, Simard wrote, "If they wanted to make me change my mind by throwing me in prison, they really blew it."

Marc Carbonneau returned from France in May 1981, and Yves Langlois in June 1982. Both men arrived at Mirabel Airport; both were immediately arrested and charged with conspiracy, kidnapping, forcible confinement and extortion; and both pleaded guilty to all charges, Carbonneau at his one-day trial on May 23, 1982, and Langlois on September 28 of that same year.

Carbonneau had worked as an apartment handyman while in exile in Paris. He had plastered and painted, installed carpets and repaired sinks and toilets, among other things. Langlois had trained as a nurse's aide and then landed a position with the French Red Cross. He had also volunteered at a South Shore senior citizen's centre in the few weeks between his return and his trial.

Judge Yves Mayrand presided over the trials of both men. He concluded that Carbonneau had been a marginal figure in the kidnapping and he took a sympathetic view of him. "Marc Carbonneau was the only member of the group who was a real worker and who had actually experienced the social inequalities he had fought for several years," Mayrand said. He cited Carbonneau's involvement with the Mouvement de libération du taxi and his efforts to improve the lot of his fellow drivers. "He followed the democratic processes," Mayrand continued. "He knocked on doors in vain. His misfortune was that of a man who sincerely tried but had lost hope in achieving social change by traditional methods.

"I am convinced that Marc Carbonneau has suffered more than the others and that his experience has been sadder and had nothing of the adventure or the glorious crusade of which certain young idealists dream."

Mayrand noted that Carbonneau was approaching fifty and would have a difficult time rebuilding his life and therefore imposed a sentence of twenty months in jail followed by 150 hours of community service.

Mayrand sentenced the thirty-four-year-old Langlois to two years less a day followed by community service. Judge Mayrand had presided over the trials of all the kidnappers of James Cross, and many Montrealers thought he was far too lenient. The judge responded to their criticism at the conclusion of Langlois's trial. "I have opted for moderation and balance, giving weight to understanding and hope rather than rancour and vengeance," he told the court. "We have decided to have confidence in the accused. We have taken a calculated risk with them. Until now, they have responded positively and have been successfully reintegrated into their communities. Now that we can turn the page on these historic events, we continue to believe that this was the best approach to take."

Fifteen

WHAT BECAME OF THEM?

THERE THEY WERE, BROTHER AND sister, right there on the front page of *Le Devoir*, Louise (now Lanctôt, not Cossette-Trudel) and Jacques, clean shaven, balding, his face fuller and heavier than it had been in January 1979 when he stepped off the plane at Mirabel and surrendered to Canadian authorities. The *Le Devoir* story appeared on May 5, 1984. By then, Lanctôt and his sister and all the other former *felquistes* had served their sentences or been paroled or had returned from exile, and a remarkable number of them had spent time in prison or self-imposed isolation abroad.

Eighty-three militants and twenty-three sympathizers had been convicted of criminal offences—bombings, bank robberies, murders and kidnappings being the most serious—and they had spent a cumulative total of 282 years behind bars. Those who had chosen exile had spent a total of 134 years in Cuba or France or Algeria. And afterward, *Le Devoir*'s Nathalie Petrowski wrote, they had disappeared without a trace. "How can you give body and soul, day and night to a cause—independence, Marxism, class struggle, feminism, armed struggle—how can you revolt, plant bombs, rob banks . . . then suddenly abandon everything?" she asked. "Militancy is, above all, a way of life, a state of mind, a romantic ideal, a philosophy that wants to remake the world. And when the world refuses, society does not follow, what happens?

"What do you do with your life?"

Jacques Lanctôt, then thirty-eight, was working long hours as the proprietor of the publishing house VLB éditeur, writing a novel and, on nights off, going to the movies or the theatre. "This is no longer the time or the place for militancy," he told Petrowski. "There are no longer big movements, nor journals like *Parti-Pris* to create serious debate. Quebec has become a leisurely society."

His sister Louise, two years younger, was employed in the Health Records Centre at the Université de Montréal. She had published her memoir, *Une sorcière comme les autres*, in the fall of 1981, held a press conference upon publication and then fallen from view. She no longer wanted anything to do with her brother or "the fallen heroes of the revolution," as she put it. In her youth, she had dreamt of revolutionary glory. "I wanted to smash in the doors," she said. "But I made myself sick. Militancy is a false vision of reality. . . . Militants marginalize themselves and have a limited view of things. It is necessary to be in the middle of things to change society."

Other ex-*felquistes* hadn't adjusted quite as well. Petrowski met Pierre-Paul Geoffroy at an art gallery that displayed paintings produced by inmates. They shook hands. His hand was sweaty and he wore the expression of a wounded man. "When you're eighteen," he said, "you have an ideal and after that it's a straight line to get there. Nothing can stop you. You revolt, you reject all forms of authority and you settle accounts with society." He had been the FLQ's most prolific and dangerous bomber. He could handle a bomb but not the daily degradation and violence of prison. Prison had destroyed his youthful recklessness. He had scarcely left the halfway house where he resided for a year or so after being paroled. "Outside, you're supposed to be free except that you don't know what to do with your freedom," he said. "You're frightened. Everything moves too fast. You no longer have confidence in yourself."

Charles Gagnon, one of the intellectual firebrands who had inspired Geoffroy and others, was forty-five and living with friends when Petrowski met him. He had no home, no family, no children. Gagnon had spent the better part of five years in jail or out on bail, fighting one charge or another. He and his collaborator, Pierre Vallières, were arrested outside the United Nations building in New York in September 1966 and charged with murder in connection with the death of Thérèse Morin, the sixty-four-year-old secretary who died in the LaGrenade Shoe Company bombing. Gagnon and Vallières were among the first persons arrested under the War Measures Act and they spent eight months in jail—charged with seditious conspiracy, among other things.

When his legal travails were behind him, Gagnon changed directions. He recognized that Quebeckers would never support FLQ-style violence, but he remained committed to independence and socialism. In 1972, he founded En Lutte!, a pan-Canadian, Marxist-Leninist organization that promoted a worker-led revolution. En Lutte!, or In Struggle!, published a bi-monthly journal called *En Lutte!*, as well as pamphlets and brochures. It also ran small bookstores in Montreal, Quebec City, Toronto and Vancouver, and organized conferences and debates. Membership peaked at four hundred and the annual budget grew to eight hundred thousand dollars.

Gagnon served as secretary general until the organization folded in 1982. Afterward, he spent several months in Mexico before returning to Montreal, where he pursued a doctorate in political science at UQAM. But he ran out of money and was ineligible for bursaries, his supervisor rejected his thesis and his dream of an academic career evaporated. "Once, everything seemed possible," he told Petrowski. "There were certainties, like capitalism would collapse under the weight of its contradictions. Today, no one dares affirm that seriously." He had learned some hard lessons. "You invest fifteen to eighteen hours a day for several years in social causes and you take account afterward and you have nothing," he added. "I still have the inclination to rebel and struggle except that, with age, one becomes less naive and more prudent."

Gagnon died on November 17, 2005, at the age of sixty-six and a tribute held in his honour the following March drew three hundred people. He was celebrated as an "indomitable dissident," an "incorrigible and doctrinaire Marxist" and an "activist and thinker who never renounced his convictions."

His former friend and collaborator—Pierre Vallières—was less steadfast. Vallières had once been Quebec's angry young man. He had loathed the stodgy, church-dominated society of his youth, and the Quiet Revolution proved too quiet for him. He had embraced the violent path of the FLQ. He had unleashed all his pent-up rage in *Nègres blancs d'Amérique*, and his book had inspired others to turn to violence. He had adhered to his belief in violent revolution through the years he spent in prison awaiting trial, defending himself or appealing his convictions. In October 1970, he had been ready to lead college and university students out of their classrooms and into the streets until the War Measures Act was proclaimed.

Vallières was detained until late June 1971. He was released on a promise to appear, but promptly disappeared and skipped court dates. The remnants of the radical left expected he would emerge rejuvenated and revive the FLQ. Instead, he published a long essay in *Le Devoir* in December 1971, in which he rejected terror and announced that he was joining the Parti Québécois. His admirers felt betrayed. Gagnon repudiated him and their friendship ended. "It was a hard thing for me to break with the FLQ," Vallières later told an interviewer. "It had been my life for such a long time. It was like breaking away from a passion."

But Vallières did break with his past. He worked briefly on a federally funded Local Initiatives Project in Mont-Laurier, a town in the Laurentians, 150 kilometres north of Montreal, and he continued to write, publishing six works of non-fiction in the space of a decade.

When *Le Devoir*'s Petrowski caught up with him, Vallières was forty-six. He suffered from arteriosclerosis, he had quit smoking, his shoulder-length hair was greying and, several years earlier, he had accepted that he was gay. They met at a bar in Montreal's gay village at the east end of Ste-Catherine Street. "Nothing has changed," he assured her. "I continue to be detached, an outsider, on the margins. That is my only constant." He no longer had any faith in politics or political parties or terrorism. "You can plant bombs everywhere but such violence is laughable against the violence of the powerful," he said. "It [terrorism] is the violence of the desperate and the powerless."

Vallières suffered a major heart attack in early December 1998, his second in less than two years. He lapsed into a coma, never recovered, and died at age sixty, two days before Christmas. He had fought for gay rights, women's rights, respect for Indigenous people and the environment, and friends and admirers praised him as a man of courage and compassion driven by a hatred of injustice.

Jacques Cossette-Trudel discussed his life with an interviewer on October 5, 1985—the fifteenth anniversary of the day he and his comrades kidnapped James Cross. He was thirty-seven and living in ritzy Outremont on the northern flanks of Mount Royal. Robert Bourassa, Jérôme Choquette and Claude Ryan all resided there as well. "I see them in the street sometimes," he told *The Globe and Mail*'s Richard Cléroux. "They do their best to avoid me."

"I've kept all my ideals," he continued. "I have remained a Communist. I still believe nothing will change without violence. But after you've said that what then? Well, you have to live so you go out and work."

He had landed a job as an information officer in the City of Montreal's social services department after being released from prison early in 1980. He and his wife Louise had split up, but shared custody of their two children. Cossette-Trudel no longer associated with his former comrades and later wrote a long, unflattering essay that appeared in the October 1990 issue of the literary review *Liberté*. He portrayed some of his fellow kidnappers as egotistical and deluded. "The months preceding the October Crisis had been the unacknowledged theatre of hot struggles for hegemony within the FLQ," he wrote. "The kidnapping of Cross and the Chénier Cell's treacherous blow were, in the end, just the ultimate manifestations of the secret wrestling match between Jacques Lanctôt and Paul Rose who, since the fall of 1969, had been the unchallenged cocks of the walk within the FLQ." Furthermore, he stated, they had all held to the misguided belief that "a colonized people, seeing its youth move to action, would be swept up in liberating imitation."

Cossette-Trudel displayed a remarkably cavalier attitude toward the two men taken hostage. "As for the British diplomat sequestered by the Liberation Cell, his greatest misfortune was doubtless to miss the bridge game planned for the evening of October 5 and to eat Quebec food for 59 days. Eat shepherd's pie for 59 days. My Lord!" Cossette-Trudel confessed to having wept secretly on the night that Pierre Laporte was murdered. "Not for the death of Laporte . . . but for lost innocence," he said. "The great Quebec party, begun in 1960, was ending. There was nothing more for the *felquistes* to do except disappear. . . ."

Some of the kidnappers lived quietly and guarded their privacy. They granted no interviews, even when reporters from *La Presse* managed to locate them on the twentieth anniversary of the abductions. Jacques Rose was living in the Laurentians and renovating homes. Marc Carbonneau resided in Montreal and worked as a handyman and renovator "when he is not on his sailboat, which is moored in Halifax," *La Presse* reported. Yves Langlois was described as very private and working in a Montreal hospital. Bernard Lortie had gone his own way and had little or no contact with the ex-*felquistes* and was said to be a small farmer who grew produce and raised poultry.

On the other hand, Paul Rose granted a long interview to journalist Ann Charney not long after his release, and her glowing profile ran in the February 1984 issue of *Saturday Night* magazine. Rose had enrolled at UQAM and had put his organizational skills to work on behalf of the patients at a long-term care facility in the city's east end. He and several fellow students had received a forty-thousand-dollar provincial grant and had used it to build gardens raised to a level that would allow those in wheelchairs to work the soil.

"Paul is a real miracle worker," said Françoise Perrault, a sixty-eight-year-old woman who suffered from severe arthritis. "He can motivate people whom no one has been able to reach for years. . . . He's always gentle, always smiling. We're lucky to have him." Annie Dubé, an occupational therapist, similarly noted, "When I look at what Paul is doing here I find it hard not to admire him. His gentleness, his kindness and his sensitivity are truly remarkable."

Rose later pursued a doctorate in sociology and economics at the Université du Québec à Rimouski and taught at the institution. He worked as an organizer for the Montreal central council of the Confederation of National Trade Unions. He married; had two children, a son Felix and a daughter Rosalie; contributed occasionally to *L'aut'journal* (*The Other Journal*); and in 1994 tried to run for a seat in the National Assembly.

Rose was president of the provincial New Democratic Party. He entered the race as the party's candidate in the Longueuil constituency of Marie-Victorin, and his brother Jacques ran in Iberville, another South Shore riding. Both Roses were unsuccessful. Jacques received 645 votes—1.79 percent of those cast—and finished fifth in a field of six. Paul never made it onto the ballot. Quebec's election law stipulated that anyone sentenced to two years or more in prison could only become a member of the Assembly after their sentence had expired. Paul was serving two life sentences and would never be eligible to hold a seat, and the chief electoral officer Pierre F. Côté disqualified him.

If Rose was disappointed, he kept it to himself and worked with his customary energy on behalf of other candidates. *Le Devoir*'s Sylvain Blanchard accompanied him on a round of door-knocking and the two chatted amiably. "I regret nothing," Rose said. "Not 1970, not the kidnappings, prison, the suffering, nothing. I did what I did. Faced with the same circumstances today, I would do exactly the same thing. It was not an error of youth."

"A man has been dead for twenty-four years," Blanchard said.

"Pierre Laporte died because of the War Measures Act," Rose replied. "Without that law he would still be alive."

Rose died on March 14, 2013, at age sixty-nine after suffering a stroke, and Francis Simard passed suddenly from a ruptured abdominal artery on January 10, 2015, at age sixty-seven. He too was unrepentant to the end. "There were four of us involved and we were all responsible for what happened and it was not an accident," Simard told one interviewer. "What counts is why. You don't kidnap a man for nothing."

"I would never boast about October 1970," he said on another occasion, "but we wanted to make a revolution and I'm proud of that."

Simard never held a regular job or pursued a career. He had two daughters, Renée-Louise and Émilie, with his first partner. His second, Béatrice Richard, was a Paris-born journalist, military historian and member of the faculty at the Royal Military College in Saint-Jean. Simard assisted with her research when he wasn't absorbed with his own projects and interests. He acquired an extraordinary collection of Québécois literary and historical works and became renowned among friends and associates for his deep and extensive reading of Quebec history.

Simard collaborated on the production of two feature films with the director and screenwriter Pierre Falardeau, a militant separatist who became one of his closest friends. Simard wrote the script for *Le Party*, a 1989 prison drama about an escape that occurs during a social event. He and Falardeau wrote the screenplay for a fictionalized account of the kidnapping crisis, as seen from the perspective of the Chénier Cell. The film, simply called *Octobre*, was co-produced by the National Film Board and released in 1994.

James Cross returned to England after he was released, and in 1971 the Queen made him a Companion of the Most Distinguished Order of St. Michael and St. George. He held a number of senior positions in the British civil service, but never again worked abroad. When he retired in 1980, he was undersecretary, principal establishment officer, with the Department of Energy, a position equivalent to that of a deputy minister in the Canadian federal government.

Cross turned down all requests for interviews on the tenth anniversary of the October Crisis, and was no more receptive when *The Globe and Mail's* London correspondent, John Fraser, tracked him down in October 1985. He was living in Lymington, a coastal town in Hampshire, in the south of England, and greeted Fraser, rather coolly, on his doorstep. "Good Lord, not this business again," he said. "Surely you people can supply all the words for me just as well as I can. I mean, you do it all the time anyway."

Cross had visited Canada in 1981 to see old friends and colleagues, and he returned in 1990 to participate in two TV programs about the kidnapping crisis. He paid a third visit in 1995 at the invitation of the family of Pierre Laporte, and he attended a twenty-fifth anniversary memorial Mass. Cross never forgot the ordeal he had endured, nor did he forgive his abductors. "I don't think about it every day," he told an interviewer in 2010, "but it comes back to me when I hear about other situations where people have been taken hostage or deprived of their liberty." As of this writing, he was in his mid-nineties and still living in the south of England.

Jacques Lanctôt was in his early seventies at the time of writing, but had not settled into a serene and contented old age. *"Il est sans le sous, et vit pauvrement,"* a friend of long standing confides. He is broke and living in poverty—and this after a long and distinguished career as a publisher. Lanctôt acquired VLB éditeur in 1984 and ran it for nearly a decade before selling to Groupe Sogides Inc., a division of Quebecor Media. He had a falling-out with his new corporate overseers and in 1996 left to form his own publishing house, Lanctôt éditeur, mortgaging his Outremont condo to finance it.

Lanctôt published dozens of writers and over seven hundred titles. He launched the career of Dany Laferrière, the Haitian-born novelist, essayist and poet who in 2013 became only the second black person and one of the few non-French citizens elected to the Académie française, the nearly four-hundred-year-old institution charged with protecting the sanctity of the French language. He published a biography of Lucien Bouchard written by the late Michel Vastel, as well as one hundred volumes of a historical series entitled Études québécois (Quebec Studies) under the direction of Robert Comeau.

However, the publishing house he founded in his own name failed to generate sufficient revenues to cover Lanctôt's debts and other obligations, and in 2005 he sold it. One year later, he unloaded his condo, and with the proceeds he purchased a triplex in the Plateau-Mont-Royal district. He fulfilled a long-time dream and opened a bookstore-café, which he called Utopia, after a phrase from Victor Hugo—"Utopia today is reality tomorrow"—but that venture failed after six months.

He resurfaced in September 2007 as the author of a blog that appears several times a month on the Quebecor-owned website www.canoe.ca. Lanctôt had yearned for a public podium ever since the broadcast of the Liberation Cell's manifesto during the October Crisis, but acknowledged in his opening piece, "This opportunity has come along at a very sad moment in my life." He then went on to share with readers all the misfortune that had befallen him in recent years before ending on a happier note. "But, I should say that life has been good to me, despite all the vagaries and surprises," he wrote. "Imagine, four marriages, three divorces, eight children [since grown to nine] and multiple moves."

Acknowledgements

I first met Robert Côté several years ago while researching a magazine article on the October Crisis. Robert was open, generous and possessed of a remarkable memory and equally remarkable stories from his days as head of the Montreal Police Department's bomb squad. He was just as generous when I began this book. He opened his personal archive of police reports, books and government documents and chauffeured me around Montreal pointing out where bombings had occurred and where the hostages had been held. He also introduced me to fellow officers who shared their memories and, in some cases, their documents. It is thanks to them that I came to appreciate the scale and scope of terrorism that this country endured at the hands of the FLQ. Thanks also to Robert Demers, who shared his memories of the failed negotiations with Robert Lemieux.

I would like to thank family and friends who encouraged me throughout by reading all or parts of the manuscript, including my wife Hélène, sister-in-law Luanne Larose, Steve Hopkins and Gordon Pavey.

Every writer needs an editor and I am fortunate to have a very good one in Tim Rostron.

Thanks also to Amy Black, Publisher of the Doubleday Canada Publishing Group, for her support and copy editor Tara Tovell, who did a great job with a challenging manuscript.

Sources

In preparation for this book I drew on contemporaneous newspaper reports, author interviews, previously unpublished police documents, government reports, works written by former *felquistes,* the memoirs of former police officers, government officials and politicians, and the work of other historians.

I interviewed a number of retired police officers—Robert Côté, Julien Giguère and Gilles Forgue among others—as well as political figures such as the late Jérôme Choquette, his former Quebec Cabinet colleague William Tetley, now also deceased, Marc Lalonde and Robert Demers.

I was able to read police documents, including incident reports, witness statements and confessions. All are now in the hands of collectors who recognized their historical value and rescued them when the Montreal Police Department conducted one of its periodic purges.

A remarkable number of former *felquistes* wrote accounts of their lives and deeds—most notably Pierre Vallières, his collaborator Charles Gagnon, the kidnappers Francis Simard, Jacques Lanctôt and his sister Louise Lanctôt—and I have drawn from these and others.

As for newspapers, I relied mostly on *The Gazette, La Presse* and *Le Devoir,* and to a lesser degree *Montreal-Matin, Le Petit Journal* and *The Montreal Star.*

INTRODUCTION

He was a native of Trois-Rivières . . . Pierre Laporte: *The True Face of Duplessis* (Harvest House Ltd., 1961)

"How do you expect me to follow the rules?" ibid

Ministers rose when he entered the Cabinet room . . . Conrad Black: *Render Unto Caesar: The Life and Legacy of Maurice Duplessis* (Key Porter Books, 1998)

He knew by name party officials . . . ibid

He was firm believer in . . . Dale C. Thompson: *Jean Lesage and the Quiet Revolution* (Macmillan of Canada, 1984)

Roman Catholic clergy were pervasive . . . Black: *Render Unto Caesar*

Autonomy meant opposition to . . . ibid

"I am dangerously well." Laporte: *Duplessis*

"The people deserve this victory." *Le Devoir*, June 23, 1960

The Liberal platform contained . . . Thompson: *Jean Lesage*

They called their movement the Rassemblement . . . Louis Fournier: *F.L.Q.: The Anatomy of an Underground Movement* (NC Press Ltd., 1984)

In the winter of 1962, Lévesque launched . . . Thompson: *Jean Lesage*

"I note one president, seventeen vice-presidents . . ." Graham Fraser: *Sorry I Don't Speak French: Confronting the Canadian Crisis That Won't Go Away* (McClelland & Stewart, 2006)

André Laurendeau, editor of *Le Devoir* . . . *Gazette*, December 8, 1963

But Gordon was an irresistible target . . . *Gazette*, December 12, 1963

CHAPTER ONE

"Young man, if you want to be successful . . ." Robert Côté: *Ma Guerre Contre le FLQ* (Éditions Trait d'Union, 2003)

"During a nocturnal raid . . ." Fournier: *F.L.Q.*

"What bomb squad, lieutenant?" Côté and Plante as quoted in Côté: *Ma Guerre*

He was a big, rotund man with a personality . . . ibid

CHAPTER TWO

Villeneuve was just nineteen . . . Gustave Morf: *Terror in Quebec: Case studies of the FLQ* (Clarke, Irwin & Co., 1970)

Hudon had recently turned twenty-one and . . . ibid

The city was building two . . . Côté: *Ma Guerre*

His name was Georges Schoeters . . . Morf: *Terror in Quebec*

As for Schoeters . . . *La Libra*, January 6, 2013

CHAPTER THREE

The founders and their . . . Claude Savoie: *La Véritable Histoire du FLQ* (Les Éditions du Jour, 1963)

"One can put one's mind at ease . . ." Bernard Smith: *Les Résistants du FLQ* (Les Éditions Actualité, 1963)

"We will look for the Hudons . . ." *La Cognée*, October 1963

In an article . . . *La Cognée*, November 1963

"The pre-revolutionary phase is . . ." *La Cognée*, April 15, 1964

"The blows that the Armée de libération du Québec . . ." *La Cognée*, April 30, 1964

"Each time one of ours is . . ." *La Cognée*, May 31, 1964

CHAPTER FOUR

"Here is the first task . . ." *La Cognée*, July 15, 1964

The ARQ had set up a base camp . . . Fournier: *F.L.Q.*

His name was François Schirm and . . . Morf: *Terror in Quebec*

"These hotheads . . ." *La Cognée*, July 15, 1964

Schirm led his recruits north to . . . Morf: *Terror in Quebec*

Edmond Guénette, 20 . . . ibid

Cyriaque Delisle, 27 and . . . ibid

He was married and . . . ibid

CHAPTER FIVE

They peppered the . . . *La Cognée*, November 30, 1964

"THE MEMBERS OF RIN ARE . . ." *La Cognée*, February 1, 1965

They had a special loathing . . . *La Cognée*, March 1, 1965

Earlier in 1965 . . . *La Cognée*, January 1, 1965

Militants launched three attacks . . . *La Cognée*, June 15, 1965

They had been supplied with . . . *Le Petit Journal*, July 25, 1965

Noël and Bourdon followed a trail . . . ibid

CHAPTER SIX

Henceforth, there would be . . . *La Cognée*, January 3, 1966

Volume one, number one denounced . . . *La Cognée*, University Edition, October 1965

"We are at the root of the attack . . ." *La Cognée*, June 16, 1966

"There was a body in front of . . ." Service de la Police de la Ville de Montréal

Mathieu had been part of a gang . . . Morf: *Terror in Quebec*

By mid-1967 most had been sentenced . . . ibid

Rhéal Mathieu was arrested in October 2000 . . . From the *National Post*, Monday, October 18, 2000, and July 6, 2000

CHAPTER SEVEN

His cell measured five feet by seven . . . Charles Gagnon: *Feu sur l'Amérique: Écrits Politiques (Volume I, 1966–1972)*

He always stood first in his class . . . Gagnon: *Feu sur l'Amérique*

Vallières was the oldest of three boys . . . Pierre Vallières: *Nègres blancs d'Amérique* (English translation, McClelland & Stewart, 1971)

Vallières was an angry young man . . . ibid

Gagnon wrote letters . . . Collected in *Gagnon: Feu sur l'Amérique*

"'This book,' he continued . . ." Vallières: *Nègres blancs*

CHAPTER EIGHT

Lévesque released a six thousand-word manifesto . . . Peter Desbarats: *René: A Canadian in Search of a Country* (McClelland & Stewart, 1976)

It was put to a vote . . . ibid

It was called *La Victoire* . . . Fournier: *F.L.Q.*

Radio-Canada had four reporters on hand . . . Mr. Trudeau is still there . . . *Le Lundi De La Matraque: 24 Juin 1968* (Éditions parti pris, 1968)

Housewife and spectator Monic Cournoyer swore . . . ibid

Raymond Lanteigne, a merchant, attended . . . ibid

A Jesuit priest, Father Jacques Couture . . . ibid

Reggie Chartrand gave a long . . . ibid

"The 24th of June 1968 . . ." ibid

CHAPTER NINE

Detective-Sergeant Robert Côté endured one . . . Côté: *Ma Guerre*

The first bombs in this new wave . . . *Rapport Générale, Service de la police de Montreal, Explosion d'une bombe, Victoria Precision Works, 2901 rue Rouen* and *Rapport Générale . . . Examen sur une scene d'explosion, 20 aout 1968*, by Robert Côté.

Côté observed those three letters . . . *Rapport Générale . . . Explosion et découverte d'explosifs, 8123 Saint-Denis, 8 septembre 1968*, by Robert Côté

The porch was heavily damaged . . . *Rapport Générale . . . Explosion d'une bombe, 916 ouest boul. Gouin, 18 septembre 1968*, by Robert Côté

The bombers launched their November campaign . . . *Rapport Générale . . . Dommages a la Proprieté (Explosion d'une bombe) 4 novembre 1968*, by Robert Côté

He and his fellow officers were lucky . . . *Rapport Générale . . . Explosion d'une bombe, 17 novembre 1968*, by Robert Côté

It comprised eight sticks of dynamite . . . *Rapport Générale . . . Découverte et désamorçage d'une bombe, 5915, boul. Pie IX, 13 décembre 1968*, by Robert Côté

CHAPTER TEN

Côté scarcely noticed any of it, though . . . Côté: *Ma Guerre*

One contained ninety-six sticks of dynamite . . . *Rapport Générale . . . Désamorçage dés trois bombes et saisies d'explosifs, 3 mars 1969, 3775 St. Dominique, appt. 3*, by Robert Côté

"I thought about this type of action" . . . and that ended the session. Declaration de Pierre-Paul Geoffroy, 4 mars 1969

"The reason we are in jail . . ." *FLQ; un projet révolutionnaire; Lettres et écrits felquistes (1963–1982)* Textes rassemblées par R. Comeau, d. Cooper et P. Vallières, VLB éditeur, 1990

Geoffroy never disclosed the identity . . . Fournier: *F.L.Q.*

On May 5, 1969, Charette and Allard . . . *Le Petit Journal*, August 17, 1969

CHAPTER ELEVEN

It had been placed at the rear . . . *Rapport Générale* . . . *Explosion d'une bombe, 4970 Place de la Savanne, 2 mai 1969,* by Robert Côté

Côté and his officers conducted . . . *Rapport Générale* . . . *Explosion d'une bombe, 5135 ouest boul. Masionnneuve, 16 juin 1969,* by Robert Côté

Shortly after 5:00 a.m . . . *Rapport Générale* . . . *Explosion d'une bombe, au 5700 rue Des Plaines, 29 septembre 1969,* by Robert Côté

Gilles Forgues, a lieutenant-detective . . . Author interview with Gilles Forgues, November 2015

"We (Jocelyn and I) put the bomb . . ." Declaration de Georges Dubreuil, 3 mai 1972

CHAPTER TWELVE

"Not all *péquistes* are terrorists . . ." Fournier: *F.L.Q.*

The numbers involved in clandestine activity . . . Gérard Pelletier: *The October Crisis* (McClelland & Stewart, 1971)

That was clear from an anonymous . . . ibid

The first occurred on Sunday, May 24 . . . *Rapport Générale* . . . *Explosion d'une bombe, 300 rue St-Sacrement, 24 mai 1970,* by Robert Côté

At 10:20 a.m., a small bomb . . . *Rapport Générale* . . . *Explosion d'une bombe, 5000 ouest Boul. Jean Talon, Canadian General Electric, 28 mai 1970,* by Robert Côté

Five minutes later . . . *Rapport Générale* . . . *Explosion d'une bombe, 4565 rue Queen Mary, Hôpital Queen Mary, 28 mai 1970,* by Robert Côté

The author, a Brazilian revolutionary . . . Carlos Marighella: *Minimanual of the Urban Guerrilla*

CHAPTER THIRTEEN

"We were discussing the week ahead . . ." James Cross interview, British Diplomatic Oral History Programme (www.chu.cam.ac.uk.), Churchill College, Cambridge University

Rose explained their motives . . . Ann Charney: *Defiance in Their Eyes: True Stories from the Margins* (Vehicule Press, 1995)

Rose spent his early years . . . ibid and www.uniteouvriere.or/index/php/prisonniersFLQ

Lanctôt grew up in . . . *Jacques Lanctôt: Confessions d'un ex-felquiste*, by Monique Roy, *Chatelaine* magazine, Oct. 1990

Lanctôt and Rose met . . . Charney: *Defiance*

"It finally reached the point . . ." ibid

"We had to find a way . . ." Francis Simard: *Talking It Out: The October Crisis From Inside* (Guernica, 1987)

Paul Rose later told . . . Charney: *Defiance*

"The farm was huge with . . ." Simard: *Talking It Out*

The failure of the Burgess plot was . . . ibid

"The moment one of these missives . . ." George Radwanski and Kendal Windeyer: *No Mandate but Terror: The Story of Canada's Kidnapping Crisis* (Simon & Shuster of Canada, 1971)

The authors described . . . Fournier: *F.L.Q.*

On Saturday morning, he phoned . . . Mitchell Sharp: *Which Reminds Me: A Memoir* (University of Toronto Press, 1994)

The purchase of several series . . . Simard: *Talking It Out*

Rose Rose later testified . . . *Allô Police!*, November 15, 1970

Investigators later retrieved postcards . . . Jean-Francois Duchaîne report

"That moment was something special . . ." Simard: *Talking It Out*

Early the following afternoon . . . Duchaîne report

"Chambly riding was next to the . . ." Simard: *Talking It Out*

"We didn't need to discuss . . ." ibid

They donned disguises and left . . . Declaration de Paul Rose, December 29, 1970, by Constable Jean Boilard of the Sûreté du Québec

"Jacques called the Laportes . . ." ibid

"I was waiting for my sister to . . ." Declaration de Mde. Louise Laporte, 46, 111 Berkley, St. Lambert, October 10, 1970

"I was on the porch and . . ." Declaration de Mde. Pierre Laporte, age 47, 725 Robitaille, St. Lambert, October 10, 1970

"The vehicle took off quickly and . . ." Declaration de Claude Laporte (35 Janvier 1953), 111 Berkley, St. Lambert, October 10, 1970

"The lurid red of police cruiser flashers . . ." Radwanski and Windeyer: *No Mandate but Terror*

"He had no idea . . ." Simard: *Talking It Out*

Paul Rose left at 7:30 a.m . . . Duchaîne report

"My dear Robert . . ." (pgs. 40–41) Radwanski and Windeyer: *No Mandate but Terror*

"I am for negotiating . . ." William Tetley: *The October Crisis, 1970: An Insider's View* (McGill-Queen's University Press, 2007)

"We wish to save . . . He is us, we are him . . ." Radwanski and Windever: *No Mandate but Terror*

Rose boarded a Montreal-bound . . . Duchaîne report

The Vennes dropped . . . ibid

"Newsmen sat along three sides . . ." (pgs. 54–55) Radwanski and Windever: *No Mandate but Terror*

Later that day, Lemieux and . . . Éric Bédard: *Chronique d'une insurrection appréhendée: La crise d'octobre et le milieu universitaire* (Les Éditions du Septentrion, 1998)

Vallières addressed more than . . . ibid

"The hall was full of smoke . . ." Carole de Vault with William Johnson: *The Informer: Confessions of an Ex-Terrorist* (Fleet Books, 1982)

Most of the students refused . . . Bédard: *Chronique*

"Dear patriots," Lemieux began . . . Radwanski and Windeyer: *No Mandate but Terror*

He held another . . . ibid

"Mr. President," Laurin said . . . Tetley: *The October Crisis*

On Sunday morning, October 11 . . . Gordon Robertson: *Memoirs of a Very Civil Servant: Mackenzie King to Pierre Trudeau* (University of Toronto Press, 2000)

The War Measures Act was . . . Ron Haggart and Aubrey E. Golden: *Rumours of War: Canada and the Kidnap Crisis* (New Press Toronto, 1971)

In October 1970 the police wanted . . . Duchaîne report

"No one, I think, ever assumed . . ." Gérard Pelletier: *The October Crisis* (McClelland & Stewart, 1971)

"The preponderant element . . ." ibid

"Every organized community . . ." ibid

"With the letters in hand . . ." Robertson: *Memoirs*

Julien later told the journalist . . . Haggart and Golden: *Rumours of War*

Curiously, the most sensible assessment . . . Tetley: *The October Crisis*

The kidnappers had acted hastily . . . Simard: *Talking It Out*

"Laporte cracked . . ." ibid

"He didn't move . . ." ibid

Lortie left for Montreal . . . Duchaîne report

"I arrived around 7:00 or 7:30 . . ." Declaration de Paul Rose

This was a complete fabrication . . . Duchaîne report

Only Jacques Rose . . . Simard: *Talking It Out*

"On the morning of October 17 . . ." Duchaîne report

They found traces of . . . ibid

The first break occurred . . . ibid

Therrien, it turned out . . . ibid

Then Bolduc, Charette and two other . . . ibid

There were, at the moment . . . ibid

The bottom, left hand panel . . . Simard: *Talking It Out*

"There were a lot of . . ." Interview with James Cross, conducted by J. M. Davey
   of the Prime Minister's Office, December 5, 1970

On October 22, Lanctôt's wife . . . Duchaîne report

One morning in the first week . . . de Vault: *The Informer*

"The days we spent as lovers . . ." ibid

She says she was recruited . . . ibid

"I was excited . . ." ibid

She says he proposed . . . ibid

"Suddenly the door opened . . ." ibid

McLeery and his partner . . . Duchaîne report

Then, in the space of . . . Duchaîne report

"There was a lot of crying . . ." Jacques Lanctôt: "Mon plus bel arbre de Noël,"
   December 25, 2009

Denise Quesnel put them up . . . Duchaîne report

It was pitch black and chilly . . . Simard: *Talking It Out*

Viger knew the Rose brothers . . . Duchaîne report

"Two of us carried out . . ." Simard: *Talking It Out*

Viger had come to their attention . . . Duchaîne report

"The first had been a . . ." Simard: *Talking It Out*

Their first stop was . . . Jacques Lanctôt: *Les Plages de l'exil* (Les Éditions internationales Alain Stanké, 2010)

He met an attractive . . . ibid

In mid-December, the Cuban . . . Louise Lanctôt: *Une sorcière comme les autres* (Éditions Quebec/Amérique, 1981)

"The days are long . . ." ibid

Jacques Lanctôt had managed . . . ibid

"During that first year . . ." ibid

"The commandant arrived . . ." Jacques Lanctôt: *Les Plages*

"We had a short . . ." Louise Lanctôt: *Une sorcière*

In order to . . . ibid

The arrival of the Cross kidnappers . . . Pierre Charette: *Mes Dix Années d'Exil à Cuba* (Éditions internationales Alain Stanké Ltée., 1979)

The Cuban authorities then moved them . . . ibid

Deliverance arrived unexpectedly . . . ibid

They learned on the afternoon . . . ibid

One morning in February . . . ibid

The exiles spent the afternoon and . . . ibid and Jacques Lanctôt: *Les Plages*

He adapted to their slower . . . **several weeks on a sugar plantation** . . . ibid

He was sent to an all-male camp . . . ibid

"Quebec seemed . . ." ibid

"It was necessary to fight . . ." Louise Lanctôt: *Une sorcière*

She had withdrawn . . . ibid

Cossette-Trudel and his wife . . . Louise Lanctôt: *Une sorcière*

"There is a time for everything . . ." Jeff Sallott: *Nobody Said No: The Real Story About How the Mounties Always Get Their Man* (J. Lorimer, 1979)

Both husband and wife were . . . ibid

Louise Cossette-Trudel gave birth . . . ibid

"I said to myself . . ." Jacques Lanctôt: *Les Plages*

"Since our group was . . ." ibid

The Cossette-Trudels left Cuba . . . Louise Lanctôt: *Une sorcière*

He sat at an oval table . . . Jacques Lanctôt: *Les Plages*

They shared a washroom . . . ibid

In the summer of 1975 . . . Louise Lanctôt: *Une sorcière*

But Lanctôt remained a . . . Jacques Lanctôt: *Les Plages*

"What instability we experienced . . ." Louise Lanctôt: *Une sorcière*

Paul Rose had done more . . . *Dossier Paul Rose* (Éditions du CIPP, 1981)

In their first communique . . . ibid

In March 1978, *Le Devoir* published . . . ibid

"When the political prisoners become eligible . . ." ibid

The campaign began with . . . ibid

"We have not detected any . . ." ibid

CHAPTER FIFTEEN

Eighty-three militants and . . . *Dossier Paul Rose.*

"It was a hard thing for me . . ." Charney: *Defiance*

"I've kept all my ideals . . ." *The Globe and Mail*, October 5, 1985

"Paul is a real miracle worker . . ." Charney: *Defiance*

"There were four of us . . ." *Le Journal de Montreal*, October 17, 2000

He had two daughters . . . *La Presse*, January 10, 2015

"Good Lord, not this . . ." *The Globe and Mail*, October 5, 1985

He launched the career . . . *Les Chroniques de Jacques Lanctot*, www.fr.canoe.ca, June 12, 2008

However, the publishing house . . . ibid, September 5, 2007

Index